Mathematics Across the Curriculum

Also available from Continuum

Mathematics Across the Curriculum

Problem-Solving, Reasoning and Numeracy in Primary Schools

Sue Fox and Liz Surtees

continuum

Continuum International Publishing Group

The Tower Building   80 Maiden Lane
11 York Road   Suite 704
London SE1 7NX   New York, NY 10038

www.continuumbooks.com

© Sue Fox and Liz Surtees 2010

British Library Cataloguing-in-Publication Data
A catalogue record for this book is available from the British Library.

ISBN: 978-1-4411-2356-5 (paperback)
      978-1-4411-5940-3 (hardcover)

Library of Congress Cataloging-in-Publication Data
Fox, Sue. Mathematics across the curriculum : problem-solving, reasoning, and numeracy in primary schools / Sue Fox and Liz Surtees.
   p. cm.   Includes index.
ISBN 978-1-4411-5940-3 (hardcover) -- ISBN 978-1-4411-2356-5 (pbk.)
1. Mathematics--Study and teaching (Primary) 2. Numeracy--Study and teaching (Primary) 3. Education, Primary. 4. Curriculum planning. I. Surtees, Liz. II. Title.

QA135.6.F69 2010
372.7--dc22

                                                    2009037923

Typeset by Newgen Imaging Systems Pvt Ltd, Chennai, India
Printed and bound in Great Britain by CPI Antony Rowe Ltd, Chippenham, Wiltshire

Contents

Appendices

Acknowledgements

We would like to thank Rachel Wilby, Lin Savage, Michael Fox, Helen Faulder and Chris Thompson for their help and support. We would also like to thank all the children whose enthusiasm and engagement with the mathematics within this book provided a constant source of inspiration.

Preface

This book is written to help you to ensure that your pupils will be inspired and challenged. They will enjoy their mathematics and be successful and they will not switch off, as was Gardner's fear (1976, p.xi)[1] that 'a teacher of mathematics, no matter how much he loves his subject and how strong his desire to communicate, is perpetually faced with one overwhelming difficulty: how to keep his students awake.'

1   Gardner, M. (1976) *Mathematical Carnival* London: Allen and Unwin Ltd.

Introduction

The aim of this book is to inspire those of us involved in the teaching and learning of Early Years and Primary mathematics to have the desire and confidence to teach mathematics. It is written in such a way that this can be achieved through giving a high profile to problem-solving activities in the daily mathematics lesson and by using and applying mathematics in the wider curriculum.

Changes and developments in Primary Education as it applies to mathematics since 1989

There have been massive changes and advances in both the legal framework and non-statutory guidance, bringing responsibilities for children's learning and their wellbeing closer together. A summary of these developments, starting with the National Curriculum (1989), and with special emphasis on the requirements for teaching mathematics, is provided in a chart in Appendix 1. This tracks the progressive emphasis on the desirability of a curriculum developed by well-trained and inspirational mathematics teachers who are capable of building problem solving, investigations, creativity, and real-life experiences into their mathematics and teaching throughout the curriculum.

Following a number of years of a somewhat structured approach to mathematics teaching, creative and cross-curricular work is being advocated by the Qualifications and Curriculum Development agency (QCDA), the Primary National Strategy (PNS) and the Department for Children, Schools and Families (DCSF). They all stress the importance of children experiencing enjoyment, fun and achievement through a relevant, challenging and rich curriculum.

This will involve children in their work and inspire them to do well and experience success. The Rose Report (DCSF, 2009a, p.15) recognizes the importance of teaching discrete subjects but also understands the benefits of knowing when to 'marshal content from different subjects into well planned, cross-curricular studies' because it 'helps children to use and apply what they have learnt from the discrete teaching of subjects'.

The focus of the book

In the book, evidence from a range of recent research is used to emphasize the importance of such an approach to teaching and learning with a blend of excellent discrete mathematical teaching and creative and cross-curricular work.

Christine Gilbert, the Chief inspector of Schools stated in December 2008 that future Ofsted inspections would 'crackdown' on boring teachers and recognized that there was a close connection between bad behaviour and lack of motivation in class. Future inspections were to emphasize the importance of good teaching and learning.

The Williams Report (DCSF, 2008, p.62) highlights concerns, taken from Ofsted and PNS findings, that there was a need to 'strengthen teaching that challenges and enables children to use and apply mathematics more often, and more effectively than is presently the case in many schools'. In order to be part of the 'highly skilled and motivated workforce' envisaged in the Williams Report (DCSF, 2008) the teacher needs to be comfortable with the twenty-first-century educational requirements.

This book encourages students, newly qualified teachers and more experienced teachers and practitioners to successfully plan and teach interesting mathematics so that children can experience and enjoy their schooling and the magic of mathematics. This could be through the discovery of patterns from shapes and number; completing an investigation; or experiencing the sheer enjoyment of having worked through a problem and discovered a solution. As Pratt (2006, p.15) stressed, 'rather than simply learning mathematical knowledge and then learning to apply it . . . children need to *be* young mathematicians; to engage in mathematical activity/understanding *from* this.' The importance of mathematics in the extended schools provision is also a feature of the book and is a relatively new area for creative mathematical teaching and learning, involving parents and the wider community. This book will support students as they work towards achieving the requirements of initial teacher training (ITT) and meeting the required standards. It will also be of use during the induction period for new teachers as they demonstrate that they have continued to meet the standards of Qualified Teacher Status (QTS), and meet the core standards during induction. The book will help them to have the confidence to work in a practical, relevant and cross-curricular way, while still meeting the requirements of the National Curriculum (NC) and PNS mathematics. It will help them to be aware of current curriculum development from the Qualifications and Curriculum Development Agency (QCDA).

Who this book is for

This book is written to provide support and ideas for:

- students training to teach in the Primary sector
- teaching Assistants working for a Foundation Degree
- newly qualified teachers wishing to broaden their teaching skills
- any teacher wishing to be more adventurous in their teaching generally
- any teacher wishing to be more adventurous in their mathematics teaching and to lessen their reliance on commercial schemes
- a mathematics coordinator wishing to develop the use of mathematics across the curriculum
- teaching assistants working with teachers to enrich the curriculum
- practitioners in the wider sector, working with parents and other professionals to enhance and extend children's mathematical learning
- Early Years Practitioners – Early Years Professional status.

The organization of the book

Chapters 1–3

The first chapter is an overview of the necessary ingredients for successful mathematics teaching and learning that is in line with the requirements of QCDA and DCSF.

Chapters 2 and 3 focus specifically on an analysis of mathematical thinking and problem solving and how to work with children as young mathematicians so they have no fear of failure. The components of using and applying mathematics are identified together with strategies to help both teachers and children develop their skills as problem solvers. A variety of problems are included, some of which can be used as they are presented and others will require adaptation for a specific group of children.

Examples of children's work is included to illustrate different areas of problem solving. While it is impossible to include all types of problems that could be used in the classroom, those chosen provide good starting points with a wealth of additional material available from websites included within the appendices.

Chapters 4–10

These are concerned with the recognition of mathematics across the curriculum from the Foundation Stage to Year 6. They illustrate how valuable and relevant mathematical work can be carried out within other subject areas as well as being an integral part of the PNS mathematics planning for the year. The focus is very much on using and applying mathematics in new situations. There is a discussion about the rationale and desirability for cross-curricular work. This is followed by case studies in different subject areas and a brief list of suggestions for the development of similar work.

Case studies have the following elements:

- a brief introduction of specific issues and recent research
- a study of a project completed in the classroom
- teacher's comment on the project
- a grid of the mathematics content
- possible misconceptions and difficulties
- a grid referencing the other curriculum areas covered
- a list of other similar topics that could involve relevant mathematics work.
- A bibliography and useful websites

The Impact of the Extended Services on the Teaching and Learning of Mathematics is in Chapter 11 together with examples of Study Support work and proven ways of achieving parental involvement both in school and the wider community.

Where appropriate, references to the *Independent Review of the Primary Curriculum, Final Report* (DCSF, 2009a), are referred to as the Rose Report and those relating to the *Independent Review of Mathematics Teaching in Early Years Settings and Primary Schools Final Report* (DCSF, 2008), as the Williams Report.

A summary of educational developments since the introduction of the National Curriculum of 1989, and the relevance of these to mathematics, can be found in Appendix 1.

The Exemplification of Training and Development Agency (TDA) Standards, as they relate to mathematics, compiled by National Centre for Excellence in the teaching of Mathematics (NCETM) are in Appendix 2. These core standards will be of particular interest to trainees. More experienced teachers should also look at the additional guidance given on the website in order to review their practice, inform their career decisions and identify their professional development needs.

References and further reading

Department for Children, Schools and Families, Williams (2008) *Independent Review of Mathematics Teaching in Early Years Settings and Primary Schools Final Report* London: DCSF Publications.

—Rose (2009a) *Independent Review of the Primary Curriculum: Final Report* London: DCSF Publications.

—(2009b) White Paper, *Your Child, Your Schools, Our Future: Building a 21st Century Schools System* London: DCSF Publications.

Department for Education and Skills (1989) *The National Curriculum (England and Wales)* London: DfES Publications.

Pratt, N. (2006) *Interactive Maths Teaching in the Primary School* London: Paul Chapman Publishing.

Websites

All website addresses were accessed on 8 July 2009.

The NCETM's presentation of the professional standards for teachers (as published on the TDA website) Available at: http://www.tda.gov.uk/teachers/professionalstandards.aspx.

The NCETM's presentation of the professional standards for teachers (as published on the ncetm website). This contains additional materials and advice.

Available at: http://content.ncetm.org.uk/tda/.

1 The Principles of Good Teaching and Learning

Mick (Mick Waters, former Director of Curriculum QCA) believes the curriculum should be treasured and valued and that it needs to be shaped to fit with children's lives. To make the curriculum work, people in schools need to set understandings of their children alongside the learning they should meet to create learning that is irresistible.

(Qualifications and Curriculum Development Agency, www.qcda.gov.uk)

Introduction to the principles of good teaching and learning

Later chapters in this book deal with the theory and content of investigational mathematical work, both in the daily mathematics lesson and the wider curriculum. How this can be made meaningful and exciting and contribute to the achievement of these twenty-first-century curricular aims will also be addressed. This chapter summarizes the various essential components of successful teaching and learning in the twenty-first century. The components are interdependent and are outlined below in no particular order of ranking:

- progress towards a twenty-first-century curriculum
- planning issues including daily lesson plans
- the requirement for inclusion
- differentiation of work within the class
- grouping
- assessment
- the value of the use of resources
- the role of Information and Communication Technology (ICT)
- display
- the role of the teacher
- the Early Years Foundation Stage (EYFS)

While reading the rest of this chapter, it would be useful to think about any mathematics teaching and learning in which you have been involved and consider how your experiences and aspirations match with what is written here.

Progress towards a twenty-first-century curriculum

In 2007, the government set out in The Children's Plan its 'ambition to make England the best place in the world for children and young people to grow up World-class schools and world-class standards are central to achieving this vision' (DCSF, 2008a).

This twenty-first-century curriculum is central to delivering the requirements of Every Child Matters (DfES, 2003b). This is the Government's vision of how professionals will work together to provide children's care in a more integrated and effective way. The aims for all children are to be safe, healthy, experience enjoyment and achievement, make a positive contribution and in time achieve economic wellbeing. The curriculum will provide the opportunity for all children to develop essential knowledge, skills and competences through a broad, balanced and creative curriculum in which the children are willing and active learners. They will be independent and reflective and creative learners who can work as part of a team or individually.

The Qualifications and Curriculum Authority (QCA) (2007) stresses the principles of a good curriculum design in which the centrality of secure understanding of literacy and numeracy is recognized and that there is provision for depth and breadth in work which is in tune with the child's personal and academic development. QCA is also reinforcing the concept of the curriculum as the entire planned learning experience both in school and the extended school day. This not only includes the lessons that children have during the school day, but also the activities and events that take place out of school. These are as much a part of the curriculum as the lessons and will encourage a commitment to learning to continue through life.

Good teaching and learning will ensure achievement of the three primary curriculum aims that the children are successful learners, who enjoy school, make good progress and achieve; confident individuals who can lead safe and happy lives; and responsible citizens making a positive contribution to school and society.

The Rose Report (DCSF, 2009a) is an independent review of the primary curriculum in the twenty-first-century and is based on the aims and values of the Children's Plan and provides the framework for Primary education from 2011. The report considers two key areas: how to provide a broad and balanced curriculum to ensure a rich education for children and how to best adapt this curriculum as children progress through primary education.

It advises ministers on how the primary curriculum needs to change in order to:

- ease the transition from early years into primary schools
- sharpen the focus on mathematics and English
- give teachers more flexibility to design and deliver a curriculum relevant to the school

The Rose Report (DCSF, 2009a) proposes six areas of learning that dovetail well with the EYFS framework (DCSF, 2008d) to ease transition from the Early Years Curriculum to Key Stage 1 and then from Key Stage 2 to Key Stage 3. The National Curriculum (NC) is to be retained as a statutory entitlement for all children and is aligned within the new areas of learning. These areas of learning open the door to crossing current curriculum boundaries when desirable and thus reduce curriculum overload caused by teaching solely discrete subjects. See Table 1.1.

The Rose Report also proposes that ICT be taught both discretely and through its application across the whole curriculum to deepen understanding. The expectation is that from

Table 1.1 Chart showing the continuum from EYFS to Key Stage 1

Six areas covered by the early learning goals 2008	Areas of learning – Rose 2009
Problem solving, reasoning and numeracy	Understanding mathematics
Knowledge and understanding of the world	Scientific and technological understanding Historical, geographical and social understanding.
Creative development	Understanding the arts
Personal, social and emotional development Physical development	Understanding physical development, health and wellbeing
Communication, language and literacy	English, communication and language Plus – ICT across all areas of learning

Source: DCSF, Rose, J., *Independent Review of the Primary Curriculum Final Report* London: DCSF Publications, 2009a, p.44.

these areas of learning, the school designs its curriculum to ensure the centrality of literacy and numeracy and ICT, opportunities for depth and breadth of study, commitment to personal development and recognition of the importance of the learning experience being in tune with child development.

There is not just one way to teach successfully. A good teacher uses a range of discrete subjects and cross-curricular teaching. As the Rose Report stresses, challenging subject teaching should take place alongside equally challenging cross-curricular studies. 'Ofsted and the QCA report that some of the most effective learning occurs when connections are made between subjects. The proposed curriculum framework will make these connections more explicit and the planning for them more manageable' (DCSF, 2009a, p.13, para 15).

The latest phase of progress to a twenty-first-century curriculum is the White Paper (DCSF, 2009b) *Your child, Your Schools, Our Future: Building for a 21st Century Schools System* in which the Government states again the desire for every child to succeed. The curriculum is to be more flexible, with the schools having more autonomy, building on the successful developments of the previous ten years.

Planning issues including daily lessons

Good planning involves a continuum of planning, teaching, assessing children and evaluating lessons, with the teacher making adaptations where beneficial. It is at this point that the potential for working across the curriculum can be accommodated.

Schools are to build on the successes of the 2006 Primary Framework for mathematics in the Primary National Strategy (PNS). In this, there was a simplification of the structure of the objectives from the National Numeracy Strategy (NNS) of 1999. There were seven strands of learning that gave a broad overview of the mathematics curriculum in the primary phase. These strands were related to the 1999 National Curriculum for England: Key Stages 1–4 (NC) and were not equally weighted.

Early Years Foundation Stage (EYFS)

Many of the principles of teaching and learning mathematics in Key Stages 1 and 2 are also applicable to the Early Years, for example, the use of ICT, differentiation and inclusion.

The curriculum area of Problem Solving, Reasoning and Numeracy (DfES, 2008b) is split into three sections, with problem solving underpinning each one. The three sections are:

- numbers as labels for counting
- calculating
- shape, space and measures

The learning is planned for through play and continuous provision activities, stemming from the individual child's interests. There is an emphasis on the learning environment so that explorative play takes place inside and outside the classroom and a lot of the learning and understanding of concepts comes from child-initiated exploration and tasks. The use of resources, real-life situations and practical tasks are the core of all mathematical learning, rather than the abstract.

The Williams Report (DCSF, 2008b) has also emphasized the importance of mathematical mark making, time and capacity in young children's learning. Children should have the opportunity to develop these skills through adult-led and child-initiated experiences in a play-based approach. Practitioners are advised to give particular attention to the uniqueness of individual children, positive relationships, enabling environments and learning and development when planning for and delivery of good quality mathematics. Planning from children's interests, using systematic observations, is a key factor of planning in the Early Years and assessment largely consists of observation, photographic evidence and conversation with the child rather than written work.

Key Stages 1 and 2

The PNS planning was organized into five blocks: (A) counting, partitioning and calculating; (B) securing number facts, understanding shape; (C) handling data and measures; (D) calculating, measuring and understanding shape; and (E) securing number facts, relationships and calculating.

Each block always incorporated some or all of the five themes of using and applying mathematics; solving problems, representing, enquiring, reasoning and communicating. These provided the framework for planning.

The Rose Report recommends that teachers should continue to use the PNS frameworks for planning purposes but with the new legislation of the 2009 White Paper there will no longer be any central bureaucracy to support this. Schools can use its structure when appropriate, and adapt and develop it to suit the needs of the children being taught. While there is much of the NNS and PNS worth retaining, now the emphasis is on planning to teach in order to facilitate learning rather than an emphasis on planning to teach for tests.

The three-part lesson

The three-part lesson has always been an integral part of daily mathematics. An important development in planning is the relaxing of the format of what had become the standard lesson: oral/mental starter, main teaching activity, plenary. The three-part lesson plan was adopted with rigour with the introduction of the NNS but it was never the intention for this to be adhered to, to the exclusion of all other lesson formats. In fact it was suggested in the NNS that the 'outline structure of a typical lesson should not be seen as a mechanistic recipe to be followed. You should use your professional judgement to determine the activities, timing and organisation of each part of the lesson to suit its objectives' (DfEE,

1999b, p.15). This view of lesson planning was reinforced by DfES (2003a, p.16) 'there is no particular format or length required by Ofsted or local authority inspections.'

The three-part lesson structure undoubtedly has many positive features and is a valuable frame for a mathematics lesson, but as Adhami (2003, p.66) warned, that although the standard lesson format can be useful, 'it can be interpreted in a ritual sense and, so that largely unrelated classroom episodes at the start and the end of the lesson are seen as the norm.'

Adhami (2003, p.66) argues that the 'reformulation' of both the three-part lesson and the 'notion' of the lesson objectives with a purposeful balance of 'instruction and practice, investigation and problem solving and thinking challenge lessons need a different type of lesson objective and a different structure'.

So while not by any means advocating the abandonment of the three-part lesson, it is worth thinking about when another approach may be more meaningful in the light of the mathematics being taught and the children's learning objectives.

The requirement for inclusion

An inclusive curriculum involves all children in the class, enabling them to contribute to ongoing activities.

All schools have a responsibility to provide for all pupils a broad and balanced curriculum that must be both relevant and challenging. The NC (DfEE, 1999a, pp.30–31) states that there are three principles for developing this statutory requirement. They are as follows:

- setting suitable learning challenges for all children so that teachers 'take account of any gaps in pupils' learning' and the needs of those 'whose attainment falls significantly below the expected levels at a particular key stage' or those pupils 'whose attainments significantly exceed the expected level of attainment within one or more subjects within a key stage'.
- responding to children's diverse learning needs through planning their 'approaches to teaching and learning so that all pupils can take part in lessons fully'. There must be a 'creative effective learning environment' in which the pupils feel valued, safe and motivated to learn. Teachers must ensure that they provide equal opportunity through the teaching approaches and that assessment and target setting is at the heart of planning and learning.
- 'overcoming potential barriers to learning and assessment' for children with special educational needs or a disability or those children for whom English is a second language.

Any class has children with a wide range of ability, knowledge, skills, learning styles, interests and expectations. The teacher's understanding of the needs of all the children in the class must be met through that awareness and their skills to plan and teach appropriately.

Building on earlier work and using previously successful teaching styles is helpful, as is the skill of finding work that is of interest to the child thus stimulating the wish to learn. Some children will have gaps in their learning and the teacher should ensure that the child's work is of the correct level but in line with the area of learning of the rest of the class. Use can be made of catch-up programmes such as 'overcoming barriers'. Similarly the needs of the more able should be planned for with challenging work, by extending the breadth and depth of study within individual subjects or by planning work which draws more deeply on the content of different subjects.

Differentiation of work within the class

Thoughtful and realistic differentiation ensures that all pupils can enjoy a rich and wide mathematics curriculum and experience success.

The NNS (DfEE, 1999b) states that differentiation should be manageable; usually no more than three levels of work in the same area of mathematics. Differentiation is not about providing able children with more of the same, an extra work sheet or larger numbers. Nor is it about limiting the experiences of those with learning difficulties. Differentiation is not about speeding through the curriculum with able children, any more than it is about giving those children needing more support 'a watered down version' of the work or 'palming them off' with a worksheet. Differentiation by task or outcome is a means of including all children in ongoing work that is appropriate to their needs and ability.

Differentiation by outcome

This implies that the same task will be accomplished by the whole class but with different levels of expectation of expertise and therefore of the quality of the completed work. Rich tasks which have a range of potential extension activities, or which the pupils can naturally develop for themselves, enable all children to work on the same mathematics.

Differentiation by task

This can be achieved within the framework of the whole class by ensuring that each task contributes to the ongoing work and is of the correct level for the child. For example, during a lesson studying 3-D shapes, a group could be working with construction kits to build nets of polyhedra, while an able child could use a computer program to develop understanding of the parallel and perpendicular faces and edges of solid shapes.

This form of differentiation would seem preferable because of the importance of sharing finished work and all having a valid contribution to make.

Differentiation by support

Differentiation can be provided by the extra support of resources or Teaching Assistant (TA). The TA can help children of all abilities in certain circumstances and it is important to remember that an able child can benefit from such support and not always to plan for the TA to work with the lower ability groups. The TA could be responsible for most of the class while the teacher concentrates on a single group.

Able children

Koshy (2001, p.30) recognizes that able children show 'persistence and stamina while carrying out investigations. They respond positively when they are given problems and investigations with open-ended outcomes. They may resent time constraints and imposed restrictions.' Able children require the opportunity to use their skills, knowledge and understanding in different contexts within a secure and flexible learning environment. They require opportunities to analyse ideas, extract principles, reason and theorize, and while doing so, they will develop their creative and critical thinking, problem-solving skills and ability to evaluate their work. The teacher must ensure that there is sufficient challenge in all subjects. *Excellence and Enjoyment* (DfES, 2003a, p.42) reminds teachers of the requirement to provide provision for gifted and talented children in all subjects 'including PE and sport, music and modern foreign languages'. Here is undoubtedly an opportunity for investigative work across the subjects involving mathematics. It is unhelpful to assume that able children can 'work on their own' as they need to be taught mathematical skills in formal lessons and have interaction with the teacher. However they need to spend less time consolidating the work and they can be given work providing the opportunity to work on tasks in some depth. Their learning objectives could be tracked forward to provide expectations with suitable challenges.

Children with special educational needs

There is a danger of children with Individual Education Plans having limited access to a rich and wide mathematics curriculum. The targets for these pupils may address knowledge of number and calculations to ensure they have the knowledge and understanding of basic fact, skills, concepts and strategies but they may miss out on the wider issues involving mathematics. However those pupils requiring extra support can readily work with the rest of the class. Ofsted reports confirms that the NNS has had 'a positive impact on the teaching and learning of pupils with special educational needs with the Numeracy Strategy providing a clear structure for planning and assessing their progress' (DfES, 2003a, p.40). Almost all pupils with special educational needs are included in the literacy hour and the daily mathematics lesson. This requires care being given to their specific needs be it extra or different resources, or their role within a group activity, their physical needs or the elimination of a potential barrier to successful learning. It may be that an adaptation of the lesson objectives is incorporated in the lesson plan so that their learning challenges are suitable and tracked back to provide suitable objectives. Their tasks could be planned for a shorter time. If tasks are open ended and in real contexts, the differentiation will be by outcome enabling the children to work at their own pace and level. Help can be provided in the form of a learning ladder so that the order and organization of the tasks are given as support, especially in an investigation or problem-solving activity. It is important that these pupils experience the challenge of interesting mathematical work and different ways of recording work. So, with the professional skills of the teacher, their questioning and provision of extra resources or support, it is possible for children to work within the framework of the lesson and not be limited in their learning. They can be included in, and enjoy a rich and wide mathematics curriculum. An illustration of this point is the work of an 11 year old with learning difficulties. She had a genuine interest in farming in general, and poultry in particular, and this led to some original and interesting investigative work in the same area of mathematics as the rest of the class. She gathered examples of the different types of eggs on her farm; bantam, hen, duck, goose, turkey and added to that an ostrich egg from a local Ostrich farm. The intention was for her to draw these eggs taking into account their relative sizes. However she chose to measure their girth with a tape measure, height with calipers and mass with electronic kitchen scales. The difficulties of recording the measurements were overcome and block graphs drawn to illustrate these measurements. The graphs were used by other members of the class in further work of comparison of bird/size of egg etc. There followed an excellent display complete with photographs of the birds and the farms.

Grouping

Making sure that children who are working together are compatible and that they have the opportunity to work in a range of groupings. This can be an important factor in encouraging successful teaching and learning.

Askew and Wiliam (1995) noted that a general agreement exists among researchers that collaborative work between pupils has a positive effect on learning. There are occasions when the whole class is taught as one unit particularly when setting the scene for new work or recapping an ongoing topic. During a lesson, it can be useful to bring the class together to discuss a successful or troublesome development. The successful starting points of a child's work can be discussed and in doing so others can be helped to 'get going'. Also in an atmosphere of sharing and support, a misconception that has arisen can be remedied. The types of grouping can be a crucial element in the success of a project. Three typical groupings are considered here.

Grouping according to ability

It is possible to give ability groups different tasks within one project. The groups then report back to the rest of the class their ideas, results and conclusions. In this way, a project can be completed with everyone participating in some way towards the end result. Donaldson (2002, pp.38–39) recognized that differentiation is more manageable and interaction is effective with others of similar ability working on the same task. However she understood the potential problem, that 'if constantly in the same group they will identify their mathematical potential with the level of the group they are in'. This could lead to a lack of challenge, a point supported by Williams (DCSF, 2008b, p.67), with a warning that there is a risk that 'children may languish in the lower sets and experience a restricted version of the curriculum'.

> *Working in ability pairs* – this is good for quality interaction, assuming of course, that the pairing is compatible and there is not a dominant partner or a lack of goodwill! Sometimes the teacher will wish a child to work with another for a specific reason such as explaining a computer program or because of a child's shyness in larger groups. This can lead to support, increased confidence and excellent work from the pair.
> *Mixed ability grouping* – is another option that can, as stated by Donaldson (2002, p.39), 'provide a refreshing change of context, less able learn from more able with the more able required to discuss and explain and clarify their own thoughts'.

Whatever the grouping, it can be helpful for the children to have a short time at the start of the work to think independently, a time for thinking about how to proceed before coming together as a group. This will prevent a dominant member taking over with their ideas, or silence as nobody has thought out a possible way forward!

Assessment

Jones and Allebone (2000, p.206) remind us that 'assessment of the children, their attainment and potential, is an essential aspect of providing a differentiated curriculum. It is in fact a central and vital aspect of any curriculum planning.' There are two forms of assessment: assessment *of* learning (or summative assessment) and assessment *for* learning (AfL) (or formative assessment).

Assessment *of* learning (or summative assessment) provides a summary of the children's achievement and attainment at a particular time such as during Standard Assessment Tests (SATS). Linked with careful tracking, this provides valuable insights into children's progress and provides evidence of successful teaching and learning. AfL (or formative assessment) is recognized as central to good classroom practice and as such is embedded in planning. Black and Wiliam (1998, p.2) refer to formative assessment as 'all those activities undertaken by teachers, *and by their students assessing themselves,* which provide information to be used as feedback to modify the teaching and learning activities in which they are engaged'. The next step in learning can also be identified together with ways of best achieving success.

Assessment for learning strategy (2008): assessing pupils' progress (APP)

QDCA is working with the National Strategies and Department for Children, Schools and Families (DCSF) to ensure that AfL is more widespread, systematic and consistent through the development and extension of the range of APP materials available. As Rose states, this support for AfL will 'enable teachers to recognise secure evidence of children's learning in essential areas, and make consistent periodic assessment of children's strengths and weaknesses in relation to national standards and use this information to plan for better learning and further progress' (DCSF, 2009a, p.85).

The AfL Strategy, (DCSF, 2008b, p.4) states that AfL will ensure that:

- every child knows how they are doing, and understands what they need to do to improve and how to get there. They get the support they need to be motivated, independent learners on an ambitious trajectory of improvement;
- every teacher is equipped to make well-founded judgments about pupils' attainment, understands the concepts and principles of progression, and knows how to use their assessment judgments to forward plan, particularly for pupils who are not fulfilling their potential;
- every school has in place structured and systematic assessment systems for making regular, useful, manageable and accurate assessments of pupils, and for tracking their progress;
- every parent and carer knows how their child is doing, what they need to do to improve, and how they can support the child and their teachers.

The aim of this new structured approach is to give teachers the confidence and ability to reduce reliance on standard testing as the main source of evidence for achieving National Standards. By using the APP procedures and resources to assess accurately, teacher will have a clear understanding of the needs of the children and be able to make judgements on pupils' progress. It will also improve the quality of feed back for children and their parents.

It helps teachers to fine-tune their understanding of learners' needs and to tailor their planning and teaching accordingly, by enabling them to use diagnostic information about pupils' strengths and weaknesses to improve teaching, learning and pupils' progress. With the information, they will be able to make reliable judgements related to national standards and track pupils' progress.

The result will be assessment that makes:

- an *accurate* assessment – knowing what the standards are, judging pupils' work correctly, and making accurate assessments linked to NC levels;
- a *fair* assessment – knowing the methods used are valid;
- a *reliable* assessment – ensuring that judgements are consistent and based on a range of evidence;
- a *useful* assessment – identifying barriers to pupil progress and using that information to plan and discuss the next step in learning.

- a *focused* assessment – identifying areas of a child's learning where there are block which might, for example, benefit from the attention of one-to-one tuition,
- for *continuity* of assessment, enabling better transfer between years and 2008b, p.5).

APP resource materials include collections of assessed pupil work that exemplify attainment at different levels. There are also assessment guidelines sheets to support teachers in tracking pupil progress assessments from levels 2 to 5.

The assessment guidelines for each Attainment target of the NC are organized into a number of Assessment Focuses (AFs). The AFs for using and applying mathematics are problem solving, communicating and reasoning. The Primary Framework for mathematics organizes learning objectives into strands that also map onto the NC. Teaching should be planned in relation to learning objectives, not the APP AFs. Combinations of learning objectives work together to provide evidence for certain AFs.

There are APP Assessment guidelines for problem solving, communicating and reasoning for Levels 2–3, 3–4 and 4–5. Training teachers to use APP began in 2008 and is to be fully in place by 2011.

Assessment that includes the child then is even more valuable because of the accompanying discussions. Black and Wiliam (1998, p.9) remind us that self-assessment is a skill that needs to be taught, and children must have a clear idea of the objectives, the targets for their work.

Learning objectives

The term learning objective is widely used in planning and assessment. The objectives are what the children are expected to learn as opposed to what they are going to do. Objectives should be shared and referred to at the start and during the lesson enabling children to understand the purpose of their task, and to plan an appropriate approach to the work. Success criteria displayed in the classroom can help the children to understand the learning objectives of the lesson and provide a focus for successful learning in language that is appropriate for the age of the children. The success criteria enable children to judge and self assess whether or not they have met the learning objective for the session. They can also provide a prompt for teacher and child discussion. It is generally agreed that success criteria are most effective if the children generate them themselves, as this gives them ownership of their learning. Asking for the children's ideas and words before they start work or during teaching enables the teacher to build up what the children have to do in class to complete the work and what they will learn.

The important issue is that the children are clear about what they are to learn and understand how they are going to achieve it. With this clarity, confusions over the terms learning outcome, learning intention, learning objective (used by the NNS) and success criteria can be overcome.

Hussey and Smith (2003, pp.357–368) propose a model that acknowledges the need for 'teachers to have intended learning outcomes (ILOs) in order to make sense of teaching and learning' but also suggest the idea of 'emergent learning outcomes' (ELOs). While the contribution of ILOs and ELOs varies, they argue that the ELOs 'contribute to the overall development as autonomous, self-managing learners'. So, it is important to recognize that some achievements may not have been in the intended learning goals but are equally important and valid and require recognition. Indeed, this is a view shared by Lee (2006, p.44) who prefers the term 'learning intention'. This is because of 'the implied flexibility; this is what it is intended we learn in this lesson, not what must or even could be learnt'. However she concedes that is it sensible to use the same terminology as the NNS-learning objective.

If the activity is meaningful and the children are able to work independently, the teacher has the opportunity to focus on an area of learning and observe, question and assess as well as analysing written work, looking at the strategies, workings and procedures. It is while working on tasks and responding to effective questioning that children demonstrate the range of their knowledge, understanding and skills. Both the teacher and the children make judgements about this learning and how it can be improved and developed. Teachers, children and peer groups are engaged in dialogue, demonstration, reflection and decision-making and assessment of ongoing work. Through this interaction, formative assessments are made.

Helpful marking and feedback of work are crucial. As Black et al. (2002, p.8) stressed, it is important not to focus solely on performance, with rewards for getting work done successfully but also give pointers for future work and guidance for improvements and developments. They make the point that feedback in the form of comments either orally or written have a much greater effect on the children with them engaging 'more productively in their work'. Any worries on the part of the teacher that the absence of marks would be detrimental have proved unfounded as 'neither parents nor Ofsted inspectors have reacted adversely'.

If marking is completed in the presence of the child, then it has extra value. It should be a balance of recognition of both learning and performance goals together with targets to help the child to plan for their next steps. A structured approach to setting targets is not at odds with an integrated and exciting curriculum, as at the planning stage, the teacher is able to use such discussions to make decisions about learning to focus as well as the way in which the curriculum content is delivered.

In conclusion – children need to know how well they are doing, where the areas for improvement are and how this can be achieved. Parents also need to be kept informed so that support for the child and the school can continue at home. Every teacher needs to know how to make sound judgements about each child in order to facilitate planning for progression. Schools need to have a good assessment system in place so pupil progress can be tracked.

Learning must be focused on the needs of all pupils and effective assessment enables the teacher to plan for the next phase of how the children are taught and learn, so a progressive circle of planning and assessment is perpetuated.

The value of the use of resources

The use of resources can and should be relevant, exciting and so enhance and extend teaching and learning.

First a cautionary tale about the use of resources,

> Hammer School left its mark on my mental life, though. I got into a crying jag over the notion of minus numbers. Minus one threw out my universe, it couldn't exist, I couldn't understand it. This, I realised tearfully, under coaxing from an amused (a mildly amazed) teacher was because I thought numbers were *things*. In fact, cabbages. We'd been taught in Miss Myra's class to do addition and subtraction by imagining more cabbages and fewer cabbages. Every time I did mental arithmetic I was juggling ghostly vegetables in my head. And I when tried to think of minus one I was trying to imagine an anti-cabbage, an anti-matter cabbage, which was as hard as conceiving an alternative universe. (Sage, 2000, p.30)[11]

Liebeck (1984, p.16) stated that a child 'must progress through a sequence of abstraction'. This sequence is as follows:

- E – *experience* with physical objects
- L – spoken *language* that describes the experience
- P – *pictures* that represent the experience
- S – *symbols* that generalize the experience.

She asserts that, young children need to experience the physical objects and the spoken language as it is through practical, interactive work that young children learn.

Similarly, Hughes (1986) showed how the use of resources, in this case bricks in a box, helped a young child succeed with addition and subtraction calculations. The child was unable to do them when asked in an abstract manner without the bricks and was clearly unhappy with the task. Hughes believed the bricks gave the child a helpful visual image as the child could calculate accurately even when the bricks were out of sight in the closed box.

However, it is important to recognize that it cannot be guaranteed that the use of a resource or game will automatically develop mathematical understanding.

Threlfall (1996) suggests that while teachers can assume that the use of the apparatus supports the learner in their understanding, it is possible that they are merely learning how to manipulate the equipment or that they have missed the mathematical significance of the resource. Delaney (2001, p.124) concurs with this view and states that 'there is no mathematics actually in a resource' but that 'the mathematics is brought to the resource by those who interact with it or is developed by them as they use it to support or challenge their thinking.'

A recent illustration of this was provided by a Year 2 child who, when shown a set of coloured 2-D shapes, confidently announced that the red shape was a circle. As it was a triangle, the

---

1   (c) 2000 Lorna Sage. By kind permission of HarperCollins Publishers Ltd.

teacher asked for an explanation. This was given, 'because it's the same colour as the shape on the poster'. A classroom poster indeed had a red circle. The child was focusing on the irrelevant attribute of colour.

Think of a tidy set of plastic 3-D shapes hidden in a classroom cupboard, then think of a collection of baked bean tins, cheese triangle boxes, Toblerone boxes, Smartie tubes, match boxes, icing sugar boxes and any posh chocolate boxes from Christmas and you will see which collection has the most potential for exciting work, looking at attributes, making nets and creating displays. Can the children find a box that is really a cube? Investigate the proportions of the three cornflake boxes. If the range was increased, what would be the dimensions of larger/smaller sizes?

While advocating the effective use of resources and group interaction, it is important to know the children well enough to respect their learning style when appropriate, and not force a child to work in a particular way if he/she is uncomfortable. The main learning styles are Visual (seeing and reading), Auditory (speaking and listening) and Kinesthetic (touching and doing) (VAK) and the Primary curriculum will inevitably require the use of all these learning styles. So, accepting that the VAK model is desirable for teaching and learning, then the appropriate use of resources has an important part to play in the Primary classroom. Resources can be categorized into two main groups, namely, structured and unstructured. To this I would add a third group namely, inspirational resources.

Structured apparatus – such as Dienes base 10 apparatus is recognized by Bottle (2005, p.87) as 'designed specifically as an embodiment of a particular mathematical conceptual structure and therefore manipulations of the materials by the child or teacher directly reflect the equivalent mathematical manipulations within that structure. They are designed to eliminate distracting features.'

Unstructured, general mathematics resources – such as arrow cards, measuring tools, number lines and multi-link can be used by the teacher to model, explain, motivate and support the learning process. Children continually use such resources, all of which should be readily available in the classroom. Organization of resources is important as they should be saying to the child, 'come and use me.' Drawers and cupboards should be labelled with words or pictures. Small apparatus such as dice can be hung in washing machine tablet bags and frequently used equipment stored on top of units or in the centre of work tables. Easy access is essential to avoid 'off task' behaviour and time wasting. We all know children who can spend an hour finding a ruler!

Number squares, lines and tracks, calendars and a range of clocks can be displayed for use when helpful. 'Washing lines' can display money, numbers, shapes and sequences. Such general resources are equally relevant to Years 5 and 6 if used appropriately. They should never be thought of as solely for the use of young or less able children.

Games with some mathematical content, such as snakes and ladders, can be valuable for consolidation, reinforcement and enjoyment.

Inspirational resources

This refers to those resources not immediately categorized as 'mathematical'. If well used, they can help to develop understanding of mathematical concepts and are a source of discussion and questioning for both teacher and children. A child fitting different sized toys into different sized boxes for the role play toy shop is learning about relative sizes and capacity as well as extending mathematical vocabulary. A class of Key Stage 2 children preparing ingredients for baking are engaged in accurate measurement of mass.

Probably the most exciting resource is the one that triggers interesting work. It can be a 'found' resource where the teacher recognizes its potential. A map of Tobermory, the town on the Isle of Mull that was used for filming the children's programme Balamory, led to work on routes, distances and compass points together with ferry charges and costs of Balamory memorabilia.

Current events provide many opportunities to interest children and involve them in exciting mathematical work. When the *Angel of the North* sculpture was first erected in Gateshead, it created a lot of publicity and literature. It also created a great deal of potential for work involving scale, measurement of length and mass. High-profile adventures involving routes and distances (such as a recent canoe journey from North to South Poles) can be utilized to provide a rich source of directional work and the calculation of distances. A recent newspaper article on Big Wheels gave the heights, passenger capacity, journey time and year of opening from a Wheel in Vienna that opened in 1897 to the Beijing Great Wheel 2009. Think of the potential in this article for using and applying the knowledge, understanding and skills of data handling, measurement, time as well as elements of history, English and geography.

Charts, timetables and other written information are a good starting point for investigations. A table of flight times to Egypt was taken from a travel brochure (so it was the real thing) and used for determining flight times, working out possible holiday dates and costs for a family including 'extras' such as hot air ballooning while on holiday. Differentiation was achieved by the use of correction fluid to delete superfluous data and the complexity of the investigation undertaken.

The Rose Report recognized that teachers are 'skilled opportunists' and an example of this was heard on Radio 2. During the programme there was a light-hearted experiment to find the coffee cup with the best insulation. Four cups were tested with sensors: paper, china, polystyrene and ridged card. The next day, the presenter Chris Evans received the results from a similar experiment conducted in a school. The class had collected the data from the experiment, interrogated it and presented it in graph form. Science, ICT, mathematics in the form of data handling all combined in a memorable spontaneous activity.

The initial stimulus could be a small 'happening' but the teacher must recognize its potential. For example, before his departure from Chelsea, Jose Mourinho stated in an interview, that Chelsea seemed to need 20 shots at goal before succeeding in scoring. This would provide an excellent starter for a lesson. One goal needs 20 attempts so how many attempts for 5 goals? 60 shots, how many goals? This is painless multiplication or division of 20.

Books as a resource

There are story books, poems and songs that provide a rich source of mathematical stimulus right through the Primary phase. They can contain mathematical vocabulary, pictures and story lines with mathematical theme and are guaranteed to provide an extra, meaningful dimension to teaching and learning. McVarish (2008, p.10) used *Maths Curse* (Scieszka, 1995) as an example of a humorous story book in which children are helped to believe that 'their world is filled with mathematical ideas essential to helping them become confident problem solvers and mathematical thinkers.'

There are poems that ensure all learners know a mathematical fact, as in this poem taken from *One, Two, Skip a Few!* (Barefoot Books, 1998).

> Eight eights are sixty four,
> Multiply by seven.
> When it's done,
> Carry one
> And take away eleven.
> Nine nines are eighty one,
> Multiply by three.
> If it's more,
> carry four
> And then it's time for tea.

I defy any member of a class knowing that rhyme not to know that $9 \times 9 = 81$ and $8 \times 8 = 64$. A list of tried and tested books is provided in Appendix 3.

Pictures and photographs

These are an open-ended resource, with lots of potential for use in the classroom to provide children with stimulating, challenging and creative learning opportunities. Oxfam has an extremely useful section on the use and display of photographs in which the importance of mathematics is specifically recognized. Oxfam (no date) suggests that

> photos can support work on collecting, representing, and handling data, and developing under-standing of shapes, spaces, and measurement. Photos can also provide opportunities to discuss and describe patterns. Information from photographs can be gathered, sorted, and recorded in the form of different types of graphs, tables, and charts. Encourage the use of language appropriate to maths: words and phrases such as bigger than, next to, as short as, in, under, how much, altogether, come naturally when discussing photos. This will help to develop an understanding of mathematical language in a wider context.

The role of ICT

ICT together with literacy and numeracy form the core of the new curriculum and as such should be prioritized both discretely to capture its essential knowledge and skills and through its application across the whole curriculum. Rose (DCSF, 2009a, p.69)

Bennett (2006, p.1) stated that by planning for the 'powerful ICT tools' in mathematics 'the quality of your teaching and children's learning will improve. Similarly by contextualising the children's ICT experience in meaningful mathematical projects, children's ICT capability will be enhanced and extended.'

Indeed mathematics in the classroom has changed with the availability of a wide range of ICT resources. Williams and Easingwood (2003, p.6) refer to the computer as a 'value added' component of teaching and learning as it provides an extra dimension to the classroom. They cite as their example, the ability of the computer to create a graph when a child has entered the necessary data thus enabling him to concentrate on the interrogation of the graph. It goes without saying that a child must have had previous experience of creating a graph by hand so the process and requirements of such work are understood. This was also the view of Carter (1998, p.199) who stated that

> there is little enquiry based work that cannot be enhanced with ICT. For example the use of data bases, spreadsheets, data logging equipment or the internet will certainly be an advantage in cases where the pupils are asking geographical questions, making observations or recordings and investigating data from fieldwork and secondary sources.

This statement is equally true across other curriculum areas. So by embedding the use of ICT throughout the primary curriculum so that the children are 'using technology to develop deeper cognitive skills', by Year 6 they will be 'well on the way to harnessing technology for life long learning' Williams (DCSF, 2008a, p.71).

Appendix 4 has a summary of the expectations of the use of ICT within the NC for mathematics programmes of study.

The use of display

Display is a powerful visual aid to the learning process.

The use of display can support and reinforce children's knowledge and understanding of a new topic, theme or concept. It can ensure that they focus on the ongoing work and give them a sense of ownership over their educational environment. Work displayed raises self-esteem and gives a sense of achievement. A cross-curricular display, with visual mathematical potential inbuilt, can also show the connections between different areas of learning and prompt interest and enquiry.

Following a class visit to a Buddhist temple, the garlands of flags seen there were researched and the colours were found to represent space – White, wind – Green, fire – Red, water – Blue, earth – Yellow. This was used as a starting point for work with repeating patterns made from paper, beads and multi-link. Accuracy was essential as this was a 'real' pattern with meaning. There were also photographs of Buddhist artefacts exhibiting symmetry and tessellation. There were questions and tasks to complete as part of the display including flags to make requiring careful measuring. Creative, interactive mathematical displays in the classroom are not common and so an opportunity to provide exciting visual stimulus is missed. With careful planning, one display can show a wide cross section of mathematical work and pose interesting questions as well as linking with other curriculum areas.

Think about the theme of triangles. The possibilities are endless:

- examples of the different triangles
- investigations of Pascal's Triangle
- triangular numbers
- internet investigations leading to the display including Haberdasher's Puzzle (four polygons that make an equilateral triangle or a square)
- internet investigations leading to the display including Sierpinski's triangle (an ever-repeating pattern of triangles could provide the basis for some creative art/mathematics)
- creative art with tessellating triangles
- pyramid nets
- triangular prism packaging of a famous chocolate- and its net
- what and where is the Bermuda triangle?
- triangles in bridge designs – why is this?

Once the theme is decided upon, the interconnecting ideas cascade, providing opportunities for internet research and a range of work with all children having something to offer.

The role of the teacher

Good teaching should make learning an enjoyable and challenging experience for all the class and the teacher.

Of course the teacher has responsibility for the components of teaching and learning already discussed in this chapter but we will now look specifically at the teacher's role and the interaction between teacher and children.

The Williams Report (DCSF, 2008f) states that it is recognized that as well as the need for sound understanding of successful classroom practice and subject knowledge, there is the third ingredient, namely the teacher's own enthusiasm for the subject. Teachers with positive attitudes to the teaching of mathematics are much more likely to adopt a problem-solving and enquiry-based approach. Enthusiasm is essential and is generally regarded as infectious. If you reflect on your work in the classroom that has been successful it will be partly because you personally have enjoyed it. The children will also be aware of this.

McVarish (2008, p.8) recognized the teacher's role as one of providing 'opportunities in classrooms and throughout the day that required observation, wonder and a time for children to make decisions on their own without constant direction from the teacher'. She saw this as a far cry from the historical view of mathematics as a 'discipline of right answers, formulas and procedural rules' (McVarish, 2008, p.4).

Similarly, the NNS (DfEE, 1999b, p.11) recognized that 'high quality direct teaching is oral, interactive and lively. It is not achieved by adopting a simplistic formula of "drill and practice" and lecturing the class, or by expecting the pupils to teach themselves from books. It is a two way process in which pupils are expected to play an active part by answering questions, contributing points to discussions, and explaining and demonstrating their methods to the class.'

Enabling the children to become active learners is not easy. If a class has not been used to making decisions and taking risks, then exciting investigations will not happen overnight and both teacher and pupils will experience failure and frustration. Koshy (2001, p.89) discusses three teaching styles that will be used by a confident teacher at appropriate times:

- The first style of teaching is where the teacher imparts knowledge to the class. The children acquire facts and learn skills by going through the correct sequence in the correct order without much interaction through discussion. This could be while instructing the children in the use of a new piece of equipment.
- Secondly, a more interactive teaching style 'will involve some discussion between teacher and pupils and some open ended questioning. A certain amount of negotiation of learning will take place during the teaching sessions. Instruction will include whole-class teaching of problem solving skills and the application of formulae. Children will construct their own understanding from what is said in the classroom and place it in a personalised enclosure of knowledge.'
- In the third style, the teacher takes on the role of a facilitator enabling the learners to 'put forward their own hypotheses, test them and make generalisations.' Koshy stresses that this does not mean 'free, non-directed play which assumes the self-discovery of mathematical ideas.' The teacher provides the necessary work in mathematical processes and sets challenging tasks matched with their level of understanding during which the children use and apply their mathematical knowledge, understanding and skills. Much of this can be taught through teacher questioning, discussion and mutual decision-making.

Similarly O'Sullivan et al. (2005, pp.18–19) believe that children can be 'active learners' of mathematics. 'They need time and space to make links between existing understanding and new learning. This requires their teacher to be fully aware of their existing understanding. Children need to make mistakes and evaluate their strategies in a secure and challenging classroom environment. They need confidence to ask their teachers questions. They need to be aware of what, when and how they are learning.'

McGuinness (1999, pp.19–20) advocates that the teacher should ensure that there is a 'a rich diet of open ended and closed tasks which do not always specify a recognised method, non-routine questions which allow children to take risks and search for meaning, and those with too much or not enough information which encourages critical evaluation'.

Questioning

The use of questioning is crucial in helping children to 'understand mathematical ideas and use mathematical terms'. There are both closed questions where there is either one correct answer as in 'what is five add four?' and open questions where there is a challenge such as 'can you tell me two numbers that add up to nine?' Both have their own use but an open question can be the starting point of an investigation whereas the closed question is mainly for checking facts.

McVarish (2008, p.45) recognized four types of questioning which she described as: verbal worksheets, problem-solving questions, teachable moment questions and information-driven questions.

The first requires only limited thinking from the children, for example what is 4p plus 5p? The last, posed by either the teacher or pupil, simply requires a straightforward answer. In contrast, a 'problem solving' question such as 'How much will it cost for the class to go bowling?' requires a high level of thinking. Similarly a question posed by a pupil, such as 'How many hours are Tescos open on a Sunday?' when seized on by the teacher, as a 'teachable moment' requires higher order thinking skills from those attempting to find an answer.

The problem-solving question will lead to the children making decisions as to how to collect the data, how to organize this and then how to display and interrogate the data. Similarly, the Teachable moment question will require further investigation. 'What are the opening hours on Sunday?' could lead to questions such as 'how are they different from the rest of the week?' and 'who could be questioned to find helpful information?' It is the 'teachable moment' when the opportunity for mathematics could easily be overlooked.

McVarish (2008, p.45) correctly believes that it is in classrooms where the mix of questions are of the nature of problem-solving and teachable moment questions that learning extends 'beyond facts and recall' and requires 'children to think, analyze, posit, wonder and synthesize.'

Praise and rewards

A somewhat overlooked but important aspect of the teacher's role is that of giving praise and rewards to encourage and reward successful learning. It is worth thinking about the statement from Askew and Wiliam (1995, p.18) that 'many studies have found that teachers regarded as more effective than average use *less* praise than their less successful colleagues.'

They believed that 'the quality of praise is at least as important as its quantity' and warn that if 'praise is used infrequently, given, uncritically and without enthusiasm, and expressed in very general terms, then it is at best ineffective and, at worst, can have damaging consequences for pupil learning.'

The reverse applies and too much praise is also meaningless. They identify three important facets to the successful use of praise.

- It must be 'contingent: the praise must depend on some particular thing that the pupil has done rather than the pupil's general performance'.
- It must also be 'specific' so the pupil understands 'what aspect of their work is being singled out'.
- The praise must also be 'credible'. It must be 'sincere; praise that follows a "formula" (i.e. always expressed in the same way) or which sounds insincere is likely to be ineffective, since pupils can "see through such praise very quickly."'

Specific praise during a lesson can also be used as a pointer for other children who are lacking in ideas and direction. The teacher can ask the class to pause in their work, focus on and praise a specific piece of work giving reasons for its success. This would refocus other children and give them ideas and inspiration for their own work.

In conclusion – we are using the work by Csikszentmihalyi (1992) to sum up the messages from this chapter. Recreating his Diagram of 'Flow' to suit the Primary curriculum, a child with appropriate challenge works successfully, a child with inappropriate challenges, is unsuccessful in his/her work. See Figure 1.1.

With low skills and appropriate challenges, a child can make progress and with a continuum of careful planning and teaching matching the child's achievement, can work towards achieving high skills, high challenge and high levels of success.

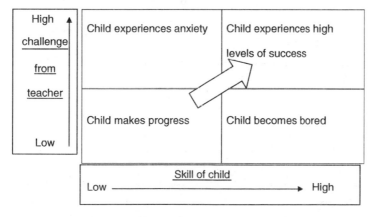

Figure 1.1 An adaptation of 'Flow' by Csikszentmihalyi (1992) to illustrate the importance of matching appropriate challenges to a child's skill level in primary education.

A skilful teacher knows how to plan, assess children's learning, evaluate their teaching and knows how to ensure all the children are included and are comfortable with their work and their classroom setting.

A skilful teacher ensures the match of skill and challenge is suitably balanced thus facilitating learning. The children will question and challenge, make connections and see the relationship between different areas of learning. They will plan, explore, evaluate and have open minds and enjoy the fun and success of their work.

References and further reading

Adhami, M. (2003) 'From lesson objectives to lesson agenda: flexibility in whole – class lesson structure' in Thompson, I. (ed.) *Enhancing Primary Mathematics Teaching* Maidenhead: Open University Press, pp.65–77.

Askew, M., Brown, M., Rhodes, V., Johnson, D. and Wiliam, D. (1997) *Effective Teachers of Numeracy* London: King's College.

Askew, M. and Wiliam, D. (1995) *Recent Research in Mathematics Education 5 – 16.* London: HMSO.

Barefoot Books (1998) *One, Two, Skip a Few! First Number Rhymes* Bristol: Barefoot Books.

Bennett, R. (2006) *Learning ICT with Maths* London: David Fulton.

Black, P., Harrison, Lee, C., Marshal, B. and Wiliam, D. (2002) *Working Inside the Black Box Assessment for Learning in the Classroom* London: NFER Nelson.

Black, P. and Wiliam, D. (1998) *Inside the Black Box: Raising Standards through Classroom Assessment* London: King's College.

Bottle, G. (2005) *Teaching Mathematics in the Primary School* London: Continuum

Briggs, M. (2007) *Creative Teaching: Mathematics in the Early Years & Primary Classroom* London: David Fulton.

Carter, R. (ed.) (1998) *Handbook of Primary Geography* Sheffield: Geographical Association.

Csikszentmihalyi, M. (1992) *Flow, The Psychology of Happiness* London: Rider.

Delaney, K. (2001) 'Teaching Mathematics Resourcefully' in Gates, P. (ed.) *Issues in Mathematics Teaching* London: Routledge Falmer, pp.123–147.

Department for Children, Schools and Families (2007) *The Children's Plan – Building Brighter Futures* London: DCSF Publications.

—Williams, P. (2008a) *Independent Review of Mathematics Teaching in Early Years Settings and Primary Schools Final Report* London: DCSF Publications.

—(2008b) *The Assessment for Learning Strategy* London: DCSF Publications.

—(2008c) *A Commitment from the Children's Plan* London: DCSF Publications.

—(2008d) *Statutory Framework for Early Years Foundation Stage* London: DCSF Publications.

—(2008e) *Developing Assessment for Learning in Mathematics – Classroom Practice into Action* London: DCSF Publications.

—Rose, J. (2009a) *Independent Review of the Primary Curriculum Final Report.* London: DCSF Publications.

—(2009b) *Your Child, Your Schools, Our Future: Building for a 21st Century Schools System* London: DCSF Publications.

Department for Education and Employment (1999a) *The National Curriculum Handbook for Primary Teachers in England* London: DfEE Publications.

—(1999b) *The National Numeracy Strategy: Framework for Teaching Mathematics from Reception to Year 6* London: DfEE Publications.

Department for Education and Skills (2000) *The National Numeracy Strategy Mathematical Vocabulary* London: DfES Publications.

—(2003a) Excellence *and Enjoyment a Strategy for Primary Schools* London: DfES Publications.

—(2003b) *Every Child Matters – Summary* London: DfES Publications.

Donaldson, G. (2002) *Successful Mathematics Leadership in Primary School* Exeter: Learning Matters.

Gardner, M. (1976) *Mathematical Carnival* London: George Allan and Unwin.

Hughes, M. (1986) *Children and Number* Oxford: Blackwell.

Hussey, T. and Smith, P. (2003) 'The uses of learning outcomes' *Teaching in Higher Education* 8(3): 357–368.

Jones, L. and Allebone, B. (2000) 'Differentiation', in Koshy V., Ernest P. and Casey R. (eds) *Mathematics for Primary Teachers* London: Routledge Falmer, pp.196–209.

Koshy, V. (2001) *Teaching Mathematics to Able Children* London: Routledge Falmer.

Lee, C. (2006) *Language for Learning Mathematics Assessment for Learning* Berkshire: Open University Press.

Liebeck, P. (1984) *How Children Learn Mathematics: A Guide for Parents and Teachers* Harmondsworth: Penguin Books Ltd.

McGuinness, C. (1999) Available at: http://www.dfes.gov.uk/research/data/uploadfiles/RB115doc.

McVarish, J. (2008) *Where's the Wonder in Elementary Math?* Abingdon: Routledge.

O'Sullivan, L., Harris A. and Sangster (2005) *Reflective Reader Primary Mathematics* Exeter: Learning Matters.

Oxfam (no date) Available at: http://blogadmin.oxfam.org.uk/coolplanet/teachers/photopps/abphopp.htm.

Qualifications and Curriculum Authority (2003) *Learning to Learn. Key Aspects of Learning across the Curriculum* London: DCSF Publications.

—(2007) *Futures in Action Building a 21st Century Curriculum* London: QCA.

—(2009) *The Assessment for Learning Strategy* London: DCSF Publications.

—http://www.qcda.gov.uk/6169.aspx for details of the government's vision of the 21st Century curriculum.

Qualifications and Curriculum Development Agency [online] Available at: http://www.qcda.gov.uk/8665.aspx [accessed 16/12/09].

Sage, L. (2000) *Bad Blood* London: Fourth Estate.

Scieszka, J. (1995) *Maths Curse* Harmondsworth: Penguin Books Ltd.

Threlfall, J. (1996) 'The role of practical apparatus in the teaching and learning of arithmetic' *Educational Review* 48(1): 3–12.

Waters, M. (2007) Available at: www.qca.org.uk/qca_8665.aspx.

Williams, J. and Easingwood, N. (2003) *ICT and Primary Science* London: Routledge Falmer.

Websites

All website addresses were accessed on 31 July 2009.

Oxfam. Available at: www.oxfam.org.uk.

Becta recognizes that a key feature of ICT is to enhance other curriculum areas and this site provides informed advice. Available at: http://schools.becta.org.uk http://schools.

Overcoming barriers in mathematics – helping children move from level 1 to level 2 Available at: www.nationalstrategies. standards.dcsf.gov.uk/node/165293.

National Curriculum Subject teaching/ICT. Available at: http://curriculum.qca.org.uk/key-stages-1-and-2/learning-across-the-curriculum/ictsubjectteaching/index.aspx.

The statutory inclusion statement and guidance on inclusion in subjects relating to the 1999 National Curriculum programmes of study and attainment targets. Available at: http://curriculum.qca.org.uk/key-stages-1-and-2/inclusion/index.aspxthe.

National Centre for Excellence in the Teaching of Mathematics (NCETM) has an excellent Online Primary Magazine and much, much more. Available at: www.ncetm.org.uk.

Using and Applying Mathematics Across the Primary Curriculum

2

Chapter Outline

Using and applying in mathematics has five themes: communication, reasoning, enquiry, representation and problem solving. In this chapter, we examine the first four of these and the combined contribution they make to successful use and application in mathematics. They each contribute to the success of problem-solving activity, the focus of Chapter 3. As Hardy stated in 1941,

> A mathematician, like a painter or poet, is a maker of patterns. If his patterns are more permanent than theirs, it is because they are made with ideas. (Hardy, 1941, cited in Pickover, 2005, p.142)

Introduction to using and applying mathematics since 1989

In the National Curriculum (NC) (1989), the first Attainment Target (Ma1) was using and applying mathematics. This gave the impression that it was a separate area of mathematics rather than an essential part of all areas of mathematics. Some teachers would have specific, somewhat structured, using and applying lessons, often at the end of a module of work involving one of the other areas of the programme of study.

The NC (1999a) recognized this weakness and placed using and applying mathematics at the beginning of each programme of study. As a result of this, Ma1 as a separate unit disappeared and became part of Ma2 as using and applying number (Key Stages 1 and 2), part of Ma3 as using and applying shape, space and measures (Key Stages 1 and 2) and part of Ma4 as using and applying data handling (Key Stage 2).

The National Numeracy Strategy (NNS) (1999b) did not follow this pattern. Rather, using and applying mathematics became an 'add on' at the end of teaching a particular topic. Using and applying mathematics skills, knowledge and understanding became 'solving problems', namely 'making decisions, reasoning and generalising about numbers and shapes'. Problems involving 'real life', money or measures were very much of a type, with their purpose being to allow children to apply what they had learnt in previous lessons. There tended not to be any connections across the areas of mathematics or with other subjects or life beyond the classroom.

The Primary National Strategy (PNS) (2006a) followed the lead of the *Excellence and Enjoyment* (2003) document and stressed the importance of children being excited and engaged in their learning. One of the aims of this framework gave using and applying mathematics a higher profile and re-established its importance. There is a wide range of supporting materials for teachers, and guidance on the potential for combining mathematics with other subject areas. The five using and applying themes of the PNS: communication, reasoning, enquiry, representation and problem solving, had in-built clear progression.

Recommendation 9 of the Williams Report (DCSF, 2008, p.62) was that part of the forthcoming Rose Review of the Primary Curriculum (2009a) that should examine 'the concept of "use and application" more generally across the subjects, to assess whether the mathematical or other aspects of the curriculum needed mending'. Indeed, the Rose Report (DCSF, 2009a) emphasized the desirability of a blend of high-quality discrete subject teaching and exciting cross-curricular work. Children must have opportunities to use and apply their mathematical skills, knowledge and understanding in both focused mathematics work and in work across the curriculum.

While the White Paper (DCSF, 2009b) removes the expectation that schools will adhere to the structure of the PNS, schools will continue to use and adapt the contents of it in order to further develop excellent teaching and learning and deliver the statutory requirements of the NC. Therefore, the five areas of using and applying mathematics continue to be an absolutely essential component of mathematics in the primary school.

Communicating (see also Chapter 8 – Mathematics and English)

Table 2.1 shows progression within the communicating theme of the using and applying mathematics strand of the PNS from the Foundation Stage to Year 6/7 (DfES, 2006b, p.3).

Table 2.1 Progression within the communicating theme of the using and applying mathematics strand of the PNS from the Foundation Stage to Year 6/7

Foundation	Describe solutions to practical problems, drawing on experience, talking about their own ideas, methods and choices
Year 1	Describe ways of solving puzzles and problems, explaining choices and decisions orally or using pictures
Year 2	Present solutions to puzzles and problems in an organized way; explain decisions, methods and results in pictorial, spoken or written form, using mathematical language and number sentences
Year 3	Describe and explain methods, choices and solutions to puzzles and problems, orally and in writing, using pictures and diagrams
Year 4	Report solutions to puzzles and problems, giving explanations and reasoning orally and in writing, using diagrams and symbols
Year 5	Explain reasoning using diagrams, graphs and text; refine ways of recording using images and symbols
Year 6	Explain reasoning and conclusions, using words, symbols or diagrams as appropriate
Year 6/7	Explain and justify reasoning and conclusions, using notation, symbols and diagrams; find a counter-example to disprove a conjecture; use step-by-step deductions to solve problems involving shapes

Source: DfES *Renewing the Primary Framework for Mathematics Guidance Paper: Using and Applying Mathematics* London: DfES Publications, 2006b, p.3.

Lee (2006, pp.15–16) discusses how the language of mathematics uses words in three categories:

- *'words that have the same meaning in everyday language as they do in ordinary English* – the words that are used to set mathematics in context
- *words that have a meaning only in mathematical language* – hypotenuse, isosceles, coefficient, graph, take moments
- *words that have different meanings in mathematical language and natural language* – difference, odd, mean, volume, value, integrate'.

It is important to recognize these three categories, as language can be a considerable barrier to children's learning, whether it is their ability to communicate with their peers or the teacher's ability to communicate with them. Pratt (2006, p.2) recognized the importance of communication as 'learning fundamentally involves people communicating about ideas with one another'. The skills of communication identified in the NC (2000) were listed as those of speaking and listening and reading and writing. To this, we would add the many forms of illustrating.

Hymer and Michel (2002) looked at the importance of discussion and questioning where teachers and learners were 'provided with the opportunity to make balanced judgements and exercise careful, discerning choices. To do that there is a need for all members of the class to feel emotionally safe. This is only possible within a climate of mutual respect where the students feel there are fair boundaries that create social order.' There must be opportunities for children to

- work in a variety of ways including collaboratively and autonomously;
- plan and organize work;
- learn the language of emotions and thinking;
- be creative;
- make choices about their learning. (Hymer and Michel 2002, p.56)

Too often the emphasis is placed on communication between child and teacher. However, children need to understand the importance of communicating for themselves such as jotting down key information in a problem that they can return to. They need to communicate with their peers while discussing strategies required for an investigation, and have the confidence to involve a wider audience of both adults and children in such an environment. Billington et al. (1993, p.40) recognized that 'when children are encouraged to work collaboratively on mathematical activities, they discuss and share their ideas; they talk more freely and increase their language proficiency; they take greater risks in posing questions; they develop better strategies; they support one another in their learning. Moreover children working in this way are more likely to openly express doubts about their understanding.'

They also stressed that 'language learning is a never-ending process. Children of all ages need support for meaning, through doing, observing and sharing.' In such a climate of collaborative discussion, children will initiate conversations with adults as well as with their classmates'.

It is important not to overlook opportunities for children to discuss their mathematics with visitors, such as governors, to the school. We have a clear memory of a Year 6 girl, unaware that she was talking to one of Her Majesty's Inspectors (HMI), who at the time was overseeing primary mathematics in England, carefully explaining the intricacies of Egyptian multiplication to her.

The NNS Mathematical Vocabulary Book (DfEE, 1999c, p.4) reminds us of the importance of the use of a wide range of mathematical vocabulary and advocates 'a structured approach to the teaching and learning of vocabulary'. New words should be introduced in context and in practical situations. These words should be used repeatedly in discussions, and the teachers should phrase questions to encourage their use. Having the correct vocabulary enables children to put their reasoning into words efficiently and accurately.

The importance of questioning in the understanding of mathematical ideas is of paramount importance. The Mathematical Vocabulary Book (DfEE, 1999c, pp.4–6) lists the different types of questions used by teachers as follows:

- To recall facts – how many fours are there in sixteen?
- To apply facts – what unit would you use to measure this milk?
- To hypothesize or predict – about how many buttons are there in the jar?

- To design and compare procedures – how would you add 99 to 45?
- To interpret results – which is the most common eye colour?
- To apply reason – how do you know that it is an isosceles triangle?

Teachers should use a combination of both open and closed questions. Closed questions, such as *what is 4p add 1p* have only one correct answer. Open questions, such as *how many ways can you make 5p using different coins* have more than one answer and provide more of a challenge as children think of different answers according to their ability.

Reasoning

Table 2.2 shows progression within the reasoning theme of the using and applying mathematics strand of the PNS from the Foundation Stage to Year 6/7 (DfES, 2006b, p.3).

The NC (DfEE, 1999a, p.22) recognized that the skills of reasoning 'enabled pupils to give reasons for opinions and actions, to draw inferences and make deductions, to use precise language to explain what they think and to make judgements and decisions informed by reasons or evidence'.

The Guidance Paper (DfES, 2006b, p.11) asserted that 'reasoning involves some understanding of "logical rules": knowing what and when things are the same or different; recognising what equivalence means and how to express, for example, equivalent number sentences or

Table 2.2 Progression within the reasoning theme of the using and applying mathematics strand of the PNS from the Foundation Stage to Year 6/7

Foundation	Talk about, recognize and recreate simple patterns
Year 1	Describe simple patterns and relationships involving numbers or shapes; decide whether examples satisfy given conditions
Year 2	Describe patterns and relationships involving numbers or shapes; make predictions and test these with examples
Year 3	Use patterns and relationships involving numbers or shapes, and use these to solve problems
Year 4	Identify and use patterns, relationships and properties of numbers or shapes; investigate a statement involving numbers and test it with examples
Year 5	Explore patterns, properties and relationships, and propose a general statement involving numbers or shapes; identify examples for which the statement is true or false
Year 6	Represent and interpret sequences, patterns and relationships involving numbers and shapes; suggest and test hypotheses; construct and use simple expressions and formulae in words then symbols (e.g. the cost of c pens at 15 pence each is 15c test pence)
Year 6/7	Generate sequences and describe the general term; use letters and symbols to represent unknown numbers or variables; represent simple relationships as graphs

Source: DfES, *Renewing the Primary Framework for Mathematics Guidance Paper: Using and Applying Mathematics* London: DfES Publications, 2006b, p.3.

calculations.' It also involves understanding implication so that children recognize that the 'multiples of 6 are also multiples of 2 and 3 or a quadrilateral with four right angles means its opposite sides are equal'.

The Guidance Paper (DfES, 2006b, p.11) further reminded us that children need to be taught how to reason. 'Children are often too quick to make assumptions about what they *think* they see rather than critically appraise the information, context and situations they are *given*. Children need to be taught how to record their thinking and reasoning in mathematics as they describe, replicate and create patterns and explore properties and relationships. These skills of recording, using objects, pictures, numbers or shapes, help children to see what *is* and begin to consider what *might be*. They help children to clarify what is the same and what is different. They help children to collect evidence when testing general statements or to predict and propose new hypotheses.'

There can be too much emphasis on recording. Initially what children need to do is to verbalize their reasoning, again the use of groups or pairs is useful. Children need to talk about what they are doing and then modify their thinking in the light of questions and ideas the teacher and other children raise. This highlights the importance of plenaries where the whole class comes together to discuss problems and possible solutions in a supportive environment.

The ability to reason is closely linked to being able to make the connections that Askew et al. (1997) identified as being so important. So, for example, the teacher, introducing the concepts of addition and subtraction (or multiplication and division) together, as opposed to separate areas of learning, is helping to establish those connections. From the foundation stage these connections can be made: if plastic ducks can fly into a bowl, they can equally well fly out again!

A classroom that embraces the ethos, 'it's ok to be wrong' is essential. It is crucial that children are given the opportunity to explain their reasoning and that they are not left feeling they've 'got it wrong'. However, as children get older they need to be made aware that while the answer they have given is eminently sensible it may not be what the author of the problem had intended.

The result of a teacher modelling their own reasoning can also be highly beneficial for children. A way to achieve this naturally is to introduce some activities and investigations to which the answer is genuinely not known. This way the teacher and children model their reasoning together. With young children, a puppet can replace the teacher. If the puppet needs 'help', this focuses attention away from a child's misconceptions while the class works together to help the puppet to sort himself out. It is also good fun.

The PNS also stressed the importance of children having access to the correct mathematical vocabulary and language so that they are able to share their reasoning with others. Unfortunately, 'most lessons do not emphasise mathematical talk enough; as a result, pupils struggle to express and develop their thinking' (DCSF, 2008, p.5).

Du Sautoy (2008, p.96) reminds us that 'a mathematician is a pattern searcher'. It is important that opportunities are made for very young children to experience and make sense of pattern using practical resources such as coloured beads on a string. The initial challenge for young children is to copy simple patterns. Here an adult helper can ask questions like, 'how did you know you needed to put the red bead next?' The next stage is to ask the children to extend the pattern, supporting with questions might be, what comes next? If this is followed by the requirement for children to explain *why* they have decided a red bead comes next, then they are building strong foundations for the number and algebraic patterns that follow. The search for pattern is an automatic human response (psychologists refer to this as 'gestalt') and like all such responses need to be used frequently and developed to its full potential.

The creation of patterns by the children is an area sometimes overlooked with an emphasis on work with existing patterns. The child can create the pattern for someone else to work out and then continue.

Later, pattern work moves away from attributes such as colour, size and shape and towards number, although initially it should have a concrete representation of some sort. The teacher must however be aware that a young child who can extend sequences of numbers such as 2, 4, 6, 8, might just remember the sequence without actually understanding its relevance in a particular activity. A well-known example of this is the child who successfully colours in a hundred square showing the two times table by concentrating solely on the striped pattern created and not the underlying mathematics.

An interesting example combining both resources and number pattern is provided by tins of beans that are stacked as shown below creating a triangular number sequence. See Figure 2.1.

Questions that follow might be:

If there are 5 tins on the bottom layer, how many tins will there be in the stack?
Can you explain the pattern?
What if there were 8 tins on the bottom layer?
Older children can be challenged further:
What if I told you there were 55 tins in the stack, could you tell me how many tins there would be in the bottom layer?
If we write the total number of cans in each stack, what is special about these numbers? (You are introducing triangular numbers.)

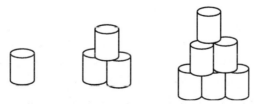

Figure 2.1 Pattern of baked bean tin stacking.

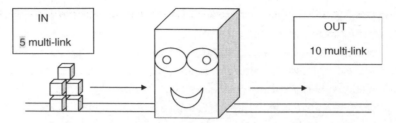

Figure 2.2 Cardboard box function machine.

Number pattern work can be developed with the use of a Function Machine, either of the cardboard box variety or from a computer program such as Ambleweb Function Machine. The Robot requires a hole at the back through which the teacher can add multi-link as the 'conveyor belt holding the multilink passes through the robotic Function Machine'. See Figure 2.2.

What happened to the multi-link in the Robot? The children will give different answers, 5 was added or the number was doubled. Both are potentially correct, so the procedure has to be repeated. This time 3 multi-link went in and 6 came out, then 4 went in and 8 came out. Clearly the number was doubled.

This home-made piece of equipment was one of the most frequently borrowed by students who also used it creatively in other mathematical areas such as with 2-D and 3-D shapes – in went a square and out came a cube, in went a triangle and out came a triangular prism. What was the function of the Robot? He was also used in Literacy for plurals, prefixes etc.

Enquiring

Table 2.3 shows progression within the enquiring theme of the using and applying mathematics strand of the PNS from the Foundation Stage to Year 6/7 (DfES, 2006b, p.3).

The NC (DfEE, 1999a, p.22) recognized that the skills of enquiry 'enable pupils to ask relevant questions, to pose and define problems, to plan what to do and how to research, to predict outcomes and anticipate responses, to test conclusions and improve ideas'.

This theme in the using and applying mathematics strand involves children in being able to plan, make decisions, organize work, justify and interpret results and give reasons for their conclusions. The questions and line of enquiry ideally will have come from the children, but may also be presented by the teacher. Through discussion, uncertainties can be resolved and new lines of enquiry developed.

These may well be drawn from any of the other strands and, depending on the questions, involve varying degrees of independent decision making and reasoning. What is important is that the children can formulate a line of enquiry to support their work and show how they arrived at this working plan and how they could follow it through. The teacher has a crucial role here in helping the children to pose questions, select relevant information and make decisions and decide on a fruitful line of enquiry.

Table 2.3 Progression within the enquiring theme of the using and applying mathematics strand of the PNS from the Foundation Stage to Year 6/7

Foundation	Sort objects, making choices and justifying decisions
Year 1	Answer a question by selecting and using suitable equipment, and sorting information, shapes or objects; display results using tables and pictures
Year 2	Follow a line of enquiry; answer questions by choosing and using suitable equipment and selecting, organizing and presenting information in lists, tables and simple diagrams
Year 3	Follow a line of enquiry by deciding what information is important; make and use lists, tables and graphs to organize and interpret the information
Year 4	Suggest a line of enquiry and the strategy needed to follow it; collect, organize and interpret selected information to find answers
Year 5	Plan and pursue an enquiry; present evidence by collecting, organizing and interpreting information; suggest extensions to the enquiry
Year 6	Suggest, plan and develop lines of enquiry; collect, organize and represent information, interpret results and review methods; identify and answer related questions
Year 6/7	Develop and evaluate lines of enquiry; identify, collect, organize and analyse relevant information; decide how best to represent conclusions and what further questions to ask.

Source: DfES, *Renewing the Primary Framework for Mathematics Guidance Paper: Using and Applying Mathematics* London: DfES Publications, 2006b, p.3.

It is quite possible for young children to formulate questions they want to know the answers to. It can be helpful to use the K-W-L technique.

What do I *Know*?	(What is the pupils' prior knowledge).
What do I *Want* to know?	(The pupils set their learning goals).
What have I *Learnt*?	(The pupils reflect on their learning and look forward to the next challenge).

An illustration of such an open line of enquiry is of a child investigating the addition of odd and even numbers. The child

- knows the number names of the odd and even numbers and that in a two or three digit number, it is the unit digit that determines whether a number is odd or even
- wants to discover what happens to the results of addition of two numbers
- learns that even + even = even; even + odd = odd; odd + odd = even

The child can then investigate further to find out why this is always the case.

Interestingly, an identical investigation is discussed by Ofsted (2009, p.9), however its example was regarded as a 'pseudo-investigation' as the teacher had cut corners and had already identified the rule for the class to confirm thus creating a closed question. 'Does odd minus odd give an odd or even answer?' This 'meant that pupils never engaged with the possibility that there might be no consistent rule' thus limiting the scope of the investigation.

Very often, if a child identifies one thing that appears to be related in some way to the question, then he has gained entry to the problem. It may be that this piece of information is not relevant in the long run but simply provides a starting point. Having thought about everything he knows, he can then begin to ask the question, 'what do I want to know?' This may well be with the help of the teacher initially. Charts, graphs, diagrams and lists can be employed to help in the organization of information and to help with the organization and interpretation of this information. Finally having either reached a solution or reached the point where no further progress is possible it is important to think about and discuss what has been learnt. This often surprises children, particularly when they have failed to reach a full solution. This reflection may give rise to further questions or it may simply give rise to the feeling that time has not been wasted and that a degree of success has been achieved.

Let us consider a geographical topic on the environment and rubbish, and questions posed by the children. *What do the children in our class throw away?* is relatively easy to answer. *How much of each thing do we throw away each week?* takes longer but gives rise to considerable potential in mathematical terms, while *what does the Queen do with her rubbish?* is probably outside the scope of most classrooms although a solution might be sought through input in a literacy lesson with a well-written letter.

Children, if they are used to using and applying their mathematics, will quickly find questions that are readily answered, those that are difficult to answer and those that are impossible to answer given the tools available to them.

Representing

Table 2.4 shows progression within the representing theme of using and applying mathematics strand of the PNS from the Foundation Stage to Year 6/7 (DfES, 2006b, p.3).

Mathematical ideas can be represented with words, pictures, photographs, objects and symbols. They can be regarded as the 'working tools' (DfES, 2006b, p.8) of problem-solving activity through which the children move from the 'real world' into the 'mathematical world'; with the help of calculations, diagrams, jottings or graphs that they understand. These are then used to find a mathematical solution to the problem.

The children *model* the problem in mathematical terms, solve the problem and then use reasoning to return to the real world. Older children also need to be able to make predictions, estimations and hypotheses.

Children may model in many different ways but need to be encouraged to develop effective strategies for this. This could be through teaching sessions where the children develop their own mathematical models based on real-life situations they have observed.

The chart taken from the *Guidance Paper: Using and Applying* (DfES, 2006b, p.9) clearly shows the movement from the 'real world' to the 'mathematical world' from the initial recognition of a problem, the decisions about how to present and use the available information, the problem-solving activity and then the arrival at a solution. See Figure 2.3.

Table 2.4 Progression within the representing theme of using and applying mathematics strand of the PNS from the Foundation Stage to Year 6/7

Foundation	Match sets of objects to numerals that represent the number of objects
Year 1	Describe a puzzle or problem using numbers, practical materials and diagrams; use these to solve the problem and set the solution in the original context
Year 2	Identify and record the information or calculation needed to solve a puzzle or problem; carry out the steps or calculations and check the solution in the context of the problem
Year 3	Represent the information in a puzzle or problem using numbers, images or diagrams; use these to find a solution and present it in context, where appropriate using £.p notation or units of measure
Year 4	Represent a puzzle or problem using number sentences, statements or diagrams; use these to solve the problem; present and interpret the solution in the context of the problem
Year 5	Represent a puzzle or problem by identifying and recording the information or calculations needed to solve it; find possible solutions and confirm them in the context of the problem
Year 6	Tabulate systematically the information in a puzzle or problem; identify and record the steps or calculations needed to solve it, using symbols where appropriate; interpret solutions in the original context and check their accuracy
Year 6/7	Represent information or unknown numbers in a problem, for example in a table, formula or equation; explain solutions in the context of the problem

Source: DfES, *Renewing the Primary Framework for Mathematics Guidance Paper: Using and Applying Mathematics* London: DfES Publications, 2006b, p.3.

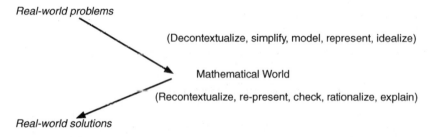

Figure 2.3 Mathematical problem solving moving between the real world and the mathematical world. (Taken from DfES 2006b, p.9).

Children seem able to solve calculations such as 112 ÷ 8 but struggle when presented with a real-life problem such as how many tables for 8 can you set with 112 beakers? Indeed this has been a concern of Ofsted and was also identified in the Williams (DCSF, 2008, p.69) in that while mathematics taught in schools was 'age appropriate', the lack of opportunities to apply and use mathematics meant that when 'faced with real-life mathematical problems' children did not know what to do.

This is in direct contrast to the research findings of Nunes and Bryant (1996) in Brazil who discovered that street children were able to solve problems in the real world but struggled when given formal written calculations to solve.

It could be thought that there was a basic problem with what the PNS called a 'real world' problem in that is contrived and patently so. It is difficult to reconcile the phrase 'real world' with the parentheses that suggest it is only 'pretend' real world.

If there are 15 boys and 13 girls in the class, how many exercise books will the teacher need if each child uses 2 a term? This is classed as a 'real world' problem but is really just a word problem. Compare this with:

What is the best way to cut the cardboard sheets (to save wastage) so that each member of the class has a calendar base the same size as A4 paper?

At the beginning of December, that is a real problem to be solved involving an understanding of area, scale and the measurement of length with the need to record information and find solutions.

Lee (2006, p.15) notes that, ' "real world" problems are introduced in order to demonstrate that mathematics is accessible, real and tangible. However, the power of mathematical ideas is that they are abstract and not contextual and it will help pupils if they become aware of this.' Children may be given access to 'real world' problems that use real data or they maybe given 'word problems' that may appear to be 'real' but in fact result in children bringing in their own experiences.

Of course there is a place for word problems but working in a creative and cross-curricular manner presents many opportunities to use *real* problems that *really* need solving. Alternatively, make use of pure mathematical problems to solve for the sheer enjoyment of the beauty of mathematics.

How to develop mathematical work that gives children the opportunity to use and apply their mathematical knowledge, skills and understanding

Billington et al. (1993) divided using and applying mathematics into three distinct areas: practical tasks, real-life problems and investigating within mathematics itself. This is a useful distinction as it suggests guidance on how and where teachers might best embed using and applying mathematics within each of the stands.

- *Practical tasks.* The strands of understanding shape and space and measures provide many opportunities for embedding using and applying mathematics through practical tasks. For example making beds from Lego for the three bears or designing and constructing a scale model of the Parthenon would combine a practical task with the opportunity to use and apply mathematical work such as the understanding of the attributes of 3-D shapes, scale and measurement.

- *Real-life problems.* Halving or doubling a recipe prior to baking at school is necessary mathematical work without which there would be too many or too few cakes.
- *Investigating within mathematics itself.* Using magic squares as a starting point for a lesson that focuses on the skills of 'Knowing and using number facts' clearly fits the bill for an investigation within mathematics itself.

Teaching style

The preference of the teaching style of the teacher has relevance to the successful problem solving of the children. Askew et al. (1997, p.24) make distinctions between the beliefs that teachers hold as follows:

Connectionist: numeracy teaching is based on dialogue between teacher and pupils to explore understandings. Being numerate involves being 'both efficient and effective'. The links between the different areas of mathematics are important and should be made explicit and misconceptions should be recognized and discussed during lessons, thus improving understanding.

Transmission: numeracy teaching is based on verbal explanations so that pupils understand teachers' methods. Problem solving follows after learning these ways of working. Great emphasis is given to the use of paper and pencil methods of working and recording, sometimes at the expense of efficiency of working.

Discovery: numeracy teaching is based on practical activities so that pupils discover methods for themselves. 'Whether or not the method is particularly effective or efficient it is not perceived as important' (Askew et al. 1997, p.29). See Table 2.5.

The NNS (1999) encouraged transmission teaching. The three-part lesson focused on whole-class oral work and mental calculation, followed by a main teaching activity which included direct whole-class teaching, and ended with a whole-class plenary. Emphasis was placed on learning tables and number bonds, practicing different mental calculation strategies before embarking on lengthy expanded methods of calculation. Each year was split into three terms with a strict timetable of topics for each tem. The number of days for each topic was limited and topics were revisited on a regular basis. This highly structured method of teaching primary mathematics on a daily basis led, in some instances, to a rise in standards. However, for many schools the strict guidelines left teachers feeling that maths was being taught in a vacuum even though advice *not* to do this was included within the NNS.

Table 2.5 Summary of the three main teaching styles

Teaching style	Application
Connectionist	Approached through challenges that need to be reasoned about
Transmission	Approached through 'word' problems: contexts for calculating routines
Discovery	Approached through using practical equipment

Source: Adapted from Askew et al. *Effective Teachers of Numeracy* London: King's College London, 1997, p 32.

Prior to the NNS (1999b) many primary schools embraced topic work where maths could be linked, should the theme be suitable, or taught, often by transmission methods, at another point in the week when it was not. Some schools chose to let all children work at their own pace, either from textbooks, work books or work-cards. Other classrooms embraced the idea of discovery mathematics where topics were introduced through a series of investigations and children were left to work at the important parts for themselves. Askew et al. (1997) found that the most effective teachers were those who used a connectionist approach. These teachers believed that it was important to make connections between different areas of mathematics and between mathematics in the same area. They emphasized the importance of developing mental calculation strategies, as did the NNS, and they also recognized the importance of questioning to enable children to verbalize their own reasoning and to draw out misconceptions. They also used approaches that encouraged discussion, in whole classes, small groups or with individual pupils. This is an active form of learning with new ideas being based on and developed from existing understanding.

The PNS (2006) offers teachers a less prescriptive framework. In many ways it attempts to keep many of the features of the NNS (1999b) and as Askew et al. (1997) discovered, we would be unwise to lose some of these, for example, mental calculation skills and effective and efficient methods for calculating. However, in contrast to the NNS (1999b), it does encourage a more connectionist approach. Lessons are planned within blocks, across different areas of mathematics and teachers are encouraged to embed mathematics within other curriculum areas. The importance of using and applying mathematics allows plenty of scope for discovery mathematics albeit with a teacher who has a clear understanding of his or her role to promote discussion, identify misconceptions and provide stimulating and appropriate activities and tasks.

Therefore, by way of a summary, using and applying mathematics needs to be embedded within the teaching and learning of mathematics and as such must be an integral part of the planning and assessing processes (Williams 2008, Rose 2009a). Children need to see how they can use what they have already learnt and know how this can then be adapted and extended in new situations, 'combined into "chained links" of calculations, decisions, reasoning and communication' (DfES, 2006b, p.8). There should be opportunities in all mathematics, be it the main thrust of the lesson or a brief part of the plenary for children to use and apply their mathematical skills, knowledge and understanding in new ways.

References and further reading

Askew, M., Brown, M., Rhodes, V., Johnson, D. and Wiliam, D. (1997) *Effective Teachers of Numeracy* London: King's College London.

Backhouse, J., Haggarty, L. and Stratton, J. (1992) *Improving the Learning of Mathematics* Portsmouth: Heinemann.

Billington, J., Fowler, N., MacKernan, J., Smith, J., Stratton, J. and Watson, A. (1993) *Using and Applying Mathematics* Nottingham: ATM.

Department for Children, Schools and Families Williams, P. (2008) *Independent Review of Mathematics Teaching in Early Years Settings and Primary Schools Final Report* London: DCSF Publications.

—Rose, J. (2009a) Report *Independent Review of the Primary Curriculum: Final Report* London: DCSF Publications.

—(2009b) White Paper *Your Child, Your Schools, Our Future: Building a 21st Century Schools System* London: DCSF Publications.

Department for Education and Employment (1999a) *The National Curriculum Handbook for Primary Teachers in England* London: DfEE Publications.

—(1999b) *The National Numeracy Strategy: Framework for Teaching* London: DfEE Publications.

—(1999c) *The National Numeracy Strategy Mathematical Vocabulary* London: DfEE Publications.

—(2000) *The National Curriculum Handbook for Primary Teachers in England* London: DfEE Publications.

Department for Education and Skills (2003) *Excellence and Enjoyment a Strategy for Primary Schools* London: DfES Publications.

—(2006a) *Primary National Strategy: Primary Framework for Literacy and Mathematics London: Department for Education and Skills* London: DfES Publications.

—(2006b) *Renewing the Primary Framework for Mathematics Guidance Paper. Using and Applying Mathematics* London: DfES Publications.

Du Sautoy, M. (2008) *Finding Moonshine: A Mathematician's Journey Through Symmetry* London: HarperCollins.

Fisher, R. (2005) (2nd edn) *Teaching Children to Think* Cheltenham: Nelson Thornes Ltd.

Hymer, B. and Michel, D. (2002) *Gifted and Talented Learners: Creating a Policy for Inclusion* London: David Fulton.

Lee, C. (2006) *Language for Learning Mathematics* Berkshire: Open University Press.

Nunes, T. and Bryant, P. (1996) *Children Doing Mathematics* Oxford: Blackwell.

Ofsted (2009) *Mathematics: Understanding the Score. Improving Practice in Mathematics Teaching at Primary Level* London: Ofsted.

Pickover, C. A. (2005) *A Passion for Mathematics* New Jersey: John Wiley & Sons.

Pratt, N. (2006) *Interactive Maths Teaching in the Primary School* London: Paul Chapman Publishing.

Websites

All website addresses were accessed on 31 July 2009.

Guidance Paper: Using and Applying Mathematics. Available at: http://nationalstrategies.standards.dcsf.gov.uk/node/47324.

Function Machine Available at: http://www.amblesideprimary.com/ambleweb/mentalmaths/functionmachines.html.

Teaching Problem Solving

In this chapter we examine problem solving within mathematics itself. We will consider different types of problems, how they might be accessed by children and how teachers can create exciting lessons full of mathematical talk and positive emotions.

A teacher of mathematics has a great opportunity. If he fills his allotted time with drilling his students in routine operations he kills their interest, hampers their intellectual development, and misses his opportunity. But if he challenges the curiosity of his students by setting them problems proportionate to their knowledge, and helps them to solve their problems with stimulating questions, he may give them a taste for, and some means of, independent thinking. Polya (1945, p.19)

Introduction to problem solving

We believe that this statement by Polya is just as true today. The Guidance Paper (DfES, 2006b, p.9) states that 'solving problems lies at the heart of mathematics', and that it should be 'integrated into mathematics teaching and learning'. This is something few would argue with. As with using and applying mathematics detailed in Chapter 2, problem-solving work enables children to use their key skills, together with mathematical knowledge and understanding, while they explore ideas, pursue lines of enquiry, identify patterns, estimate, order, compare and recognize attributes. They must then communicate all this in language, using diagrams, mathematical symbols and ICT.

What exactly is a problem? This question is answered well by Sakshaug et al. (2002, p.vi) who state that it is a 'task that required the learner to reason through a situation that will be challenging but not impossible. With the problem there is a hurdle that the learner cannot immediately see how to get over or round.' In order to solve a problem a child must be challenged to make decisions about which strategies to use.

In the PNS, progression within the problem-solving theme highlights the 'increasing complexity of the problems the children tackle as they move from one-step to multi-step problems and begin to meet those problems that are more complex and where less routine approaches are needed to solve them'. See Table 3.1.

Table 3.1 Progression within the solving problems theme of using and applying mathematics strand of the PNS from the Foundation Stage to Year 6/7

Foundation stage	Use developing mathematical, ideas and methods to solve practical problems
Year 1	Solve problems involving counting, adding, subtracting, doubling or halving in the context of numbers, measures or money, for example to 'pay' and 'give change'
Year 2	Solve problems involving addition, subtraction, multiplication or division in contexts of numbers, measures or pounds and pence
Year 3	Solve one-step and two-step problems involving numbers, money or measures, including time, choosing and carrying out appropriate calculations
Year 4	Solve one-step and two-step problems involving numbers, money or measures, including time; choose and carry out appropriate calculations, using calculator methods where appropriate
Year 5	Solve one-step and two-step problems involving whole numbers and decimals and all four operations, choosing and using appropriate calculation strategies, including calculator use
Year 6	Solve multi-step problems, and problems involving fractions, decimals and percentages; choose and use appropriate calculation strategies at each stage, including calculator use
Year 6/7	Solve problems by breaking down complex calculations into simpler steps, choose and use operations and calculation strategies appropriate to the numbers and context; try alternative approaches to overcome difficulties; present, interpret and compare solutions

Source: DfES, *Renewing the Primary Framework for Mathematics Guidance Paper Using and Applying Mathematics* [Online]. Available at: nationalstrategies.standards.dcsf.gov.uk/downloader/e5f49e2d5663a1412acbc1d96623fe00.rtf (accessed on 31/07/09), 2006b, p.4.

The whole concept of problem-solving challenges elements of a traditional linear approach to teaching and learning. An approach that starts with one-step problems, then moves on to two-step problems and so on appears limited in that it does not help children decide on an appropriate strategy when faced with a new problem.

If we believe that mathematicians are problem solvers, and as teachers we want our children to be mathematicians, then we need to encourage our children to solve problems in their own way. Furthermore, we need to develop an environment, where children learn to think creatively and critically within a social framework. It is neither sufficient, nor desirable, to limit children's experience of problem solving to sets of word problems in order to assess whether they can apply skills learnt in previous lessons. Developing children's creativity in problem solving and encouraging them to think mathematically requires an appropriate learning environment to be established and nurtured by the teacher. This environment needs to include rich tasks and activities and the freedom for children to explore those activities so that they become confident, competent and creative problem solvers. It should also be a safe environment where children are not afraid to 'have a go' and possibly make mistakes.

Problem solving includes the skills of identifying and understanding the problem, planning ways to solve a problem, monitoring progress as the problem is tackled and then reviewing a solution to a problem. There could also be the potential for the child thinking about 'what next?'

Sakshaug et al. (2002, p.vi). describe the mathematical problem-solving experience as something that 'encompasses the acts of exploring, reasoning, strategising, estimating, conjecturing, testing, explaining and proving. It is a very active process for those involved. Through the problem solving, we are challenged to think beyond the point where we were when we started, we are challenged to think differently. We are challenged to extend our thinking about a situation in a way that is new or different.'

The process of problem solving

Mason et al. (1982) and Burton (1984) defined problem solving as a cyclical process with key phases of Entry, Attack and Review. Entry was considered the critical stage so that it was essential for the problem to be appropriate and accessible. It was at this point that the child was working out what needed to be done and how they would do it. Attack involved finding a way of solving the problem. This did not happen immediately as questions needed to be posed and a way of working organized. During Review, the child assessed the success of the work, the working out and the end result. As problem solving is a continuous process, there may well have been a new question to be answered as a result of the work leading to an extension activity.

Consider the following problem:

Tom and Mary make the same number of toffee apples to sell at the school fair. Tom charges 10 per cent more for his toffee apples but sells 10 per cent fewer. Who raises the more money, Tom or Mary?

In order to gain Entry to this problem a number of questions may arise for the child:

- can I read the question?
- can I understand what the question is asking me to find out?
- do I have the mathematical knowledge (in this case, a good understanding of percentages is required) to use and apply to this problem?
- if I respond negatively to any of the above do I need additional support to go forward?
- if I'm working as part of a group can other children help by reading this problem for me, we might discuss and agree on what this problem requires us to find out. However, if I have no understanding of percentages then I am likely to gain little from working through this problem and may well remain stuck.
- if I have overcome the described obstacles, I might still feel stuck and writing this down can help. At this point I either have to persist or ask for help if I am to move forward.

Whether part of a group or on my own, or with a prompt from the teacher I can start to Attack this problem if I decide to simplify it as follows:

I decided that Mary made 10 apples that she sells for 50p each. From there I can work out how many apples Tom sells (9), how much he sells them for (55p each), work out how much money they each make (Mary £5.00, Tom £4.95) and who makes the most.

It is now time to Review what I have done so far. I've found an answer but is it correct and will it still be correct if the numbers I choose change? In other words, can I generalize? At this point I need to re-enter the problem. Even if I do succeed and find a general solution that I can explain and justify, I can still look for ways to extend the problem further. What if there were three children instead of two? What if toffee apples and candyfloss were for sale? What if the percentages changed from 10 to 15 per cent?

Teaching the skills and strategies of problem solving

These skills and strategies cannot be just 'picked up' in class. Teachers need to teach them and on occasions lead specific problem-solving lessons with a focus on lines of enquiry and approaches.

The children need to know:

- how to use pictures, lists, tables, graphs and diagrams to represent a problem;
- how to organize and interpret any information they collect;
- how to skim read to find information and make brief notes as opposed to copying chunks of information;
- how to recognize the clue words in word problems and not be side tracked by superfluous information;

- how to try to solve a problem by using the structure of a similar but simpler problem;
- how to organize the results in a helpful order, but not necessarily the order of discovery;
- how to use the results to find whether there is a meaningful pattern (or not);
- how to appraise the work and think of a different approach if necessary;
- how to think of an extension or associated activity;
- how to check work and test hypotheses;
- how to present work for others;
- how to communicate the work effectively to others.

Problem posing

Problem Posing and Problem Solving are inextricably linked. Posing problems can be empowering for learners as they themselves decide the questions to be solved, thus removing the assumption that there is only one way to solve a problem and only one right answer. Brown and Walter (2005, p.5) suggest that this might provide 'the beginnings of a mechanism for confronting the rather widespread feelings of mathematical anxiety'. This approach, added to the use of the entry, attack, review and extend structure outlined earlier in this chapter provides a range of strategies which can be used by the teacher. 'Once learners feel less apprehensive, they are likely to be motivated to attempt new problems.' Understanding that there are many ways to work through a problem, and that it is the process rather than the answer that is important, increases these more positive feelings. Self assessment, with the learner reflecting on what they have learnt rather than what they have got wrong, provides a further boost to self esteem.

Brown and Walter (2005, p.126) remind us that solving a problem frequently leads to problem posing. They also make the point that 'the act of problem solving requires some reformulation of the original problem that is essentially a problem generating activity'. Thus learners who feel confident in generating their own problems are likely to feel confident and be confident in asking, of themselves and others, questions about someone else's problem. They suggest the first phase of problem posing is that of 'Accepting'. That is, while an obvious question has been presented for solution, there are often many more questions that *could* be asked. They gave an example of a standard, square, five-by-five geo-board. The first question they asked simply required the student to make a number of different shapes on the board. They then suggested harder questions that might include finding the area of the shapes created, finding the shape given the number of nails, both initial and on the boundary, and also finding the total number of non-congruent squares on such a board (Brown and Walter, 2005, pp.22–23).

Starting with answers can be part of mental and oral starters. The answer is 20, what might the question be? Numbers can be varied to suit the ability of the children. So the question could be adapted to 'using only addition and subtraction if the answer is 20 what might the question be?' To encourage a range of answers, the children can be asked to try and find a total number of different questions that corresponds to the number of children in the class. Initially give them a few minutes (this decreases with time) to come up with as many possible. Starting with less able children and working towards the more able allows for plenty of differentiation by outcome. All the answers can be written on the board and note how less able children come up with 'new ideas' as the feedback progresses.

Rather than just giving an answer, an equation might be given. For example, $6 + 4 = 10$. The children are then required to tell a number story from it. For example, 'If I have 6 mice and my friend gives me another 4, then I have a total of 10 mice.

Teachers need to be aware that although children really enjoy generating this type of question, there will sometimes be the need to step in and ask for a change of variable. (After five children choose animals and the acquisition of additional animals, it is time for a change!)

The second phase suggested by Brown and Walter (2005, p.33) is that of 'what – if-not'. This approach suggests that the child begins by examining the attributes in a situation and then considering the case where these attributes are false or altered. For example, the geo-board in the problem on the previous page is square and finite in size. However, if the board is neither square nor finite then a new range of possibilities are opened up. (In this case the geo-board is a concrete material; however other starting points may be used in a similar way.)

Take the case of this problem: Find the area of a square with sides of 10 cm.

Now consider the following:

> What if the sides were not 10 cm?
> What if the given variable was not the length of the sides?
> What if the shape was not a square?
> What if the shape was not two-dimensional?
> What if the solution to the problem was not one of area?

Can you find two new questions to pose for each of the five 'what – if-not' suggestions given above? Clearly the original question can be extended to give rise to many new questions.

Other starting points can be used rather than a simple question or problem. The teacher might use a cereal box and begin by asking the children to list some attributes and ask some questions. For example attributes might relate to dimensions of length, area and volume and shape. Questions might be simple, focused on the length, breadth and width of the box, or they may require calculations such as in finding the surface area or volume of the box. Alternatively, they could be more practical; what is the maximum mass of cereal that could fit into the box? The children then work out solutions to their own questions before being asked to extend their thinking to include notions of 'what – if-not' for example, what if the box is no longer a cuboid? This results in further problems of their own devising to solve!

Good opportunities to pose and solve problems enable children to apply their mathematics in interesting ways. By choosing the approaches to adopt, and by reasoning and refining their thinking, they reach a solution and possibly embark on another problem as a result.

Finding the right problems

If children are to develop their mathematical thinking through problem solving, it is essential that children engage with those problems even if they are not of their own making. Ready-made problems from text books or the teacher can result in the child feeling that the problems are 'given by authority' as a closed task with the child having little or no control (Brown and Walter, 2005, p.1). It therefore relies on the teacher, choosing problems with care and adapting them if necessary. As Fielker (1997, p.28) reminds us, it requires a skilled teacher to 'turn routine of those found in text books into more worthwhile mathematical activities'.

Sakshaug et al. (2002, p.vi) discuss the necessary characteristics of good problems. 'They must challenge the pupils, hold their interest and connect to a pupil's range of concepts in mathematics or other disciplines. There should ideally be a range of challenges embedded in the problem for learners who are at different levels mathematically'.

Take a lesson during which the teacher is assessing the accuracy of the children's addition and the mental strategies they employ. They could be given a worksheet but as always, some children would finish quickly unless differentiation was built in, and some would not complete the page. So the solution is to turn the activity into interesting puzzles and problems to solve in which accurate addition is necessary. The child does not know the end result and there is the potential to ask 'what if' questions. Such an example is provided by magic squares.

Magic squares problems

These provide extensive opportunities for problem solving both in primary and secondary classrooms. The problem posed is why are these squares magical? No suggestions limiting the exploration are given.

The following examples provide only a fraction of the possibilities and a basic internet search will provide a wealth of mathematical squares. See Figure 3.1.

This square uses the digits 1 to 9 and the children are challenged top find out why the square is special. (It has a 'magic' constant of 15 made by combining three numbers diagonally, horizontally and vertically.) The children will find that these digits can be arranged

4	9	2
3	5	7
8	1	6

Figure 3.1 A 3 × 3 magic square.

in a multitude, although finite, number of ways. (Alternatively the digits 0 to 8 can be used giving a magic number of 14.)

A further differentiation within the class could be the study of a magic square outside the Gaudi designed Sacrada Familia Cathedral at Barcelona. There are 310 ways of adding together 4 numbers to make 33, the age of Jesus at his death. If the children know that fact, they can then find the patterns of the groups of four numbers. They have a symmetry which adds to the beauty of this square and is part of the investigation to find the range of the symmetry. See Figures 3.2 and 3.3.

Further classroom research could be to investigate the square Dürer included in an engraving entitled 'Melancholia'. It has the added interest, that within the square is 1514, the year of the engraving.

Find this on the internet (Mathforum) then pose the questions:

Which numbers does Dürer use?
What is the constant in Dürer's magic square?
What is the sum of the four corner squares, what do you notice?
Can you find a 2 × 2 square with the same constant?
Can you find any relationship between the numbers in adjacent rows or columns?
Can you create a similar square, using the same numbers and with the same properties?

1	14	14	4
11	7	6	9
8	10	10	5
13	2	3	15

Figure 3.2 The Gaudi magic square.

1	14	14	4
11	7	6	9
8	10	10	5
13	2	3	15

Two diagonally opposite squares of four adding to 33

1	14	14	4
11	7	6	9
8	10	10	5
13	2	3	15

Two vertical lines of four adding to 33

Figure 3.3 Two examples of addition to 33 in the Gaudi square.

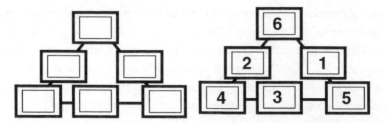

Figure 3.4 A magic triangle, the digits 1 to 6 are used so each side of the triangle has the same total. Is there more than one solution?

Magic triangles

What if not square but triangle? This will lead to further investigations where children can be asked to find their own magic triangles. See Figure 3.4.

There is sufficient challenge in this work and potential for differentiation through the selection and exploration of different squares or triangles. For some children it may be appropriate to have numbered counters to manipulate on a base board on which a square or triangle is drawn. The important point is that all children are engaged in a similar activity and will have something to contribute to the discussion.

Engagement with the problem

A key question for teachers to ask themselves before presenting a problem to children might be, 'would I be motivated to start this problem and to keep going if I found it difficult?' Engagement with the problem is essential, as lessons can flounder where children either fail to start the problem, quickly lose interest or simply give up. It is important too that the teacher is interested by a problem, as it is much easier to model enthusiastic engagement with a problem if those emotions are genuine.

Children may fail to start a problem for all sorts of reasons:

- The problem might be difficult for them to access in terms of the language or the mathematical content;
- The presentation of the problem may fail to motivate and engage;
- The child might be put off simply because they have been told to work out the problem using methods predetermined by the teacher. If as a teacher, you see problem solving as a *creative* activity, then it follows logically that freedom rather than structure is required.

The issue of children failing to engage with problems from the start, showing declining interest or simply abandoning the problem as 'too hard' is less likely to occur in a creative, open learning environment. Importantly, children should be given a choice of problems wherever possible. This is an approach advocated by a growing number of teachers and can result in huge motivational gains. Part of the success of this approach is that it enables learners to feel ownership of the problems. The notion of ownership is also in evidence when children extend an initial problem set by the teacher, or are given opportunities to pose their own problems.

This approach can help to overcome the situations where children of lower ability spend a great deal of their time on routine practice simply because problem solving can be perceived by some as beyond their capability. Ofsted (2009, p.5) recognized that in good teaching it was not just the higher attainers who worked on challenging tasks, 'non-routine problems, open-ended tasks and investigations are used often by *all* pupils to develop the broader mathematical skills of problem-solving'.

The teacher as a problem solver

As a teacher it is important to reflect on your own responses to a new problem in order to understand the feelings of a child when presented with a problem to solve.

The next time you buy a newspaper, try out their different Sudoku puzzles. Don't be distracted by the newspaper's probable claim that the puzzle is not mathematical. As Du Sautoy (2008, p.283) states, a Sudoku is a 'sophisticated error-correcting puzzle'. Its compiler has ensured that there is enough information in the Sudoku to work out the positions of the missing numbers. 'So a Sudoku is like a message in which lots of the information has been lost in transit but, thanks to the structure of the message, it is possible to reconstruct the whole message from the partial signal received.'

Consider your responses to the Sudoku problem. Could you gain 'Entry'? (This might be difficult with even the simplest if you have not attempted Sudoku before.) Did you quickly lose interest? If so, why? (Possibly the puzzle was too easy.) What was it about the puzzles you liked or disliked? How might the puzzles have been presented to you so that you would have been more interested in 'having a go'? Could you introduce these puzzles to children? What prior knowledge would they need?

Questions to ask yourself if a child will not, or cannot, start to solve a problem

- Can the child *read* the question? In the search for an interesting and engaging problem, this can be overlooked. Mixed ability grouping and pairing can help with this particular issue.
- Is the mathematical content too difficult or too easy? Problems that are perceived by children to be too easy can often fail to motivate.
- Is the context likely to be within the child's area of experience? Questions that require calculation of the cooking time for a chicken weighing 1.3 kg will seem like a pointless exercise to many children. Whereas calculating the number and size of chocolate bars required to make 200 crispie cakes for sale at the school fair might well be a real problem and thus prove more interesting and motivational especially if the information is to be used.

- Does the question take into account the children's interests? It is easy to choose football as a context and forget that this is a sport that some children actively dislike. A student recently found that few members of the class supported a football team while nearly all the class members were fans of the local speed-way team so work was planned accordingly.
- Has the question been chosen so that the children can 'apply' a specific method of calculation? In dictating a method, the problem becomes immediately confined; the dimension of 'choosing' a suitable method is lost. Moreover, any children who lack confidence in that method will be reluctant to start.
- Remember that children who favour learning styles not supported by a particular method, will also be discouraged. For example, posing the question, 'Which three consecutive numbers have a sum of eighty four?' and then imposing partitioning/compensating as the method to use is unlikely to prove fruitful! This type of problem often comes as a result of devising problems so that children can apply a method they have learnt. While to the problem poser this may seem logical, problem solvers however, rarely agree!

Making a problem accessible to children of different abilities

A class of mixed age and ability were studying square numbers and had completed a graph to show the relationship between the side of the square and the number of square units, so 1^2 has 1 unit square, 2^2 has 4 unit squares, 3^2 has 9 unit squares and so on. For those needing support, this had been completed pictorially and multi-link blocks were used. The children recognized the pattern involved in this work. See Figure 3.5.

This led to much discussion and recognition of a pattern by the children. They found that:

- the numbers involved with making the next square numbers were all odd
- the odd numbers were increased by two each time
- the question was then asked: would the next in the sequence also be two more? Would it be 1 + 3 + 5 + 7, then add 9? There was only one way to find out.

These results were made into a table to facilitate further investigation for some of the class. See Table 3.2.

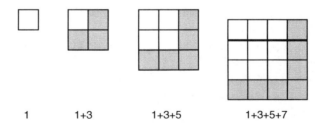

| 1 | 1+3 | 1+3+5 | 1+3+5+7 |

Figure 3.5 Coloured multi-link blocks used to develop the work on square numbers.

Table 3.2 Chart showing the results of the square number investigation

Square number	How many squares have been added?	How many more squares have been added than last time?
1		
4	3	
9	5	2
16	7	2
25	9	2
36	11	2

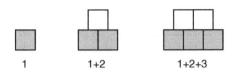

Figure 3.6 Coloured multi-link used to develop the work on triangular numbers.

Table 3.3 The design of the chart for the square and triangular numbers investigation

Natural numbers	1	2	3	4	5
Triangular numbers	1	3	6	10	15
Square numbers	1	4	9	16	25

Similar investigations into triangular numbers were developed from here; some children used practical resources and others developed a fascinating chart to show the results of the investigation. See Figure 3.6 and Table 3.3.

Differentiation and extension activities had been planned but this work had developed further than expected due to the children's interest and willingness to ask questions about the patterns as they made them and we can still recall the interest and excitement of the children when they saw the pattern of this chart. The sum of the first triangular number and the second natural number equals the second triangular number and the sum of the first and second triangular numbers is the second square number.

Others found the vertical patterns such as 2, 3 and 4 in the second column and 3, 6 and 9 in the third. What numbers would the sixth column contain?

The children were able to discuss and make generalizations from this data.

Group work

If our aim is to encourage children to think and behave like mathematicians then it is helpful to look back to the time of the Ancient Greeks, where there was support for the notion of group work. Very few mathematicians, either then or now, work in isolation. However, we need an understanding of what group work consists of as distinct from what actually occurs in many classrooms. Studies carried out have tended to find that while children may be working on the same task and seated round the same table, they rarely collaborate together to solve problems. Consequently there is little discussion particularly of the type identified by Mercer as exploratory talk. He identified exploratory talk to be where 'partners engage critically but constructively with each other's ideas' and found that this type of discussion held the greatest potential for children's learning. While children find it relatively easy to simply agree or disagree with each other they need to be encouraged to develop the skills to critically discuss problems and make constructive suggestions as to the steps they might take next. Mercer (1995, p.104) and Ofsted (2009, p.7) in their report *Understanding the Score*, recognized that mathematical discussion was a key factor in good classroom practice. 'Teachers encourage pupils to discuss mathematical problems in depth and this helps to build their confidence. In a primary school where developing pupils' understanding was promoted effectively, pupils were confident in "thinking aloud" and were not afraid to have their mistakes used to help others.'

Teachers who are committed to children working collaboratively, will, by providing interesting problems, and by modelling exploratory talk, develop quality mathematical discussion within their classrooms. Similarly, teachers who press children to explain and justify their thinking, at all stages of a lesson, will find that the same children start to challenge each other and themselves.

Some teachers may find it difficult to distinguish between the positive sharing of ideas through collaboration, and the counter productive copying of each other's work. This can be eased by the encouragement of collaboration and active learning. It is important that when the activities selected for the children provide lots of opportunities for them to think mathematically, the children are not then instructed to work quietly on their own.

Another source of anxiety for teachers can be that group or paired work will result in one child actually working and that any discussion will not be mathematical. Experience suggests that with learners of all ages neither of these things is true provided the classroom ethos and mathematical tasks are conducive to collaborative learning and are interesting and engaging for the children.

Researchers such as Askew and Wiliam (1995), have demonstrated the potential gains from group work and it would appear that regardless of age and mathematical ability, with high expectations from teachers on how children should work together and given suitable investigational tasks, there were significant gains for all learners. Once children become used to working in groups, and this may take some time, the benefits can be enormous, not only in terms of developing the children's ability to think mathematically and thus solve an increasingly complex range of problems, but also to enhance their self-esteem. An important point to think about is that very few adults live in isolation. The majority work together, learn from each other and solve problems with others. In order to do this effectively, adults need to have developed the necessary social skills and feel confident that their contributions to discussions will be valued.

An example of a problem from a content-driven learning outcome that supports collaborative learning

While the mathematical content of the following problem is focused on multiplication it involves so much more. For example, an understanding of the commutative law ($5 \times 4 = 4 \times 5$) is essential if the solver is to make sense of the problem.

Figure 3.7 is a copy of the multiplication tables up to 10×10. To prepare the problem for the children it is necessary to cut the table into 16 pieces once some of the numbers have been removed. By removing more or fewer numbers the problem can be differentiated to cover quite a wide ability range. (The multiplication tables might be increased to 12×12 or reduced to 6×6 to increase or decrease the content and level of challenge) The pieces of jigsaw are then placed in an envelope and presented to pairs or small groups of children to complete. Instructions might range from 'I want you to try and complete your jigsaw' to those that offer greater guidance such as 'look at the pattern of the units in the rows and the tens in the columns to help you complete your jigsaw'. See Figures 3.8 and 3.9.

1	2	3	4	5	6	7	8	9	10
2	4	6	8	10	12	14	16	18	20
3	6	9	12	15	18	21	24	27	30
4	8	12	16	20	24	28	32	36	40
5	10	15	20	25	30	35	40	45	50
6	12	18	24	30	36	42	48	54	60
7	14	21	28	35	42	49	56	63	70
8	16	24	32	40	48	56	64	72	80
9	18	27	36	45	54	63	72	81	90
10	20	30	40	50	60	70	80	90	100

Figure 3.7 Multiplication hundred square.

1		3	4		6	7		9	
	4	6			12	14		18	20
3			12	15			24		30
4	8	12		20	24	28	32		40
5		15	20			35		45	
6	12	18		30	36		48		60
7	14		28	35		49		63	
8		24	32	40	48	56	64	72	80
	18	27			54	63			90
10		30		50	60		80	90	

Figure 3.8 Multiplication 100 square with numbers missing.

Figure 3.9 Two cut sections (similar to pieces in a jigsaw) taken from Figure 3.8, top, left corner.

Teacher starting points, support and intervention during problem-solving activity

1 Prepare for a wide range of types and levels of problem solving

Next time you are preparing to teach a discrete area of mathematics, ensure you have a range of problems that link with it. You might find something suitable in this book, from the nrich, naace or ncetm websites, from the supplementary materials provided by the PNS, or a newspaper. The source of the problem is immaterial. Simply take the problems into the lesson for the children to work on in groups before bringing the whole class together to share a solution.

The following example shows the potential of a range of problem solving activities during the study of polyhedra with Years 5 and 6.

Group 1 Packaging boxes
The teacher had collected a range of packaging boxes from a supermarket and these were to be the starting point of the work. The group was given the challenge of recognizing the attributes of a range of polyhedra. There was a selection of cuboids, prisms and pyramids.

Product type, predominant box colour, sizes, construction material and the faces were identified and decisions made about how to record this information.

Group 2 worked with construction kits

It was involved in building the polyhedra with construction kits such as Polydron. This involved looking carefully at the attributes of the faces to ensure they would 'fit'. There were problems to solve involving triangles, where in some cases it was important that equilateral triangles were used and in other cases this was not relevant. There were discussions concerning regular and irregular polyhedra. The limitations of the construction kits were also an issue. Running short of squares, a child had made a square pyramid using two right angled triangles to make the square base. The group had to decide if it was made of six triangles but decided the two triangles making the square had lost their separate identity and become a square!

Group 3 focused on the nets of polyhedra

They set up a challenge for the class to decide which would make a cube and which would not. See Figure 3.10.

This developed to nets of other polyhedra with the class deciding on which polyhedra could be made from them. The result was a wall display of the nets and the polyhedra alongside with a brief caption of their properties. On a table in front of this display were construction kits and a challenge for others to make the polyhedra.

Group 4 identified the faces, vertices and edges of the packaging boxes

The children set about counting them accurately and time was spent deciding how to do this. The decision was made to work in pairs with one partner counting and marking with chalk and the other holding the polyhedron. Children devised their own methods of recording their results. These were then collated on the smart-board with the teacher acting as scribe and making sure that all children gave results. Discussions included why square and rectangular prisms were excluded from the list! See Table 3.4.

While studying this chart a small group had 'discovered' Euler's formula. They saw that Edges = (Faces + Vertices) − 2. They found their discovery very exciting and made a construction kit pentagonal prism and hexagonal prism to test this further.

Later work included using the formula to find the answer to such problems as 'how many vertices are there on an octagonal prism if it is known that there are 24 edges and 10 faces?'

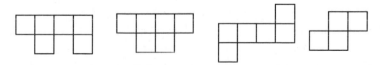

Figure 3.10 Which of these are the nets of cubes?

Table 3.4 Chart of the faces, vertices and edges investigation

Polyhedron	Number of edges	Number of faces	Number of vertices
Cuboid	12	6	8
Cube	12	6	8
Triangular pyramid	6	4	4
Square pyramid	8	5	5
Hexagonal pyramid	12	7	7
Triangular prism	9	5	6
Pentagonal prism	15	7	10
Hexagonal prism	18	8	12

2 Use 'STUCK! AHA! CHECK and REFLECT' (rubric writing)

Mason et al. (1982, p.17) terms the use of a framework of these four key words a Rubric, and later extended this to the idea of rubric writing. This follows the custom in medieval times of writing key words in the margins of books. For both a learner and a teacher, this can be enormously powerful. Writing the word STUCK! or saying the word stuck aloud appears to be extremely liberating. Instead of wallowing in a feeling of self-pity and despair, where we simply feel like giving up, we admit we are stuck and then start to look for ways to become unstuck. Parts of the benefits arise, as Mason et al. (1982) suggest, from the normality of the situation. Anyone who has experienced the feeling of panic when faced with a problem that appears too difficult, knows that this comes from feeling that it's only you who can't do the problem and all to often this results in, 'I can't do this, I'm no good at maths!' Understanding that everyone experiences this quite often is extremely encouraging!

The next word is AHA! This AHA! moment might in fact turn out to be a blind alley but nevertheless it involves solvers with the problem again. CHECK and REFLECT are equally important, particularly for young children whose initial instinct, having found a solution, is to say, 'right that's it, I've finished with this problem'. Thus rubric writing can help children to reflect on their thinking, leading to more solutions that have been verified. We fully support the assumption made by Mason et al. (1982) that this area of children's emotional well being, when solving mathematical problems, is often largely ignored. A change in that state can lead to enormous mathematical gains in children, and adults, of all abilities.

3 The teacher as a modeller

'Any application of mathematics to solve a real-life problem requires the pupil to engage in mathematical modelling, i.e. to use a piece of mathematics to model the real world situation' Billington et al. (1993, p.22).

The process of selecting the key bits of information that are needed and representing the problem, using mathematical calculations, tables or diagrams, is the essence of this process in order for the mathematics and the result to have meaning.

As well as being taught mathematical modelling in clear stages, children need to see their teachers as problem solvers, and in some cases they will see them as less than successful problem solvers! This lies at the heart of the process of the teacher modelling problem solving. Billington et al. (1993, p.25) suggest working alongside the children and 'making rough notes or diagrams, discussion mathematical ideas, and in some cases offering a possible presentation.'

For many teachers this might well happen at first by chance, a problem presented to children to solve that had not previously been looked at and where the answer appears to be elusive. If the problem proves to be too tricky, don't worry it is the process that is important. After the first moments of panic, and subsequent recognition of being 'stuck!', the teacher begins to explore the problem with the children who quickly become keen to make suggestions of their own. Eventually a solution is reached, or the lesson ends with everyone asked to give it some more thought, thinking time for both children and their teacher! For some children, having seen the teacher stuck, but persevering, will be sufficient to embolden them in their next problem-solving attempt. The first occasion can be quite alarming, particularly for an inexperienced teacher, but the rewards can be amazing and looking back at such lessons, many teachers realize that the experience was empowering for everyone. The children had seen their teacher unable to proceed with the problem and then witnessed how they attacked the problem from that point.

Similar lessons could then be planned for those children in the future, and the class with its teacher, could move towards becoming a group of mathematicians. Hitherto reluctant problem solvers became more willing to 'have a go' and less keen to give up as soon as they became stuck. Teachers would find, often to their surprise, that they were enjoying teaching more as the challenges to find new and interesting problems to share with the children were rewarded by exciting lessons full of mathematical talk and positive emotions where individuals, groups and the whole class had found solutions to problems.

Teachers have always modelled methods or proofs for children, and it is clearly important to do so as it enables them to acquire some of the necessary tools of mathematics. However, modelling goes beyond this as it is the teacher's own thinking is being verbalized and shared with children.

4 Keep the problem to be solved 'open'

This was advocated by Fielker (1997, p.27) who suggested that the problem to be solved should be 'vague'. This leaves the options for solving the problem open for the children to decide on their approach.

An example of such a problem was presented to a class as follows. There are currently eight British coins of different value (1p, 2p, 5p, 10p, 20p, 50p, £1 and £2) and the teacher asked each child to choose a total of eight coins (one of each coin, multiples of one coin or any combination of coins of different values). They were then asked to devise a series of questions using their coins. The questions were varied both in complexity and in the area of mathematics involved. There were inevitably many questions involving the values of the coins but others used their dates to order according to age, sort according to metal or diameter and one child's challenge was to choose the coins that would make a line estimated to be 5 cm or 9 cm etc. This would of course then need checking. This soon was developed to estimations of how many 1ps would be needed to go from one side of the classroom, playground or games field. How could this be estimated with a limited number of 1p coins?

5 Change something in a familiar problem

Pascal's triangle offers many possibilities for investigations. See Figure 3.11.

Open-ended exploration can be provided through challenges to look for patterns, in the diagonals, or by adding the horizontal rows.

Adopting a *what if not* stance as identified by Brown and Walter (2005) produces a whole new range of problems. For example, *what if not* 1 but 2 results in the following six rows if 2 replaces 1. Do the same pattern formations apply? See Figure 3.12.

While the mathematical content of this problem is focused on addition, it provides extension possibilities that include calculating powers of 2 as well as looking for, and making sense of patterns.

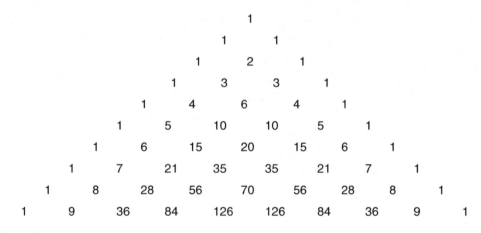

Figure 3.11 Pascal's triangle.

Figure 3.12 The 'CHANGED' Pascal's triangle.

6 Be aware of misconceptions

If the children have reached an impasse due to a mathematical misconception, then questioning should expose this allowing the teacher to offer support to enable them to move forward in the activity. Similarly teacher intervention may be necessary primarily as a tool for encouraging children to carry on with the problem when they believe they can't go any further. Talking through what they have done and what they do now, together with carefully phrased open-ended questions, often enables the children to move forward. Some specific examples of different types of questions are given by the NNS (DfEE, 1999, pp.4–6) and these include questions that can help to extend children's thinking at different times during an investigation. Sometimes a hint such as 'talk me through what you have done so far, have you thought of trying, would a diagram help . . .' can be effective. The important thing is not to lead the children or tell them the answers; this can be good, shared learning for both children and teachers! The notion of working alongside the children and thus modelling the process of investigation can also be effective. Those investigations or problems that draw the teacher in, as a result of children exploring in a way unpredicted by the teacher, can lead to a real feeling of mutual exploration, working together within a mathematical community. It is highly likely that the participants will continue with the investigation independently long after the lesson has finished!

What of the future?

A European Parliament and Council recommendation in 2006 lists eight key competences for life-long learning that are a combination of knowledge, skills and attitudes and are necessary for 'personal fulfilment and development, social inclusion, active citizenship and employment. The eight competences are:

- Communication in the mother tongue
- communication in a foreign language;
- mathematical competence and basic competences in science and technology;
- digital competence;
- learning to learn;
- social and civic competences;
- sense of initiative and entrepreneurship; and
- cultural awareness and expression.'

These are all 'interdependent and the emphasis in each case is on critical thinking, creativity, initiative, problem solving, risk assessment, decision taking and constructive management of feelings' Rose (DCSF, 2009, pp.114–115).

It is not difficult to see the beginnings of these key competences for life in primary mathematics, both in discrete lessons and across the curriculum, where children have opportunities to work on tasks requiring them to make choices, reason about problems, plan and discuss strategies, refine ideas and work collaboratively and experience success.

References and further reading

Askew, M. and Wiliam, D. (1995) *Recent Research in Mathematics* London: HMSO.

Billington, J., Fowler, N., MacKernan, J., Stratton, J., and Watson, A. (1993) *Using and Applying Mathematics* Nottingham: ATM.

Brown, S. and Walter, M. (2005) *The Art of Problem Posing* Mahwah, NJ: Lawrence Erlbaum.

Burton, L. (1984) *Thinking Things Through Problem Solving in Mathematics* Oxford: Basil Blackwell.

Department for Children, Schools and Families Rose, J. (2009) *Independent Review of the Primary Curriculum: Final Report* London: DCSF Publications.

Department for Education and Employment (1999) *The National Numeracy Strategy Mathematical Vocabulary Book* London: DfEE Publications.

Department for Education and Skills (2006a) *Primary National Strategy Primary Framework for Literacy and Mathematics* London: DfES Publications.

—(2006b) *Renewing the Primary Framework for Mathematics Guidance Paper Using and Applying Mathematics* [Online]. Available at: nationalstrategies.standards.dcsf.gov.uk/downloader/e5f49e2d5663a1412acbc1d96623fe00.rtf (accessed on 31/07/09).

Du Sautoy, M. (2008) *Finding Moonshine* London: HarperCollins.

Fielker, D. (1997) *Extending Mathematical Ability Through Whole Class Teaching* London: Hodder and Stoughton.

Hughes, M., Desforges, C. and Mitchell, C. (2000) *Numeracy and Beyond Applying Mathematics in the Primary School* Buckingham: Open University Press.

Mason, J., Burton, L. and Stacey, K. (1982) *Thinking Mathematically* Wokingham: Addison Wesley.

Mercer, N. (1995) *The Guided Construction of Knowledge* Clevedon: Multilingual Matters Ltd.

Ofsted (2009) *Mathematics: Understanding the Score. Improving Practice in Mathematics Teaching at Primary Level* London: HMSO.

Polya, G. (1945). *How to Solve It.* Princeton, NJ: Princeton University Press.

Pratt, N. (2006) *Interactive Maths Teaching in the Primary School* London: Paul Chapman Publishing.

Sakshaug, L., Ollson, M. and Olson, J. (2002) *Children are Mathematical Problem Solvers* Reston, VA: National Council of Teachers of Mathematics.

Websites

All website addresses were accessed on 31 July 2009.

National Centre for excellence in the teaching of mathematics. This is a frequently updated and edited by a variety of people. It has a lot of interesting ideas and mathematics related articles. Available at: www.ncetm.org.uk.

A Cambridge project of resources for parents, teachers and children with the aim of enriching learning. There is a new web page every month. Available at: http://nrich.maths.org/public/-

A range of up to date mathematics teaching and learning resources. Available at: http://www.bgfl.org/index.

A variety of mathematics resources and activities for primary schools. Available at: http://www.mathcats.com/explore.html.

And the teacher area for the site is available at: http://www.mathcats.com/grownupcats/.

Mathematics Across the Curriculum, an Introduction

4

Chapter Outline

Maths that is taught without reference to its power to explain real problems is a stilted maths, like learning to speak without ever having had a conversation.

(Copeland, 1991, p.3)

The primary curriculum design for the twenty-first century is a blend of challenging discrete subject teaching alongside equally challenging cross-curricular studies. This is clearly stated in the 2009 Independent Review of the Primary Curriculum, the Rose Report. So as well as teaching the skills, knowledge and understanding of separate subjects, there is an expectation that teachers will plan to complement subjects by 'worthwhile and challenging cross-curricular studies that provide ample opportunities for children to use and apply their subject knowledge and skills to deepen their understanding' (DCSF, 2009a, p.10). It is therefore essential that when planning their mathematics teachers need to embrace the fact that mathematics in other curriculum areas is no longer an optional extra.

The benefits of cross-curricular working

There have been many advocates of the benefits of cross-curricular working. Barnes (2007, p.8) gives a definition of it as '. . .when the skills, knowledge and attitudes of a number of different disciplines are applied to a single experience, theme or idea, we are working in a cross-curricular way. We are looking at the focus.' Such interesting work takes the child beyond the separate subjects in the timetable and helps to build a positive attitude to mathematics. The desirability of making links between mathematics and other subjects was recognized by the NNS (DfEE, 1999, p.16), which advised teachers to 'look for opportunities for drawing mathematical experiences out of a wide range of children's activities. Mathematics contributes to many subjects of the primary curriculum, often in practical ways.'

Haylock and Thangata (2007, p.48) recognized three different ways of looking at cross-curricular mathematics:

- '. . .other areas of the primary school curriculum can be seen as providing opportunities to apply skills and knowledge that pupils learn in mathematics lessons in purposeful activities.
- other curriculum areas can be seen as providing meaningful contexts within which mathematical concepts can be introduced or developed.
- mathematics can be seen as one of a number of curriculum areas that might come together as an extended cross-curricular project of some kind, which is not located in any particular subject area in the school timetable.'

Hughes et al. (2000, p.9) understood the problems of involving meaningful mathematical work in situations beyond the daily mathematics lesson. 'People seem to have enormous difficulty in using and applying mathematical skills and knowledge from instructions and formats in which they are learnt, to novel situations. This poses a major challenge to a key area of schooling, that key aim being to make the lessons of school applicable to the larger world of everyday life.'

Widening the scope of the mathematics curriculum should be recognized as a valuable part of the whole teaching and learning experience. Children will be learning 'not only **what** to study, but also **how** to study as part of a self disciplined, engaging and rewarding process' Rose (DCSF, 2009a, p.19).

Another benefit is that while children are working with exciting and interesting mathematical tasks, the teacher can assess their true understanding as the children can apply, consolidate and develop their skills or knowledge and understanding from one subject context to another. Mathematics previously covered in a discrete session can be revisited or new mathematics can be introduced in interesting way.

Why it is beneficial for children to use and apply their mathematical skills, knowledge and understanding in new situations

Children will see the relevance of their work during the daily mathematics lesson and develop their ability to think mathematically while applying their mathematics in new situations. Also, at the same time as developing their mathematical understanding in situations beyond the mathematics lesson, interest in the other subjects involved will be enhanced.

The children will be thinking and behaving creatively. Grey (1997, p.146) recognized the importance of creativity as part of mathematics, as his work 'revealed that children who were successful mathematically had learnt how to develop new facts from old in a flexible way'. Barnes (2007, p.135) refers to Koestler (1964) and states his definition of creativity as '*bisociation,* the often unexpected, coming together of two contrasting planes of thought'. Barnes sees this as 'central to understanding the purpose of cross-curricular learning'.

Creativity checklist

QCA also recognizes the importance of creativity and provides the following checklist of creative activity in subjects in the classroom where the children will be:

- questioning and challenging
- making connections and seeing relationships
- envisaging next steps
- exploring ideas, keeping options open
- reflecting critically on ideas, actions and outcomes

All these points are crucial for lively mathematics work where the children will be working in mathematics and other curriculum areas, using their mathematical knowledge, understanding and skills in order to solve problems, provide data and extend learning.

Mathematics for its own sake

We have argued that mathematics is a relevant and essential subject for work in other subjects and in everyday life but never forget the beauty and wonder of mathematics for its own sake. Denvir et al. (1982, pp.27–29) recognized three categories of mathematics as being 'a useful tool, part of our culture and pleasurable'.

This point about mathematics for enjoyment is also made by Fielker (1997, p.162), who, while discussing the content of his book, believed that it is not necessarily the case that children will not be interested in their mathematical work unless 'they can see a use for it'. He concedes

Figure 4.1 Example of the subtraction exercise.

that most of the mathematics in his book 'is fairly useless, but has been found to be enjoyable – like poetry, art or music'. He felt that the need for mathematics always to have a purpose was a 'myth' that was 'perpetrated by teachers who feel they cannot make mathematics enjoyable!'

Look at this simple mathematical exercise. It is difficult not to find it fascinating but other than revising accurate subtraction, it has very little purpose. Write down four numbers. Underneath, find the difference between them using the last and the first for the 4th number. See Figure 4.1.

Start with different numbers of very different values; what happens if you start with five numbers? It is guaranteed anyone trying this will have sheets of paper covered with different trials and have enjoyed the intellectual exercise!

Outside the classroom

There are many opportunities to develop exciting mathematical work in the school grounds. The DfES (2006b, p.3) published *Learning Outside the Classroom*, which aims to 'raise achievement through an organized, powerful approach to learning in which direct experience is of prime importance. This is not only about what we learn but importantly how and where we learn.' Well-planned learning experiences in the outdoors can build bridges between theory and reality and raise achievement across a range of subjects including mathematics.

The Williams Report (DCSF, 2008b, p.62) highlights concern that not enough attention is paid to building good attitudes to mathematics. 'Clearly if children's interests are not kindled through using and applying mathematics in interesting and engaging ways, and through learning across the full mathematics curriculum, they are unlikely to develop good attitudes to the subject.'

Adapting, combining and embedding mathematics within the curriculum

Following the Rose Report (2009a), schools are being encouraged, increasingly, to take responsibility for their curriculum, incorporating literacy and numeracy with other curriculum areas to provide a broad and relevant curriculum. QCA (2005) advocated the desirability of customizing the curriculum to suit the school's requirements. This can be by:

- *adapting units* from the schemes of work, adjusting plans to better meet children's needs and interests and whole school planning
- combining units from different subjects
- *embedding* aspects of mathematics in other subjects

It is then possible to 'take advantage of your school's resources or capitalise on current events and local contexts'. The aim is to make the work both relevant and exciting and thus motivate children. 'Combining units makes learning more coherent, connecting essential skills with knowledge and understanding' (QCA, 2005).

In 'Customise your Curriculum', QCA (2005) also advises that it is important to consider the following points when embedding mathematics:

- look carefully at the impact any changes will have on coverage of subjects, curriculum continuity, and children's progress
- make sure that important learning objectives and learning outcomes are not lost in the process. Leaving out key subject objectives can disrupt children's learning
- check that any changes to the focus of a unit do not lead to overlaps between different year groups' plans
- consider knock-on effects for your school's curriculum plan as a whole.

QCA provides examples that show opportunities to embed mathematical work in art and design, design and technology, history, geography, music, PE and science.

How to combine/embed mathematics within other curriculum areas

With all the requirements of planning, delivering and assessing mathematical teaching and learning it can be a daunting task to take advantage of the wealth of mathematical opportunities in other curriculum areas, whilst still meeting the curricular expectations of the other subjects.

Remember that high-quality mathematics teaching and learning incorporates three interdependent areas:

- designing the planning and application of exciting and relevant mathematical activity
- meeting the mathematical requirements of the children with using and applying strands at the centre
- using the components of the National Curriculum (NC), Ma2, Ma3 and Ma4.

With such planning, while achieving the mathematical learning objectives, the children will have extended their reasoning powers, conceptual knowledge and procedural skills without fear of failure. They will have extended their knowledge and understanding of number facts, and the rules and procedures of mathematics, developed their skills such as ordering, classifying, hypothesizing and reasoning. The teacher will have had an excellent opportunity to assess mathematical understanding while the child is using and applying their understanding in a new context. Most importantly, the children will enjoy their mathematics and see its relevance to their everyday lives.

Checklist for successful cross-curricular work featuring mathematics

- Remember that for the mathematics to be of value, it must be planned for and not be an 'add on'. However that does not mean you avoid the unexpected opportunity as it arises. So, always be on the look out for the unexpected occurrence or situation that could be a stimulus for exciting mathematical work and adapt planning accordingly.
- Do not attempt to change your way of working instantly. Ofsted (2009, p.13) recognize that 'cross-curricular and other focus or themed days can add enjoyment and value to many pupils' learning in mathematics. For example, one primary school had a maths and art week and another held a team problem-solving day.' Starting with small steps is a good way of gaining confidence.
- Ensure that the connections are essential and meaningful, an integral part of the study, with effective links, and not 'tagged on' for the sake of including mathematics in the work.
- Consider working through a topic using a planning web to see the range of subjects that could be meaningfully covered.
- If necessary, rearrange the order of the work in other subjects so they are studied at the same time as the current mathematics objectives, or rearrange the mathematics unit to fit with the other subject if appropriate to do so.
- Alternatively plan for the mathematics to be revisited during other work in another subject and use it for assessment.
- As with all mathematics, you must ensure that work is differentiated, through planning, to provide challenge at the correct level for the individual members of the class. This will prevent any possibility of the class all being given and identical mathematical task just because the work happens to be within another curriculum area.
- Make sure that you have clearly identified areas of mathematics to assess and ensure that you have recognized the different aspects of using and applying – communication, reasoning, enquiry and problem solving, in your planning. Often such activities provide an excellent opportunity for assessment.
- Check that there is a healthy balance between review of previous learning, extending new learning: chances to practise and apply skills and time for evaluation.
- Make sure that teachers of other year groups are aware of your planning if you have made any alterations to your school's curriculum planning.

- If developing a cross-curricular approach throughout the year, or indeed the whole school, ensure that each of the foundation subjects is appropriately represented.
- Consider a range of time scales. There may be a situation where a topic could be ongoing for a long time; such as during the building of a school extension or it could be a short project such as Chinese New Year where all work has a Chinese emphasis for a week.
- Remember to include the use of ICT in your planning to enhance and extend teaching and learning.
- Look beyond the four walls of the classroom for your mathematics work.

It is important to remember that the mathematics must be commensurate with the current level of understanding of the child for it to have mathematical worth. Simple mathematical activities may well be a necessary part of the work but should not be thought of as having any specifically mathematical worth. For example, the inclusion of tessellating tiles during work on the Romans or Greeks in a Key Stage 2 class does not equate with their level of understanding of 2-D shape unless there is an element of problem solving.

Do all regular quadrilaterals tessellate? If so, why?
Do irregular quadrilaterals tessellate? If so, why?
Why do hexagons tessellate but octagons do not?

Such questions, together with others suggested by the children, provide the starting point for real mathematical investigation at the mathematical level of the children. This will then support their artistic tessellations of 2-D shapes.

If you have been accustomed to always teaching in discrete subject areas, to develop a cross-curricular approach can be a daunting task and it would not be sensible to attempt to instantly change your way of planning and teaching. However, with increased awareness of the potential of making connections across the subjects, this will gradually become part of your professional skills. You will teach in the manner described by Briggs and Davis (2009, p.7) so your children can be 'creative learners of mathematics and can be innovative in their approaches to solving problems'.

In conclusion, we believe that teachers and practitioners can plan and teach interesting, creative and relevant mathematics with breadth and progression that is both challenging and accessible. This will be in the daily mathematics lesson and other curriculum areas. Children will experience the magic of mathematics be it through the discovery of patterns from shapes and numbers, the completion of an investigation, the appropriate and vital use of mathematics in another subject or the sheer enjoyment of having worked through a problem and discovered a solution.

Finally, a simple and meaningful quotation from Gwilliam (1988, p.48) who stated that 'the experience of young children does not come in separate packages, their experience is undifferentiated.'

References and further reading

Barnes, J. (2007) *Cross Curricular Learning 3–14* London: Paul Chapman Publishing.

Briggs, M. and Davis, S. (2009) *Creative Teaching, mathematics in the Early Years and Primary Education* Abingdon: Routledge.

Copeland, T. (1991) *A Teacher's Guide to Maths and the Historic Environment* London: English Heritage.

Denvir, B., Stolz, C. and Brown, M. (1982) *Low Attainers in Mathematics 5–10 Policies and Practices in Schools. Schools Council Working Paper 72* Methuen Educational.

Department for Children, Schools and Families (2008a) *Assessment for Learning Strategy* London: DCSF Publications.

—Williams, P. (2008b) *Independent Review of Mathematics Teaching in Early Years Settings and Primary Schools Final Report* London: DCSF Publications.

—Rose, J. (2009a) *Independent Review of the Primary Curriculum: Final Report* London: DCSF Publications.

—(2009b) White Paper *Your Child, Your Schools, Our Future: Building a 21st Century Schools System* London: DCSF Publications.

Department for Education and Employment (1999) *The National Numeracy Strategy: Framework for Teaching Mathematics from Reception to Year 6* London: DfEE Publications.

Department for Education and Skills (2003) *Every Child Matters* London: DfES Publications.

—(2006a) *Primary National Strategy Primary Framework for Literacy and Mathematics* London: DfES Publications.

—(2006b) *Learning Outside the Classroom* London: DfES Publications.

Fielker, D. (1997) *Extending Mathematical Ability Through Interactive Whole Class Teaching.* London: Hodder and Stoughton.

Grey, E. (1997) 'Compressing the counting process: developing a flexible interpretation of symbols' in Siraj-Blatchford, I. (ed.) (1998) *A Curriculum Development Handbook for Early Childhood Educators* Stoke-on-Trent: Trentham Books.

Gwillliam, P. (1988) 'Beyond numeracy – practical mathematics through geography' in Mills, D. (ed.) *Geographical Work in Primary and Middle Schools* Sheffield: Geographical Association, pp.48–56.

Haylock, D. and Thangata, F. (2007) *Key Concepts in Teaching Primary Mathematics* London: Sage.

Hughes, M., Desforges, C. and Mitchell, C. (2000) *Numeracy and Beyond, Applying Mathematics in the Primary School* Buckingham: Open University Press.

Koestler, A. (1964) 'The act of creation', in Barnes, J. (ed.) (2007) *Cross Curricular Learning 3–14* London: Paul Chapman Publishing.

Ofsted (2009) *Mathematics: Understanding the Score* London: Crown Copyright.

Pratt, N. (2006) *Interactive Maths Teaching in the Primary School* London: Paul Chapman Publishing.

Qualifications and Curriculum Authority (2005) *Customise Your Curriculum* London: QCA.

—(2004) *Creativity: Find It, Promote It Promoting Children's Creative Thinking and Behaviour Across the Curriculum at Key Stages 1 and 2* London: QCA.

—(2007) *Futures in Action Building a 21st Century Curriculum* London: QCA.

Williams, J. and Easingwood, N. (2003) *ICT and Primary Science* London: Routledge Falmer.

Websites

All website addresses were accessed on 31 July 2009.

For advice on ICT in specific subjects. Available at: http://schools/becta.org.uk.

For curriculum ideas. Available at: http://www.ncinaction.org.uk/sunjects/maths.ict-Irn.htm.

For interactive teaching programmes. Available at: http://www.standards.dfes.gov.uk/primaryframeworks/library/Mathematics/ICTResources/itps/

'Customise your Curriculum' – useful examples, which show opportunities to embed mathematical work in art and design, design and technology, history, geography, music, PE and science.[Online.] Available at: http://www.qca.org.uk/schemes.

Examples of pupils' work showing how the NC programmes of study and non-statutory frameworks for Key Stages 1 and 2 translate into real activities. They also illustrate the standard of pupils' work from reception to Year 6 together with the effective use of creativity and ICT across the curriculum. Available at: http://curriculum.qca.org.uk/key-stages-1-and-2/assessment/nc-in-action/index.aspx.

5 Mathematics and Scientific and Technological Understanding

Chapter Outline

Mathematics and science

Every scientific investigation or experiment is likely to require one or more of the mathematical skills of classifying, counting, measuring, calculating, estimating, and recording in graphs and tables.

NNS (DfEE, 1999, p.17)

Introduction to mathematics and science

Harlen (2006, p.3) recognizes the new use of the word 'enquiry' which refers to the considerable range of experiences that together support children in building their understanding of scientific ideas and processes. There are undoubtedly strong connections between mathematics and science. This was the view of Peterson (1999, p.24) who recognized the connections between science and mathematics, with the need for the mathematics to be used in a science investigation. 'Neither the maths nor the science are trivialised. It is not a case of trying to teach two things at once and possibly failing at both but rather generating one skill from another through an authentic link.'

Feasey and Gallear (2000, p.iv) also believe that 'at the heart of science is mathematics. Science relies on the use of mathematics to provide quantitative evidence on which scientists make comparisons, note patterns and trends, make generalisations and draw conclusions. In exactly the same way, school science relies on children's mathematical understanding as a base upon which to develop their ability in primary science.' They see the value of mathematics in scientific work in that there is a 'real reason' for the application of mathematical skills.

Ward et al. (2005) recognize the mathematical potential in the range of data collection, and interpretation involving the recognition of patterns and understanding of quantitative and qualitative data. Similarly Easingwood and Williams (2003, p.79) argue that data handling is central to successful investigational work in mathematics and other subjects. As an integral part of Primary Science, they believe that 'without it, there is little prospect of any genuine scientific investigation'.

Frobisher et al. (2007, p.7) recognize the strong link between nature and mathematics with 'much geometry to be explored in the patterns.' There is the symmetry of butterflies and leaves, the number patterns of Fibonacci spirals of fir cones and sunflowers as well as the repetition of life cycles of animals and plants. Oliver (2007, p.122) agrees that 'linking maths with the topic of living things suggests opportunities for counting and measuring. How many seeds in a pod? Do all pods have the same number of seeds?' This mathematics would be unacceptable for older children, unless the data was used as a starting point for wider investigations of a range of seeds and pods. We are reminded of some work with Year 5 children in which the children were challenged to find the diameter of a single pea. The solution was to measure the length of a row of 10 peas and then divide the result by 10! The mass of a pea was found in a similar way. Accurate division by 10 became essential.

Peterson (1999, p.24) sees two approaches to integrating science and mathematics:

- as a science investigation in which some mathematics is identified in the work. She describes an activity where lung capacity is to be found using containers, water and tubing. The accurate measurement of volume is required with the children using an appropriate unit of measure. The children's ability to use estimation, comparison, checking and recording is an integral part of the work.
- part of a lesson introduced by the teacher as 'a prepared, concomitant mathematical skill'. The example cited was a work on shadows in which the children studied the movement of the sun and 'measurement of length, awareness recording of time, and could include consideration of the changing area of shade cover or lead to projective geometry'.

Case study – growing potatoes, Years 3–4

The project is compatible with the following DfES Units from the Science schemes of work:

Unit 1B: for Year 1 – Growing plants
Unit 2B: for Year 2 – Plants and animals in the local environment
Unit 3B: Year 3 – Helping plants grow well

There was very little space in the school grounds for growing plants outside so the teacher decided to concentrate on one crop, potatoes. In order to fit with school terms, he decided to grow early potatoes in tubs.

The variety of potatoes to grow had to be chosen. This was done with the class using a collection of catalogues and the Internet. The class found this fascinating as they discovered the range of shapes, colours and varieties of potatoes. Information in the catalogues was largely in grid form and the children quickly learnt to read and extract the relevant information. Seed potatoes were sold in 1 or 2 kg packs with a range of prices and reductions for purchasing two or more packs. Working out the best deals provided the opportunity for mental calculations and recordings.

The decision was made to grow First Early potatoes in vegetable grow-tubs. The children were interested to see if there was a difference in the yields of different early potatoes so the decision was made to plant 4 different varieties in the same conditions and record the growth and mass of the crop. The varieties chosen could be planted as early as February. Using the calendar to count the potential growth time scale, they were planted in March so the initial growth period was during the Easter holidays. Records of growth and watering were kept in photographic form as well as by creating charts and graphs.

The following instructions are written. They show the potential for a huge amount of mathematics from the 3 and 5 times table while determining numbers of potatoes for different numbers of tubs, to keeping records of growth, conversion from inch to centimetre, record keeping of compost in litres, records of the complete growth cycle complete with time scale and various costs incurred in the project.

Instruction chart for growing potatoes
Each planter is suitable for between 3 to 5 seed potatoes

Place your seed potatoes in a cool light place and leave for a few weeks

until shoots grow approximately 2.5 cm (1 inch) long. For each planter you will need 40 l of good general purpose compost.

Pour approximately 10 cm (4 inches) into the bottom. Plant your seed potatoes, with the shoots or eyes facing upwards, to half the depth of the compost. Keep the compost slightly damp but do not over-water.

When the shoots have grown 7 cm (3 inches) high add another layer of compost to leave the tips of the shoots just showing, keeping the compost damp each time.

Repeat this process until the compost and shoots are 3 cm (1 inch) from the top.

The plants will produce small white or pink flowers. At this time your potatoes should be ready to harvest. Dig carefully down into the planter to see if your potatoes are ready. Remove a few potatoes at a time or tip the planter out to reveal the whole harvest.

When the potatoes were harvested, the number of potatoes on each haulm,(potato plant) above an agreed size, was counted. A basic sieve was made of thick card so that the rejected potatoes fell through and were then discarded.

The mass of potatoes on each plant was found using kitchen scales.

This was repeated with the other three varieties of potatoes and comparisons were made of the crop: differences in numbers of potatoes on each haulm, differences in mass as well as differences in shape and colour. Similarities and differences in results were discussed.

The potatoes were packed into plastic bags. Labels for the bags were designed showing a Logo, weight and variety and cost. The packs were advertised with posters and sold to parents and friends of the school. The children worked out the total cost of buying and growing and packaging the potatoes and the money from sales to see if there was an overall profit.

Teacher's comment

I was very keen that the children would experience the practical side of measuring out the capacity of water and measuring mass and height. This was so that they would 'know' what a litre of water or 500 g felt and looked like. I was keen for this to happen as I remembered during an early SAT's paper my class could not answer a question on the mass of an apple. Is an apple 40 g, 140 g or 240 g? They could have attempted a calculation but they had not 'felt' an apple in their hands and related it to what 140 g felt like.

During this project the children had the opportunity to find out about the range of varieties of potatoes and communicate what they discovered through graphs, charts, photographs and drawings. They observed, experienced and explored with all their senses and related the plant growth to other plants with which they were familiar. They were aware of Health and Safety issues involved in growing plants such as care with the use of compost and fertilizers and that 'the potato plant should be considered poisonous except the tubers when not green' (ASE, 1990). We could have grown some of the potatoes in poor conditions such as without water or sunlight but as the focus was on success and sales of potatoes this aspect was not included in the project.

There was a lasting result to this work. Such was the interest in growing plants that the school has developed a small chequerboard garden. This is made from alternate concrete paving slabs and soil and provided a number of small 'gardens' for different plants. The next project focused on Design and Technology – making small 'greenhouses' to provide good growing conditions in the spring.

It is interesting to note that this could be an excellent whole-school project with responsibilities given to the different age groups: from counting the potatoes in the Early Years classes to responsibility for the measurements and watering with Years 3–4 and the older children in charge of design and promotion. The range of mathematics involved would be wide and essential for the success of such a project.

Mathematics included in this work

Mathematics	Objective	Activity
Using and Applying	• Develop and evaluate lines of enquiry: identify, collect, organize and analyse information. Present conclusions and pose other questions to answer.	Decisions about the presentation of the results of growing and the mass of the potatoes
	• Solve one-step, two-step problems involving money and measures and carry out appropriate calculations	Costing of potatoes and finding the variety that is the 'best' value for money
Measuring	• Choose and use appropriate units to estimate, measure and record.	Measuring and recording growth of plants and finding the mass of the potatoes
		Measuring compost in litres
		Using a sieve to determine if the potato was too small for sale
Data Handling	• Construct and interpret frequency tables, bar charts with grouped discrete data, and line graphs; interpret pie charts	Prepare charts and graphs of: • growth of the potato plants • charts of profits Make conversion charts – inches/cm

Possible misconceptions and difficulties

- Care must be taken to ensure that all measurements are with appropriate tools. Ensure that children are measuring from 0 and not 1 and from the correct end of the ruler, thus ensuring accurate use of the tools used.
- There could be difficulties when reading the scales, in order to find the mass of the potatoes with lack of understanding of the intervals used. This could provide a good opportunity to highlight 'place value' with the kilogram as the 'unit' and the grams as tenths, hundredths and thousandths. Other scales may just record grams in which case they need to be adapted to kilograms and grams.
- Understanding of mass and the accurate measurement of mass was an important feature of the work. It is common for children to confuse mass and weight as the word 'weigh' is in every day usage. 'Mass can be defined as the amount of matter in an object and weight is the downward force of the object calculated as the mss multiplied by the force of gravity. Hence the units of mass are kilograms and the unit of weight is the Newton,' Mooney et al. (2001, p.55). The teacher had to re-educate the children to talk about potatoes with a mass of 2 kg.
- With records of the measurement of the growth of plants, the time scale must be considered. This could be with weekly measurements
- There could be problems with the graphs having inaccurate, inappropriate or inconsistent time scales on the x and or y axes.
- Bar charts designed to show the amounts grown by different children must have a gap between the columns as the information is discrete

Other curriculum areas included in the work

Subject	Objective	Activity
Science	• Understanding of the requirements for growth in green plants • Know plant parts and their functions • Use a range of sources of information • Use first-hand data to carry out a range of scientific investigations • Recognize health and safety issues	Ensure the conditions are right for healthy growth of the potatoes Observations, drawings and record keeping of growth of the potato plant Internet and catalogue use to research varieties of potatoes Graphs of potato yields the different varieties and analysis of the significance for future plantings. Take appropriate care when handling compost and plants.
ICT	Use the internet to search large databases and to interpret information Choose and use appropriate ICT to generate, develop, organize and present their work. Recognize relevant information and check for accuracy.	Research about potato varieties and yields. Design and print labels for packaging using Word labels facility. Make sure the information on the label is accurate.
Art and Design	Record from first-hand observation Use a range of materials and processes including ICT	Chalk or pastel still life drawings of a group of potatoes. Plant drawings
Design and Technology	Develop, plan and communicate ideas thinking about the use of the finished work	Design and print labels for the potato packaging. Design and make posters to advertise the potatoes.

Other science topics that could involve relevant mathematics work

Always ensure that the level of mathematics is commensurate with the age and ability of the children by cross referencing the PNS objectives at the planning stage.

- Natural world – leaves, butterflies, camouflage – symmetry and pattern
- Fibonacci spirals – snails, sunflowers etc. – number patterns and shapes
- Garden Centre role play area with seed packets designed by the children with relevant information about the plants, different sized plant-pots, canes for measurement work, opening times for time work and even a small coffee shop
- Life cycles – repeating pattern
- Practical work on the circulation and breathing – recordings of pulse and breathing rates before and after exercise – graphs
- Earth and Beyond – relationship between distance, speed and time. Use of calculators with large numbers
- Materials investigations such as heat insulation – Venn and Carroll diagrams for results of sorting – temperature reading
- Healthy Eating project – pie charts of food groups, bar charts of daily intake, calorie counting

Mathematics and design and technology

Making links between Design and Technology and mathematics has significant benefits for learning in both subjects. (QCA, 2006 p.1)

Introduction to mathematics and design and technology

The link to Mathematics is identified in the National Curriculum (Ma3, 4a–c) because of the importance of accurate measuring of length and angles in order to mark and cut out the materials being used in the practical work. However the use of accurate measurement, both using standard and non-standard measures, goes much further than this with the links with place value and estimation.

Hope (2004, p.27) identified the importance of practical activity for children as they learn to 'manipulate real objects to gain spatial awareness, properties of size, shape, appropriate vocabulary in which explicit mathematical links can be made'.

Orton and Frobisher (1996) discuss the importance of practical activity to give children the experiences they need to develop a good understanding of shapes. Children need to be taught to observe accurately as they handle the shapes around them. 'The aim of teaching about shapes and space in schools should enable children to become conscious of the variety of shapes around them, their size, how they are arranged, the way they may move and how they may change position and direction; in essence to understand their world' (p.133). This practical activity does not of course need to be confined to the mathematics lesson or limited to mathematical sets of shapes bearing no relationship to the real world. What better way to explore shapes than by disassembling or creating artefacts during practical activity?

Benson (2000, p.3) looks at the potential of the multi-disciplinary nature of the subject which 'provides opportunities for children to apply knowledge and understanding gained in the areas of, for example, science, mathematics, language, art and ICT. It is then that they can demonstrate a real understanding of a concept given appropriate support from the teacher in making the links.'

This view is reinforced by The Design and Technology leaflet in the first issue of Primary Subjects (CfSA Summer, 2008) that stresses that the subject is a lot more than 'just a craft activity' and that children must 'draw upon understanding from maths, science and other areas and apply it in a practical way to generate solutions'.

Hope (2004, p.28) reminds us that it must not be forgotten that Design and Technology offers opportunities for spectacular successes. 'Ticks in a maths book are nothing compared to the joy of having a box with a properly fitting lid, standing on the display shelf next to everyone else's.' A child experiencing such a glow of success knows all about the accurate measuring of length and angles, as well as the techniques of construction. There has also been the opportunity to see the purpose and benefits of using and applying mathematics in real life.

A young graduate recently reminded us of his huge 'grandfather clock' constructed in Year 5 and clearly a high spot of his years in Primary education. It had involved a lot of glue but also a lot of sensible estimation and accurate measurements!

Case study – design and make packaging boxes, Year 5

The design and technology challenge was to make two boxes of the same design but different sizes. They were to be packaging for clay work from a previous module of work, where each child created two different sized bowls. The boxed bowls could then be used as Christmas presents. The children were to include a logo showing rotational or reflective symmetry. They had to consider the safety of the bowls while in the boxes, measure them to ensure a tight fit, and choose a card of appropriate weight. They also had to design a simple fastening device.

Teacher's comment

This was an ambitious module of work as the class had a very wide ability range. As an extension activity, the more able children were given an extra challenge; the base of their box was to be a trapezium or rhombus. Those children needing extra support made their initial designs from construction kits such as Polydron and Clixi. This gave them a visual basis for their own designs of nets. They used a set square to make accurate right angles for their boxes and could choose to use a squared card for their nets. This helped to make the measurements accurate.

I used this work to assess a key objective for Year 5 'Draw and measure lines to the nearest millimetre', and for the less able children and the Year 4 objective 'to make a net of a common solid'. I was also assessing their ability to decide on the scale of the two boxes and recognize the relationship between them.

The logos were designed on the computer using the program *Revelation Natural Art* that provided an assessment opportunity for their understanding of symmetry.

The display of the boxes was excellent as the project records were kept by all the children. This included annotated photographic evidence and a short explanation of the sequence of their work.

Mathematics included in this work

Mathematics	Objective	Activity
Using and Applying	• Solve problems by measuring, estimating and calculating • Read and interpret scales on a range of measuring instruments, recognizing that the measurement made is approximate, and then recording results to a required degree of accuracy • Tabulate systematically the information in a problem or puzzle; identify and record the steps or calculations needed to solve it. • Represent and interpret sequences, patterns and relationships involving numbers and shapes; suggest and test hypotheses; construct and use simple expressions and formulae in words then symbols	Decide on the best way to adapt a net to create two identical polyhedra with a different scale Present work in the form of accurate diagrams of nets, calculating the accurate angle and side measurements Record the measurements of the two boxes to show the scale. Explain the relationship between the measurements of the two boxes in algebraic form
Shape and Space	• Describe, identify and visualize parallel and perpendicular edges or faces; use these properties to classify 2-D shapes and 3-D solids • Complete patterns with up to two lines of symmetry; draw the position of a shape after a reflection or translation (Year 5)	Use knowledge of the properties to draw 2-D shapes and nets of 3-D shapes Logo designs
Measures	• Choose and use standard metric units (cm) and use decimal notation to record these measurements • Use a protractor to accurately measure and draw the angles accurately.	Measure the bowls height and width. Estimate the dimensions for the boxes. Measure acute and obtuse angles using an angle measurer or protractor when required to while drawing the nets of the boxes. Measure out the complete nets of the boxes.

Possible misconceptions or difficulties

- There could be inaccurate measuring with the rulers not being used accurately especially starting measuring at 1 cm and not 0 cm.
- There could be confusion between centimetre and millimetre.
- There may be difficulties when using a protractor if the logo is to display rotational symmetry. For example if the design is to be of Order 3 then the initial planning must involve dividing 360° by 3.
- When making the smaller box, the child may not reduce all the measurements equally.

Other curriculum areas included in this work

Design and Technology	Investigate, disassemble and evaluate Complete practical tasks Design and make the required items.	Study a range of cardboard boxes looking at their nets, methods of joining edges and closing the lid. Test choice of card and make decisions about joining the card and securing the lids processes. Consider the measurements for both boxes. Make and evaluate the two boxes.
ICT	Use graphics package in the design processes. Share and exchange information using text and photographs	Design nets, re-size shapes. Use print-outs as part of individual recording and evaluation of work completed Use graphics to design symmetrical labels, resizing accordingly. Designing work for display – to be easily viewed and understood.

Some examples of other Design and Technology topics that could involve relevant mathematics work

Always ensure that the level of mathematics is commensurate with the age and ability of the children by cross referencing the PNS objectives when at the planning stage.

- Design and make a bridge – triangles, parallel lines and symmetry
- Apply knowledge of ratio when working with pulleys
- Design curve stitching and making parabolas
- Junk modelling for all key stages with a range of 3-D shapes (It is a good idea to deconstruct and reform boxes using glue gun, turning printed surface inwards and thus providing a plain card surface on which to paint. It doesn't take too long and the results make it worthwhile.)
- Make origami and paper aeroplanes – accurate measuring and understanding of 2-D shapes, following instructions and understanding of the vocabulary of folding
- Design street furniture with a theme linked to the neighbourhood (The designs have to exhibit symmetry. Design of street tiles involving measurement of tile and size of shapes to rotate or reflect within it and demonstrate understanding of the Order of rotational symmetry.)
- Measure distances travelled in trials of models
- Measure time taken to complete a sequence
- Accurate weighing of ingredients and measurement of the liquid for baking and make sure the oven is at the correct temperature, converting the temperature from Celsius to Fahrenheit if required
- Doubling or halving the ingredients for baking larger or smaller amounts
- Use of skills of estimation and comparison
- Design and make kites – reflective symmetry 2-D shapes
- Design and make a board game linked with a story book
- Design and make pop-up cards – measurement of length and angles

References and further reading

ASE (1990) *Be Safe* Hatfield: ASE.

Benson, C. (2000) *Teaching and Learning Design Technology* London: Continuum.

Council for Subject Associations (2008) *Primary Subjects, Making Every Child Matter* Reading: CfSA Publications.

Department for Children, Schools and Families Rose, J. (2009) *Independent Review of the Primary Curriculum: Final Report* London: DCSF Publications.

—Williams, P. (2008) *Independent Review of Mathematics Teaching in Early Years Settings and Primary Schools Final Report* London: DCSF Publications.

Department for Education and Employment (1999) *The National Numeracy Strategy: Framework for Teaching Mathematics from Reception to Year 6* London: DfEE Publications.

Feasey, R. and Gallear, B. (2000) *Primary Science and Numeracy* Hatfield: ASE.

Frobisher, L., Orton, A. and Orton, J. (2007) *Learning to Teach Shape and Space* Cheltenham: Nelson: Thornes.

Harlen, W. (ed.) (2006) *ASE Guide to Primary Science* Hatfield: ASE.

Hope, G. (2004) *Teaching Design and Technology 3–11 an Essential Guide for Teachers* London: Continuum.

Mooney, C., Briggs, M., Fletcher, M. and McCulloch, J. (2001) *Primary Mathematics Teaching Theory and Practice* Exeter: Learning Matters.

Oliver, A. (2007) *Teaching Science in the Early Years and Primary Classroom* Abingdon: David Fulton.

Orton, A. and Frobisher, L. (1996) *Insights into Teaching Mathematics* London: Cassell.

Peterson, S. (1999) 'Linking mathematics and science in the primary school' in Pinel, A. (ed.) *Teaching, Learning, and Primary Mathematics* Derby: ATM, pp. 24–27.

Qualifications and Curriculum Authority (2006) *Embedding Mathematics in Design and Technology at Key Stages 1 – 2* [Online.] Available at: http://www.cfbt.com/lincolnshire/pdf/qca-06–2359_opportunities_to_embed_mathematics_in_d_and_t.pdf (Accessed: 4 August 2009).

Ward, H., Hewlett, C., Roden, J. and Foreman, J. (2005) *Teaching Science in the Primary Classroom: A Practical Guide* London: Paul Chapman.

Williams, J. and Easingwood, N. (2003) *ICT & Primary Science* London: Routledge Falmer

Websites

All website addresses were accessed on 31 July 2009.

The *Standards* Site *Schemes* of Work materials support the *DfES* publication,

Excellence and Enjoyment. Available at: *www.standards.dfes.gov.uk/schemes3/*

Bulbs and Seeds. Available at: www.thompson-morgan.com.

www.unwins-seeds.co.uk.

In 2006, the DCSF published its manifesto 'Learning Outside the Classroom'. It set out a vision to enable every young person to experience the world beyond the classroom as an essential part of their learning and personal development. It is available at *publications.teachernet.gov.uk*.

The NCETM actively promotes the learning of mathematics outside the classroom. 'Learning Maths Outside the Classroom'. Available at: http://www.ncetm.org.uk/resources/9268.

Details of Logotron's Revelation Natural Art computer program available at: http://www.r-e-m.co.uk/logo/?comp=rna.

6 Mathematics and Historical and Geographical Understanding

Mathematics and history

From the standpoint of young learners, making links between subjects enriches and enlivens them, especially history and geography.

Rose (DCSF, 2009, p.3)

Introduction to mathematics and history

There is a strong case for making connections between history and mathematics at the planning stage. Children need to develop fully their chronological understanding in order to understand and explore historical events. So, as in mathematics, they need to learn the vocabulary associated with the passing of time and the relationship between units of time; this can be an element of historical study as they study specific periods. Also while researching times past, children need to use a range of information sources. Data about people or events can take many forms, and mathematical skills may be needed to interpret this information, be it working out the length of a reign or analysing parallel events in history.

Briggs and Davis (2008, p.91) recognize two ways to link history with mathematics. 'The first is to link with topics in history and the other is to link directly with the history of mathematics.' The connection with mathematics is also recognized by Nichol and Dean (1997). They feel that although history was generally linked to geography there are many opportunities to develop relevant work in a range of subjects including mathematics, and they cite an example of a Year 3 class creating a Roman market and selling goods at realistic prices in

Roman currency. The opportunity for shape and space work with mosaics patterns will also be there.

While children are learning about significant people, events and places from the past, an obvious connection with mathematics is in work involving chronological order, time lines and working out time spans, such as the length of a monarch's reign or a war, or estimation of the duration of an ancient war.

Coles and Copeland (2002, p.25) remind us that while it is easy to think of mathematics in history as working with time lines and chronology, they extend this view as the subject also has a 'clear role to play in enabling children to quantify primary evidence, and help then to draw conclusions and communicate their findings'. Similarly, the National Curriculum (NC) (DfEE, 1999, p.105) suggests the use of census databases 'to search for information and identify and explain patterns of change'.

Mathematics input can be on a small scale, but still have relevance to an historical topic. A good example of this was a student working with a Year 5 class. She used the history topic of the Second World War to develop some artwork that took the form of an exciting wall display of house silhouettes in the blitz. Hanging from the ceiling were model aeroplanes made from cubes, cuboids and square pyramids. These shapes were accurately measured so they fitted together to form the aeroplanes. She used the activity to assess both the children's ability to measure angles and length accurately as they made the nets of the polyhedra and also their understanding of the properties of 3-D shapes. This shape and space work was included in the mathematics planning for the daily mathematics lesson.

Case study – Florence Nightingale, Year 6

While studying Florence Nightingale as a significant historical figure, the teacher took the opportunity to develop mathematical work in handling data.

Florence Nightingale was famous for going to Turkey to help soldiers injured in the Crimean War, but she was also an accomplished mathematician using her knowledge of statistics to demonstrate that the majority of deaths resulted from the soldiers' stay in hospital rather than the injuries sustained in battle.

Thus, history and mathematics were combined in this work using historical data.

Teacher's comment

This project was 50 per cent history and 50 per cent mathematics with both aspects crucial to the success of the topic. The pupils were fascinated to see the somewhat shadowy historical figure with a lamp become a strong and vibrant character from history. Her academic strength was also a surprise and fired enthusiasm to research her life and work. It also led to general discussions on emancipation and the role of women in that period of history.

The data was constructed on a wide range of graphs and charts according to the pupils' level of understanding, and this enriched the displays of their work.

Mathematics included in this work

Mathematics	Objective	Activity
Using and Applying	• Present data in an appropriate graph. Draw conclusions from the graph • Pose and answer relevant mathematical questions • Present your work to the class, including your graphs and other data	While researching the life of Florence Nightingale and the Crimean War, focus on a mathematical aspect of her life and choose the most efficient ICT program to present your findings and results.
Data Handling	• Develop and evaluate lines of enquiry: identify, collect, organize and analyse information. Present conclusions and pose other questions to answer • Construct and interpret frequency tables, bar charts with grouped discrete data and line graphs; interpret pie charts	Make graphs and pie charts to support the investigations and findings using a range of ICT

Possible misconceptions and difficulties

The mathematical work linked with this topic is mainly handling data.

- Children may find it difficult to pose an appropriate question: too simple a question and there will be little opportunity for challenging mathematics, too complex and the relevant data may not be available.
- Problems could be caused by difficulties in processing and transferring the collected information into graph form with
  - inaccurate labelling especially with grouped data,
  - not using a key and
  - inappropriate choice of graph, for example, selecting a line graph to represent discrete data.
- Children may have insufficient time to interpret their graphs and amend if appropriate.

Other curriculum areas included in the work

Subject	Objective	Activity
History	Understand the impact of significant individuals in Victorian Britain through the study of Florence Nightingale – looking particularly at why she went to Turkey to help soldiers injured in the Crimean War and what happened as a result of her work.	Research to answer questions such as Who was Florence Nightingale? Why did Florence Nightingale go to Scutari? What was it like for Florence Nightingale working in the Crimean War? How did Florence Nightingale make things better for soldiers in the Crimean War?
ICT	Choose and use appropriate ICT to generate, develop, organize and present work. Recognize relevant information and check for accuracy.	Use a spreadsheet, for example, excel, to collect, interrogate and present data in an appropriate chart. (This may include the use of formulae to calculate means etc. for more able children.)
English Unit 1 Non-fiction Biography and autobiography	Develop a biographical style of writing, distinguishing between fact, opinion and fiction. Use appropriate grammar and language conventions.	Research, analyse and write biography combining Florence Nightingale both as a nurse and a mathematician.

Other curriculum areas that could involve relevant mathematics work

Always ensure that the level of mathematics is commensurate with the age and ability of the children by cross referencing the PNS objectives when at the planning stage.

- Investigations on the work of mathematicians such as Pascal, Fibonacci and Euler linking the time they were alive, their circumstances and their mathematics;
- Roman times – number system, tiling patterns, army organization, Hadrian's Wall distances and so on;
- Hadrian's Wall today;
- Historical buildings – symmetry in design, records of the buildings including plans;
- Egypt – pyramids, number system, measuring system;
- Use of Census material – data handling. Census data is available on the internet;
- Study units of measurements in ancient civilizations, including the introduction of 'zero'. How did this development change computation?
- The development of units of measure in our society from the Magna Carta (1215) to the present metric system. Create conversion charts;
- Study of churchyards and parish records need sensitivity but provides data for dates of birth and death, longevity, family trees;
- Study of historic voyages of discovery.

Mathematics and geography

Geography and numeracy are intimately linked. http://www.qca.org.uk/geography/innovating/keystage2

Introduction to mathematics and geography

Morgan (1998, p.5) recognizes that geography 'develops skills in thinking and reasoning and offers opportunities for discussion and group collaboration'. She also stresses the 'wide scope for a variety of forms of writing as well as a valid context for mathematics and Information and Communication Technology'.

This strong relationship between mathematics and geography is easily identified. Carter (1998, p.89) gives an obvious example of this: 'Go to any maths scheme and you are likely to find activities which draw on local investigations of traffic or houses, shops or the weather. Children need to use and apply mathematics in real contexts which are meaningful to them.'

So it is crucial to recognize the mathematics within geographical work and ensure that planning has taken this into account. The mathematics may involve revisiting work already covered in another context or it may be the introduction of a new aspect of mathematics. Whichever way round, there must be a genuine need to use the mathematics so that the activities are meaningful rather than, as Carter (1998, p.89) contends, 'second-hand exercises which characterise some maths schemes'.

Carter (1998, p.89) lists the huge range of geographical contexts in which the integral use of mathematics is essential. The following list is adapted from it:

- use of grid references and compass points for location, direction, distance, size and scale, lines of latitude and longitude with large scale maps, plans and globes;
- comparison of maps and globes in order to see how a rounded surface may be represented on a flat surface;
- understanding time zones, day and night, seasons – because the earth is a sphere moving round the sun;
- the collection, recording, presentation and interpretation of data from a geographical investigation;
- use of a wide range of measuring instruments to facilitate the accurate measure of data, such as distance, rainfall or temperature;
- the sorting, ordering and classifying of collections. Making choices about selection of criteria;
- number work involving estimation, finding totals or averages.

Links with data handling are plentiful. Chambers and Donert (1996) recognized the benefits of combining and linking units of work citing the planning of work with the theme of 'fast food' with geography, ICT and mathematics combining as children worked through a proposal for a fast-food outlet, devised a questionnaire and database to explore options, make conclusions and present and interpret data at the Local Planning Office.

Fox and Armstrong (1997) describe the central use of ICT during a geographical study with the theme of 'Changes': from plant to basket in an OXFAM shop. Information was gathered and in the form of databases, scatter graphs and line graphs, interrogated to find solutions to a range of problems involving packaging the baskets for transporting to shops.

Thomsitt (2008, p.39) notes that 'similarities and differences between countries, climate zones, historical periods, different religions, different cultures and so on all lend themselves to possibilities of working with Venn diagrams. The use of this mathematical tool could enhance the ability to appreciate similarities and differences and may well deepen knowledge and give children a greater appreciation of our global world.'

Nicholson (1994) shows how stories can provide a context for geographical work. While the book's list is somewhat dated, the ideas are fresh, with a wide range of mathematical suggestions, and would provide a good stimulus at the start of planning.

Case study – Key Stage 1, Year 2

The class had two teddy bears, Teddy Edward and Teddy Brown that 'lived' in the classroom. Children often took them home where they stayed with families, and they were included in school outings. They were used to support the Literacy curriculum with teddies' diaries being written by the children.

A child went to Australia during Christmas holidays to attend a wedding in Sydney. The teacher took this opportunity to include it in her planning, using as a guide the QCA geography scheme Unit 5: *Where in the World is Barnaby Bear?* Teddy Edward went to Sydney Australia, and Teddy Brown remained in Newcastle-upon-Tyne, England. During the holiday, photographs of both teddies were taken, and all the children were asked to keep a pictorial weather chart for the 2 weeks. The teacher and children had discussed the range of photographs to be taken in both countries.

The initial study of the photographs prompted discussion of the similarities and differences. Most obvious was the contrast of seasons and weather conditions. The Christmas Day photographs showed the Australian outdoor barbecue Christmas dinner with the family in tee shirts and shorts. This was a stark contrast to the British meal round the table, with lights on and fire lit and warm winter clothing. However, both photographs showed evidence of fun, present giving and traditional Christmas trees.

The Australian diary, kept by Teddy Edward, followed the pattern of sections of the Unit 5 geography schemes of work.

1. Which country did Teddy Edward visit?
2. Can we find it on the map?
3. What was it like while Teddy Edward was there?
4. Which places did he visit, and in what events did he participate?
5. How did Teddy Edward travel to these places?

Work in the classroom included a chart of the months showing the seasonal differences and weather charts and analysis of the weather charts. The discussions also concerned the countryside and crops grown in the two areas. Key features such as the Sage building in Gateshead and the Sydney Opera House were looked at on photographs and the architecture and usage discussed. It was noted that the tiles of the Sydney Opera House were irregular hexagons.

Travel times were discussed informally – it takes 23 hours to get to Sydney. It takes less than an hour to fly to London from Newcastle.

Teacher's comment

This work was successful as the objectives for the different subjects were met, and the children enjoyed their participation. The combination of geography, mathematics and literacy worked well with the overlap seeming natural.

The photographs were used in an interactive display that involved sorting according to different criteria. This was in addition to the graphs and charts of weather, seasonal differences and modes of travel.

The diary writing was well done as was the fact finding and recording, especially when linking Australia with the indigenous animals.

The work with road signs and the Sydney Opera House tiles was almost an 'add-on' and resulted in an excellent piece of mathematical work including the orientation of 2-D shapes.

Valuable road safety issues were aired. The children discovered the significance of the shapes and colours of British Road Signs. Signs for school were designed and erected so there was now no excuse to run down a corridor or not to know where there was 'No Entry'.

Mathematics included in this work

Mathematics	Objective	Activity
Using and Applying	Follow a line of enquiry by gathering information and explaining methods and results	Use internet, news press and email to gather information to make charts and graphs showing temperature and weather contrasts. Compare road signs
Shape and Space	• Understand the properties of common 2-D shapes. Identify them from different orientations Identify reflective symmetry	Tessellation of hexagons – roofing tiles at Sydney Opera House
Measures	• Use the four compass directions (Year 3) • Use the vocabulary of time • Revise the months and seasons (Year 1)	NSEW – position of main cities in the work in relation to one other Understand how to work out time taken during the journeys counted in hours Recognize features of the seasons
Data Handling	• Classify and organize information in simple ways	Draw Pictogram to show the different modes of transport Daily Weather chart Seasons chart

Possible misconceptions and difficulties

- Ensure that the children have considered the properties of polygons - edges, interior angles and why shapes do or do not tessellate.
- Check that the shapes are viewed from different orientations and that children have the opportunity to see irregular polygons as there is a tendency for regular polygons to be illustrated in one orientation.
- When working with compass directions, ensure there is a link between the four compass directions and right angles before introducing the 45° directions, N,S, E, W, NE, NW, SE, SW. If helpful imagine the compass as a clock face with 12 o'clock, 3 o'clock, 6 o'clock and 9 o'clock as N, E, S and W. Mnemonics such as Never Eat Slimy Worms or Naughty Elephants Squirt Water always seem helpful!
- Remember that there are two aspects to time:

  - the passing of time, which in this case is the journey that is measured in hours, days and weeks; and
  - recording time, which is this case will be the time and date when something on the journey happened and was recorded in the diary. Think about analogue and digital time.

- Pictograms display discrete data. It is important that the symbols are the same size. Think about the possibility of developing this work so that a symbol represents more than one item, for example, a car symbol represents two cars.
- Block graphs can be an alternative, in which scale is not an issue as it is the blocks (of the same size) that are counted.
- A bar chart can be used, but this requires a side scale. Columns should be separated as the data is discrete.

Other curriculum areas included in this work

Subject	Objective	Activity
Geography	Locate a variety of places at home and abroad and find places on a map	Use atlases, travel guides and wall maps to locate the places in the journey
	Recognize features of places	Comparison of the main features seen in Newcastle and Sydney
	Recognize the difference and similarities in locations of other places	Use of TV, newspaper, internet, email to gather weather information, followed by observation and discussion
	Identify types of weather that are experienced in places and seasonal change and their effects on people	From discussion, photographs and internet, think about why the forms of transport are used
	Understand the range of types of transport used to get to other places	
ICT	Gather and represent information	Internet map searches
		Internet photograph searches of main features of the area
		Plotting routes
		Graphs and charts of weather and season: contrast
		Use the information from above in individual and class work for display – adding captions
English	Combine texts and graphics	Reports on findings on seasonal and daily time differences in Australia and England
	Non fiction texts	Write weather reports for Newcastle and Sydney.
	Explanation – oral and written	Factual details of places studied
	Information texts	Diary entries for teddy Edward or Teddy Brown
	Recount	

Other geography topics that could involve relevant mathematics work

Always ensure that the level of mathematics is commensurate with the age and ability of the children by cross-referencing the PNS objectives when at the planning stage.

- Look at the Schemes of work http://www.standards.dfes.gov.uk/schemes2/geography/ in which Unit 25 of geography at Key Stages 1 and 2 (Year 1–6) is geography and numbers. This specifically links mathematics and geography.
- Plot routes from adventure climbs, sailing competitions, charity walks or cycle rides and expeditions currently in the news.
- Plan for map work with direction and scale linked with story books such as the Scilly Isles in *Why the Whales Came* by Michael Morpurgo.
- Rubbish topic (see 'Improving the Environment' topic for Year 4 scheme of work (http://www.standards.dfes.gov.uk/schemes2/geography/)
- Weather recording using instruments and a range of scales.
- Locality studies starting from the classroom, school, immediate locality.
- Use a range of locality studies such as field trips to the local shops/supermarket – for all ages from Foundation Stage to Key Stage 2. Look at stacking, price comparisons, 'offers', packaging patterns and shapes, food sources and so on.
- Sort with the similarity and differences of rocks and soils – sorting and grouping using different criteria. Tree sorts, Venn and Carroll diagrams.

- Plot routes with programmable toys.
- Use a range of scales with maps and plans.
- Use data handling during surveys.
- Use secondary sources such as weather records on the internet to compile and interrogate graphs during study of distant places.
- Link history and geography with a study of tourism in historic sites such as Hadrian's Wall: Gather information and look at transport, costs of museums, accommodation, publicity and so on.

References and further reading

Briggs, M. and Davis, S. (2008) *Creative Teaching: Mathematics in the Early Years and Primary Classroom* Abingdon: Routledge.

Carter, R. (ed.) (1998) *Handbook of Primary Geography* Sheffield: Geographical Association.

Chambers, B. and Donert, K. (1996) *Teaching Geography at Key Stage 2* Cambridge: Chris Kington.

Coles, D. and Copeland, T. (2002) *Numeracy and Mathematics Across the Primary Curriculum* London: David Fulton.

Cooper, H. (2007) *History 3–11 a Guide for Teachers* Abingdon: David Fulton. (This book contains interesting examples of cross-curricular work with a historic emphasis.)

Copeland, T. (1991) *A Teacher's Guide to Maths and the Historic Environment* London: English Heritage. (Despite its age, this book contains a lot of useful links between mathematics and history.)

Department for Children, Schools and Families Rose, J. (2009) *Report Independent Review of the Primary Curriculum: Final Report* London: DCSF Publications.

Department for Education and Employment (1999) *The National Curriculum Handbook for Primary Teachers in England* London: DfEE Publications.

Fines, J. and Nichol, J. (1997) *Teaching Primary History. Nuffield Primary History Project* Oxford: Heinemann.

Fox, S. and Armstrong, H. (1997) 'Baskets' in Govier, H. (ed.) *MICRO-SCOPE Information Handling Special* Newman College/MAPE.

Morgan, W. (1998) in Carter, R. (ed.) *Handbook of Primary Geography* Sheffield: Geographical Association p. forward.

Morpurgo, M. (1994) *Why the Whales Came* London: Mammoth.

Nichol, J. and Dean, J. (1997) *History 7–11: Developing Primary Teaching Skills* London: Routledge.

Nicholson, H. (1994) *Place in Story-Time* Sheffield: Geographical Association.

Thomsitt, R. (2008) 'Hoop hoop hurray' in *Mathematics Teaching Incorporating Micromath* November 2008 211 Mathematics.

Websites

All website addresses were accessed on 31 July 2009.

http://.www.bbc.co.uk/schools/famouspeople/standard/nightingale/index.shtml.

http://en.wikipedia.org/wiki/Pie chart.

Historical biographies of mathematicians. Available at: http://www-groups.dcs.st-and.ac.uk/~history/BiogIndex.html.

An excellent compilation of useful websites. Available at: http://www.geography.org.uk/eyprimary/geographysubjectleaders/resourcesict/usefulweblinks.

Mathematics and art and design

The connection between mathematics and art was recognized by Woodman and Albany (1988, p.iv):

> Very often, depicting mathematical patterns or relationships in a colourful and artistic way adds to a child's understanding and appreciation of them. Children may come to realise that, inherent in many artistic forms, there exists a mathematical precision too often taken for granted. Also it is hoped that children will come to appreciate that natural forms and structures can be interpreted only by using mathematical language and techniques. Symmetry is a dominant characteristic of both the natural and man made world.

Introduction to mathematics and art and design

There is a close connection between requirements of Ma3 in the Mathematics National Curriculum (NC) and areas of the Art curriculum. This can clearly be seen in the study of pattern and shape in both subjects. The Art and Design Schemes of work require the development of children's understanding of colour, form, texture and pattern. In mathematics there is the study of pattern of numbers and shapes. Symmetry, rotation, translation and tessellation together with the properties of a wide range of shapes are part of the Mathematics NC.

Planning for a module of art work with other subjects has its problems. QCA (2004, p.5) warns that 'where art and design is combined with other subjects it is more likely to be

included in a cross-curricular topic and seen as supporting a topic or an opportunity to practise skills, rather than a subject to be taught in its own right.' The following case study is very
firmly focused on Art with the mathematics not detracting from this. Indeed QCA recognizes that shape, space and measures provide excellent opportunities to study cultural expression by studying and constructing patterns form different cultures.

Case study – African fabrics, Year 4

The teacher planned this unit of work to cover the following Art and Design objectives and
used the QCA Scheme of Work Unit 3B: Investigating Pattern as a starting point:

- develop children's understanding of colour, form, texture, pattern and their ability to use materials
  and processes to communicate ideas, feelings and meanings;
- explore with children ideas and meanings in the work of artists, craftspeople and designers;
- help them learn about their different roles and functions of art, craft and design in their own lives
  and in different times and cultures;
- help children to learn how to make thoughtful judgements and aesthetic and practical decisions and
  become actively involved in shaping environments.

The potential for work in other curriculum areas was thought out on the following
planning web. See Figure 7.1.

The children studied the work of the African craftspeople, looking at how the fabric was
made and the possible influences of the designs. They used colour, shapes, pattern and texture
to develop their own ideas and feelings as they created their own fabric designs. This involved
experimenting with shapes and finding how to fit them together, how to make triangles tessellate and how to rotate and reflect patterns. This was done initially using wax crayons and ink
wash to create vibrant patterns. This was a technique remembered from Key Stage 1 days.

Each member of the class required a piece of fabric. This involved measurement and
decisions about the most economical way to cut the fabric into smaller pieces.

The class investigated print-making techniques and explored ways of combining and
organizing shapes, colours and patterns to make their fabric. They also discovered that
African craftspeople used signs, symbols and metaphors to communicate ideas and meanings. Some children designed their own symbols, relevant to their lives and experiences. The
designs required a key or brief summary to explain the symbolism.

The shop from where we had bought the African fabric samples had cut 1 m × 1.10 m
pieces of fabric into four – these were called 'Fat Quarters'. This provided a starting point for
investigational area and perimeter work.

The following problems needed investigating:

- When the fabric was cut into 4 quarters, what is the area of each new piece? See Figure 7.2.
- Would it make a difference if the quarters were long-ways? See Figure 7.3.
- How much braid would you need to edge a Fat Quarter?
- Would the length of braid be the same for the longitudinal quarters?

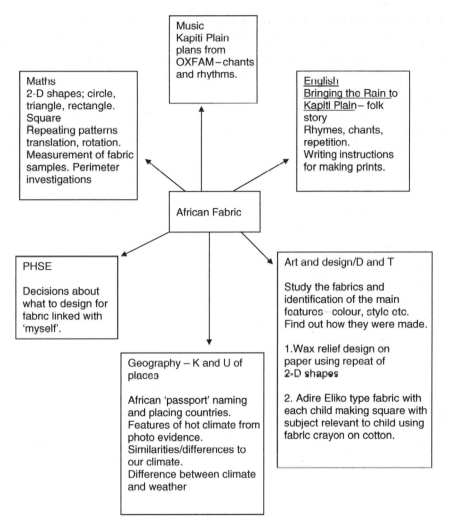

Figure 7.1 Planning web for African fabrics.

Figure 7.2 Fabric cut into Fat Quarters.

Figure 7.3 Fabric cut into quarters, lengthwise.

Teacher's comment

The impact of this work was huge. The children really focused on their tasks as they developed their ideas. They enjoyed the colourful fabrics and the photographs. The vocabulary of shape was used naturally and I was pleased that there was the opportunity for differentiation in the mathematical aspects of the work. I took the opportunity to assess the children's ability to measure accurately, and, where appropriate, to use decimal notation to record their measurements – part of Year 4 Key Objectives. The children needed to measure their templates and fabrics carefully and to record these measurements in their personal planning records. The braid measured in the perimeter investigations was used in the display of fabrics providing borders to enhance the presentations.

The designing and printing of fabric was very successful and involved a lot of mathematical discussions about symmetry and repetition. An unexpected bonus was created by the Kola nut fabric which had repeated shapes in patterns of four, illustrating rotational symmetry. A child commented that for one pattern there were four nuts, so for two patterns there would be eight nuts. This developed into a 'game' involving the four times table and illustrated how to use known facts to the best advantage.

There was a lot of discussion involving the orientation of identical 2-D shapes. Was it still the same triangle when 'upside down'?

Among the range of books used in this work, the children loved the fun of the book *Bringing the Rain to Kapiti Plain*, which has the same rhythm as *This is the House that Jack Built*. The music plan from Oxfam was successful too (despite being aimed at Key Stage 1) with its focus on rhythm providing more pattern work but this time using sound not paint.

Mathematics involved in the work

Mathematics	Objective	Activity
Using and Applying	Identify and use patterns, relationships and properties of shapes to solve a problem, present and interpret the solution in the context of the problem. Report solutions to puzzles and problems, giving explanations and reasoning orally and in writing, using diagrams and symbols.	Use the examples of the fabric, make choices about shapes that will 'fit together' and test them in drawings.
Shape and Space	Solve one-step and two-step problems involving measures, choose and carry out appropriate calculations, using calculator methods where appropriate. Suggest a line of enquiry and the strategy; collect, organize and interpret selected information to find answers. Draw polygons and classify them by identifying their properties including their line symmetry.	Make fabric sample and explain symbols, organization and methods in leaflet. 'Fat Quarters' investigation. Use the vocabulary of the properties of the polygons in the description of the fabric designed. Include line symmetry in this.
Measures	Choose and use standard metric units and their abbreviations when measuring and recording length. Where appropriate, use decimal notation to record measurements. Find the area and perimeter of rectangles.	Measure the fabric and the templates. Problem-solving work involving 'Fat Quarters' requiring decimal recording. 'Fat Quarters' investigation

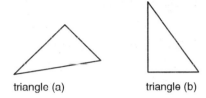

triangle (a)   triangle (b)

Figure 7.4 Triangle (a) and triangle (b).

Possible Mathematical misconceptions or difficulties

*Please note that rotational symmetry is not specifically mentioned in the PNS and only in the NC except in a general statement 'identify all of the symmetries of 2-D shapes' by Level 5. However the authors feel its inclusion is desirable and appropriate here.

- Text books tend to draw both 2 and 3-D shapes with the base parallel to the bottom of the page so if the orientation alters, the child does not recognize that the shape is the same. This was identified in early SAT's evaluations when many children failed to identify the following right-angled triangle (a) but had no problem with triangle (b). See Figure 7.4.
- Some children can find the names of 2 and 3-D shapes difficult to pronounce and remember. Ensure that recognition of the properties, similarities and differences of the shapes is securely understood. It will help to discuss the word derivations: such as 'tri' meaning 3 and 'quad' relating to four.
- Regular polygons tend to be seen so ensure that the child understands the properties and names of irregular polygons.
- A common misunderstanding is the confusion between the meaning of length and width with children assuming that length is always the longer measurement.

Other curriculum areas included in this work

Subject	Objective	Activity
Art and Design	Explore and develop ideas and experiment with stencilling and block-printing techniques to create a printed pattern. Increase critical awareness of the roles and purposes of art of different cultures.	Use the African fabric samples to design and make a piece of fabric with similar characteristics of symmetry and symbolism. Look critically at the materials and processes that were used to make it as well as where and when it was made.
ICT	Search for information using key words. Use graphics package and select tools to explore and realize their ideas and designs. Identify ways to develop images using repeating patterns.	Research types of traditional African fabrics, designs and symbolism. Create own symbols relevant to local area. Develop the initial design to a repeating pattern.
Music	Schemes of Work Unit 10: Play it again – exploring rhythmic patterns.	Create simple rhythmic patterns and perform them rhythmically using the poem *Bringing the Rains to Kapiti Plains*.
Literacy	Instructional writing	Write an explanation of the symbolism of the fabric designs. Instructions for fabric printing

Other art and design topics that could involve relevant mathematics work

Always ensure that the level of mathematics is commensurate with the age and ability of the children by cross referencing the PNS objectives when at the planning stage.

- Study of the artist Piet Mondrian – squares and rectangles
- Study of the artist Henri Matisse to include 'The Snail', a gouache of quadrilaterals
- Study of William Morris designs – symmetry.
- Study of Bridget Riley – circles, quadrilaterals and tessellations
- Study of styles of art such as cubism
- Designs from other cultures and religions – such as Aboriginal, Rangoli patterns (Woodman and Albany (1998) remind us not to undervalue these patterns by not also learning about their religious and cultural significance.)
- Beadwork designs during a weaving project – increasing patterns
- Celtic knots
- Tessellations inspired by M. C. Escher
- Study of patchwork designs such as North American Amish patterns – symmetry, tessellations and 2-D shapes
- Tangram – an old Chinese puzzle of seven polygons cut from a square and used in a range of designs in which none of the 2-D shapes overlap (Useful for story writing too, see website later.)
- Art Shop role-play area with home-made cards, framed pictures – Range of paintbrushes – Picture frames made from multi-link (think of all those investigations), colour charts etc
- Visit an Art gallery
- Various printing of tessellations, translation and symmetry
- Bayeux Tapestry inspired drawings with a sequence of time.

Mathematics and music

I listen to a lot of music when I do mathematics . . . I have this fantasy that music is actually stimulating the same part of the brain that I need for mathematics. (Marcus du Sautoy, 2008, p.33)[1]

Introduction to mathematics and music

With all the pressures on the curriculum, it could be tempting to forget the importance of music. However, as far back as 1979, Glynne Jones (p.43) stated that 'music with its unique combination of mental and physical skills, its discipline both corporate and individual, and its affirmation of delight in life, is a subject that no school can afford to ignore.'

There are strong connections between music and mathematics. Coles and Copeland (2002, p.69) recognized this and remind us that 'like mathematics, much of the structure of music is based on patterns and relationships. The patterns and relationships and sequences of sound,

---

1 (c) 2008 Marcus du Sautoy. By kind permission of HarperCollins Publishers Ltd.

notes and rhythms in music resemble those of numbers, shapes and measurements in mathematics.'

The NC recognizes many such links and by making and responding to music children should have the opportunity to develop understanding and appreciation of a wide range of different kinds of music and be taught chants and rhymes, to sing in unison and parts, to create a range of musical patterns, to understand such musical elements as pitch (gradations of high/low), duration (groups of beats, rhythm), dynamics (gradations of volume, louder/quieter/silence), tempo (different speeds) and structure (the ways different sounds are organized).

By engaging children in making and responding to music, there are opportunities to develop their understanding and appreciation of a wide range of different kinds of music. They will also develop skills, attitudes and attributes that can be identified as being helpful in supporting learning in other subject areas and that are needed for life and work. These include listening skills, the ability to concentrate, creativity, intuition, aesthetic sensitivity, perseverance, self-confidence and sensitivity towards others, all integral to successful mathematics work.

Case study – Years 2 and 3

There are a number of aims for this music project, which is an adaptation of Unit 10: *Play It Again*, of the QCA schemes of work. The teacher wanted the children to explore the nature of sound with instruments and voice and develop their understanding and awareness of rhythm. She wanted them to enjoy making music.

A start was made with clapping games. This developed into playing a clapping version of *Simon Says*. One rhythm was chosen as Simon's. The class played follow-my-leader. As the teacher clapped different rhythms, the class copied. However if she clapped Simon's rhythm, the class folded their arms.

They drew tune patterns in the air, and then Sol Fa, the system of musical notation was introduced. (The main notes of the sol-fa scale are doh, ray, me, fah, soh, lah, te, doh. Remember the Sound of Music?) Using a suggestion from Wisbey (1980), the children started with doh – touch your toes, me – touch your knees, soh – touch your waist. One person sang four or five notes using doh, me and soh, and the rest touched the appropriate part of the body. This quickly developed into a pentatonic scale – doh, me, soh, lah and doh (Pentatonic Scales feature in Unit 12: Music Schemes for Years 3/4).

At this point the children started to design and make their instruments. The children categorized them as follows: drums, gongs and bells, jingles (small items such as metal bottle tops strung together), shakers, clappers, scrapers and tuned instruments. The last category was courtesy of a father cutting copper tubing to create a glockenspiel. Drinking glasses filled with water, elastic bands stretched over lunch boxes and electric keyboards brought from home swiftly followed this. The idea had been to use the instruments to accompany known songs but quickly the children started to create their own words and music.

Children started to record their music using numbers and symbols. This was inspired by a child attempting to write the notation for Frere Jacques using a keyboard. It was as follows:

> 5675 5675 712 712 2321 75 2321 75 525 525
> The child had numbered the keys and written them in groups thus recognizing the pattern of the song.
> Compositions were performed and recorded on tape.

As the compositions developed, the children tried to write their parts using numbers, letters and symbols with position on the page indicating higher or lower notes. This lead to the development of the work using the pentatonic scale of C, E G, A and C. As before, compositions were created and played. The children were aware of the patterns both from the notes used, and the rise and fall of the music. The children used a CD-ROM to compose, write and evaluate their music increasingly using time signatures, notation and rhythm with accuracy and confidence.

Teacher's comment

Throughout this work, the children worked cooperatively with one another and enjoyed the group work and the presentations. There were many opportunities for extension work as in the case of the group who wrote and performed a 'Grave Yard poem' starting with 12 strikes of the church and then developing creative use of voices and instruments to create atmosphere while the poem was read. Over two terms, the children showed a massive development in their ability to work with rhythms, instruments and composition.

It was well worth spending the time making instruments and learning about rhythm and notation before using the CD-ROM. This then gave the children the opportunity to create sequences of sounds and rhythms and use notation to compose short pieces of music, which reinforced their earlier explorations.

There was a great deal of mathematics in this work from the patterns and the rhythm and the notation.

As well as the curriculum areas cited, this music making contributed to the physical, emotional, social, perceptual, intellectual, aesthetic and recreational aspects of the child's personality.

The child wrote:

> The pipes are made of copper. One pipe is 9 cm, then there is 13 cm, 16 cm, 19 cm 20 cm, 21 cm and 23 cm. You can hit them with big nails. Then they sound like bells.

The decision to include measurements of the tubing was made independently and shows understanding of the relationship between the length of the pipes and the pitch. See Figure 7.5.

Pipes 1	AA	BB	CC	BB	ABA	
Pipes 2	CC	DD	EE	DD	CDC	
Xylophone	CC	DD	EE	DD	CDC	
Glasses with water	11	22	11	22	112	
Drum						IIIIIIII
Clacker						IIIIIIII

Figure 7.5 Copy of child's attempt to organize the playing of an 'ensemble' using a chart to show when the various instruments were to be played

Mathematics included in this work

Mathematics	Objective	Activity
Using and Applying	• Represent the information in a problem using numbers, images or diagrams.	Make informal attempts to make a record of music on paper.
	• Identify patterns and relationship involving numbers and shapes (and sounds) and use these to solve problems.	Recognize and use the different patterns of the music.
	• Describe and explain methods, choices and solutions orally and in writing using pictures and diagrams.	Record work – both the music created and the instrument design.
Number	• Derive and recall number facts for 3 and 4 times tables.	Count and conduct in 3/4 and 4/4 time. Start to write music with reference to the number of beats in each bar.
Handling Data	• Answer a question by collecting, organizing and interpreting data using pictograms.	Sort the instruments into groups according to agreed criteria.

Possible misconceptions or difficulties

- While creating patterns of the pitch and the rhythm, the child could confuse the two aspects.
- Children will want to show notes that are held for longer and may need help to do so either by devising a symbol or introducing the crotchets and quavers.
- There could be difficulties with recognizing basic rhythms so conducting simple tunes from tapes will help with understanding of $3/4$ and $4/4$ time.

Other curriculum areas included in this work

Subject	Objective	Activity
Music	Explore and create rhythmic patterns and perform them rhythmically using notation as a support. Identify repeated patterns in different types of music	Make and use a range of instruments. Create music with homemade instruments. Create written music. Have awareness of the pattern of the music.
ICT	Use tape recorders and electronic keyboards to support work Use simple music software CD-ROM – 2Simple Music Toolkit	Work in groups or individually to use instruments creatively, adding words or keyboard as appropriate in compositions. Communicate musical ideas through performance and recordings. Further develop skills by creating sequences of sound and rhythm together with notation

Science	Discover many different sources of sounds and listen carefully to the sounds	Experiment with different materials using secondary sources and existing instruments to give ideas.
	Experiment with different ways of making sounds Adapt initial experimentation into an 'instrument' having some ideas about how the sound is created.	Make decisions about how the sounds are made.
Design and Technology	Use ideas from existing instruments to design and make a musical instrument. Evaluate the success of the instrument and play it individually or within a group.	Practical activity of designing, making and evaluating the instruments

Other Music topics that could involve relevant mathematics work

Always ensure that the level of mathematics is commensurate with the age and ability of the children by cross referencing the PNS objectives when at the planning stage.

- A wide range of topics in DfES schemes of work where the focus is on rhythm and melodic patterns.
- Mathematical links in Hanke (2003) *Music Express: A Complete Music Course for Primary Teachers*
- Measurement involved in making props for musical performances – such as puppets in East et al. (2006) *The Singing Storycloth*.
- The Rose Report (DCSF, 2009, p.41) cites 'Where in the World – Learning Journeys' as an excellent example of working across the curriculum, in this case, music and history and geography. Why not add mathematics to this with distances and population data?

References and further reading

Coles, D. and Copeland, T. (2002) *Numeracy and Mathematics Across the Primary Curriculum* London: David Fulton.

Department for Children, Schools and Families Rose, J. (2009) *Report Independent Review of the Primary Curriculum: Final Report* London: DCSF Publications.

Du Sautoy, M. (2008) *Finding Moonshine* London: HarperCollins.

East, H., Waugh, L., McManus, M. and Koralambe, J. (2006) *The Singing Storycloth* London: A&C Black.

Glynne Jones, M. (1979) *Music Education Review* Volume 2.

Hanke, M. (2003) *Music Express: A Complete Music Course for Primary Teachers* London: A&C Black

MacGregor, H. (2005) *Tom Thumb's Musical Maths: Developing Maths Skills with Simple Songs* London: A&C Black.

—(2007) *Listening to Music Elements* London: A&C Black.

Wisbey, A. S. (1980) *Music as the Source of Learning* Lancaster: MTP Press.

Woodman, A. and Albany, E. (1988) *Mathematics Through Art and Design* London: Collins Ed.

Story books linked with the art work

Aardema, V. (1981) *Bringing the Rain to Kapiti Plain* Oxford: Macmillan.

The following two books provide an excellent starting point for PHSE work. Although picture books, they have been used with great success in Key Stage 2 classes as they deal with sharing and differences and similarities in people.

Chamberlin, M., Chamberlain, R. and Cairns, J. (2006) *Mama Panya's Pancakes* Bath: Barefoot Books.

Grifalconi, A. (1986) *The Village of Round and Square Houses* London: Macmillan.

Qualifications and Curriculum Authority (2004) *Art and Design 2002/3 Annual Report on Curriculum and Assessment* London: QCA.

Websites

All website addresses were accessed on 31 July 2009.

Photographs and details on how different fabrics including mud cloth and adire are made. Available at: www.adire. clara.net.

Fabric samples and clay buttons. Available at: www.africanfabric.co.uk.

Maps of Africa. Available at: http://www.oxfam.org.uk/education/resources/.

Beadwork designs. Available at: http://www.cyffredin.co.uk.

www.oxfam.org.uk/education/resources/global_music_lesson_plans/5_.

Details of Logotron's Revelation Natural Art computer program. Available at: http://www.r-e-m.co.uk/logo/?comp=rna.

Tangram story writing and mathematics. Available at: http://bg016.k12.sd.us/tangram.htm.

An Art and Design Teachers' Kit with links to mathematics through symmetry. Available at: www.english-heritage. org.uk.

Piet Mondrian and fractions in an article with ideas to use in the classroom. Available at: http://www.ncetm.org.uk/ resources/16792.

A selection of art works for art and mathematics project including Bridget Riley, Mondrian, Suerat, Monet and Klimt. It has some excellent photographs. Available at: primary.naace.co.uk/curriculum/art/.

CD-ROM '2Simple Music Toolkit' Available at: www.2simpleshop.com.

QCA music schemes. Available at: http://www.qca.org.uk/schemes.

8 Mathematics and English, Communication and Languages

Mathematics and English

The revised primary curriculum increases opportunities for teachers to teach thoroughly and enrich all four strands of language – speaking, listening, reading and writing – and equally valuable aspects of numeracy.

Rose (DCSF, 2009, p.12)

Introduction to mathematics and English

The role of language is central to the development of mathematical competence and confidence in mathematical work. While working on mathematical investigations and problem-solving activities, there will be many opportunities for children to use and teachers to assess the full literacy range. Indeed, Ball (1990, pp.6–7) refers to discussion as the most effective 'diagnostic tool' in assessment and argued that observing and listening to children during discussion was the best way of assessing understanding and identifying and responding appropriately to misconceptions and problems.

Children will plan and record their investigations, predict possible outcomes and explain the processes used. They will discuss work with peer groups and the teacher and recount events to inform others. They will persuade others in their groups, in a positive way, to develop work along lines they have identified as helpful in the investigation, and they will explain procedures and reasons for the focus of the work and listen to the views of others.

Then they will describe what has happened and what they have seen or found out and make records of instructions and events.

The four strands, speaking, listening, reading and writing, are now considered separately.

Speaking and listening

> *Most lessons do not emphasise mathematical talk enough; as a result, pupils struggle to express and develop their thinking.*
>
> *Ofsted (2008, p.5)*

Speaking

Many years ago we saw a cartoon of a stool with two legs. Tied to the legs were the labels 'RECORDING' and 'DOING'. The caption read 'Two legs are insufficient for understanding.' Next to this was a three legged stool with the following labels tied to the legs: 'RECORDING', 'DOING' and 'TALKING'. The second caption read 'understanding requires three legs.' Indeed, throughout the Primary phase, quality oral skills are central to mathematical understanding with NNS (DfEE, 1999, p.11) describing the need for high-quality direct teaching that is 'oral, interactive and lively'. Long gone are the days of the historically praised 'nice, quiet class' working individually from books and work sheets. Bottle (2005, p.36) stresses the desirability of a classroom atmosphere with 'a lively mix of discussion, questioning, debate, and reasoning related to the mathematics in consideration'. Children will be organizing their thoughts as well as giving information about their ideas to others. It is worth remembering that even as adults, often it is whilst talking through a problem that a solution or alternative way of proceeding becomes clear.

A 'discourse community' is described by Lee (2006, p.3), in which the teacher must create a talking and learning classroom. 'The ability to talk about ideas gives the pupils the potential to be efficient mathematical problem solvers, and thereby enables them to take on more challenging work. Because the pupils can express their ideas they can control how they use them in ways that tacit learning does not allow.' To facilitate this, the teacher must work with the pupils in a way that involves them in the learning process. Lee (2006, p.99) stresses that in such a talking and learning environment, the pupils will be able to extend their understanding of mathematics as they search for, and find, answers to the problems that they encounter. 'As the pupils form their ideas into language that can be shared they change ideas that are transitory and indistinct into organised and more stable ideas, which is in itself part of the learning process.'

Children will find that they can 'do' mathematics as they use the areas of talk categorized by Wray (2006, p.9) as discussion, explanation, description, questioning and oral retelling.

The teacher's role is to enable this discussion. Fielker (1997, p.25) reminds us that the ideas should come from the children and not from the teacher with this helpful checklist.

The teacher is reminded to hold back from

1. imposing your own ideas
2. making judgements too early about what the children say
3. ignoring or dismissing ideas that you think are incorrect
4. ignoring ideas that you think the rest of the class will find too difficult
5. asking leading questions
6. giving 'hints'.

Ball (1990, pp.3–8) also recognizes the importance of discussion-based learning and described the child as a mathematical 'thinker' with 'responsibility and opportunity to develop his/her own learning'. He recognized four reasons why discussion is beneficial.

- *It develops understanding* as the children 'discuss, share and compare ideas'. If work is silent and individual, there is a danger that a child could miss the clues, misunderstand the instructions or have a limited perception of the concepts involved in the work. This would lead to failure.
- *It improves language skills* as the children articulate their ideas as clearly and succinctly as possible, using correct vocabulary.
- *It promotes social and personal skills* during interaction in group work where children take it in turn to listen, talk, support peers and learn how to give and take constructive criticism.
- *It encourages a positive attitude* as the child realizes that his/her opinion is valued and so resulting in the development of 'self-esteem' and in the child being 'comfortable' with mathematics.

In the classroom, Pratt (2006, p.33) refers to the importance of a 'high level of mathematical discourse' in good mathematical teaching where the teacher has recognized the 'importance of encouraging children to learn maths by articulating their mathematical thinking'. Children will then appreciate that ideas can at first be tentative and that discussion can lead them to extend and adapt them, keep them as a possible line of enquiry or indeed reject them.

The Williams Report (DCSF, 2008, p.64) similarly stresses the importance of 'high quality discussion that develops children's logic, reasoning and deduction skills, and underpins all mathematical learning activity'.

The PNS identifies the expectations of progression in discussion. In Year 1, children are required to describe puzzles, patterns or ways of solving puzzles or problems and give explanations of choices made and answer a question by selecting and using suitable equipment. By Year 6, children should be able to suggest, plan and develop lines of enquiry and explain both the reasoning and conclusions, using words, symbols or diagrams as appropriate. This requires the ability to articulate ideas and use appropriate vocabulary.

Talk partners are increasingly used in mathematics sessions where children focus on a current problem for a short time and then report back their findings in a class discussion.

It is valuable to spend some time discussing class 'rules' such as respecting others views and listening if someone else is talking. The children themselves can agree these rules. Hymer and Michel (2002, p.56) stress the need for children to feel emotionally safe in a 'climate of mutual respect' in order for positive work to take place through collaboration and discussion. In such an environment, the child will also be more willing to discuss doubts and misunderstanding.

The importance of good quality teacher questioning during oral work

The quality of the teacher's questioning is crucial and must extend beyond closed questioning, where the teacher poses a question for which they usually have an answer in mind. The child responds and the teacher 'accepts or rejects it' (Ball, 1990, pp.9–10).

Pratt (2006, p.42) reminds teachers to avoid IRF. (*Initiation,* where the teacher asks the question, *Response* given by the child and *Feedback* in the form of evaluation of the answer by the teacher.) This, Pratt recognizes, 'sends out a message "I will ask the questions and I will be the judge of the response."'

Recent research by Kyriacou and Issitt (2008) refers to this teacher, pupil questioning. The key findings of their research identified 'eight possible characteristics of effective teacher-initiated dialogue aimed at improving conceptual understanding in mathematics.'

1. *'Going beyond "initiate, response, feedback".'* Make use of open-ended questions.
2. *'Focusing attention on mathematics rather than "getting the answer right".'* The teacher should use the opportunity to 'get pupils involved in mathematical thinking'.
3. *Working collaboratively with pupils.*
4. *Transformative listening.* The teacher listens to the pupils 'in a manner that conveys that there is a genuine "meeting of minds".'
5. *Scaffolding.* The teacher helps the pupil to build on his/her existing knowledge
6. *Enhancing pupils' self-knowledge about using dialogue as a learning experience.* 'Pupils need to appreciate how using talk, and listening to teachers and other pupils is a learning experience'.
7. *Encouraging high quality pupil dialogue.*
8. *Inclusive teaching.* Teachers must be seen to value the contributions made by all children.

The teacher must be prepared for discussion to take a different direction to the planned lesson. However, as Ball (1990) commented, 'the experienced teacher can arrive at a pre-defined goal through an apparently child driven activity.' Clearly, in this situation, the input and skill of the teacher during the activity is central to success.

Remember too that children cannot always give speedy responses to questions and may need time to think. There will be uncertainty, false starts and even silence. Once again, the skilled teacher helps and encourages with appropriate questioning enabling the child to articulate the embryonic ideas within the working group.

Mathematical vocabulary

The use and interpretation of mathematical vocabulary is an important issue. Pimm (1987, p.75) refers to the confusion that can be caused with 'a mixture of what has been called "ordinary English" and "mathematical English"'. This creates a potential problem with a child misinterpreting a word, be it the difficulties of recognizing the 'whole' when a 'hole' is what the child is imagining or not understanding that mathematically it is possible to 'multiply' and make a smaller amount ($2 \times \frac{1}{2} = 1$). Similarly, Wood (1998, p.261) recognized that 'terms used in mathematics are "parasitic" upon words used in everyday discourse. But they have special and technical mathematical meanings which, if not *negotiated* with children in activity and discourse can cause problems.'

Clausen-May (2005, p.62) believed that 'school mathematics is steeped in hard words. Nowhere is this more evident than the Shape Space and measures curriculum. Mathematical language may present a major hurdle to pupils who could otherwise fly with the images of Shape and space, causing them instead to crash on the mass of mathematical jargon.'

She advocates spending time making sense of a word by 'demystifying it wherever you can. Pentagon, for example is simply Greek for five sides.'

The NNS Mathematical Vocabulary Book (DfEE, 2000) is helpful in that it has a list of the key vocabulary as a guide for each year. New vocabulary for each year group is in red so it is easy to see which the words to introduce are and which to revise.

Listening

Children tend to be better at speaking than listening! It is presumptuous to assume that children listen because they have been told to. Every teacher has experienced the irritation of a child asking 'what do I do?' following lengthy teacher-lead instructions! This is a reminder that listening skills need to be taught.

The teacher's voice projection is important, as is the children's understanding of basic rules of talking and listening such as respecting different views, listening before talking and only one speaker at a time.

Children listen because what is being said is interesting and relevant and they understand the context. They listen to gain information, understand the order of work to be done and the organizational details of groupings as well as during discussion. If a child has been listening, then he will have the opportunity to question and check if there is a difficulty.

The potential for a child mishearing a word is reduced if, as Wray (2006, p.91) suggests, key words are written on the board so that similar sounding words are not confused – 'ankle for angle or size for sides'.

Teachers also need to be able to listen to children. As well as encouraging discussion, teachers need to listen to children's replies. In listening to them, teachers can challenge their own mathematical thinking especially if pupils give an unexpected or complex response to a question. This should make the teacher think about how to respond appropriately to children's ideas in order to extend thinking or address misconceptions.

Poetry

Coles and Copeland (2002, p.44) draw attention to the link between poetry and mathematics. They assert that 'understanding the meaning of the language in a poem makes use of the same skills and techniques as other texts but there are additional features such as aspects of the physical layout and structure of the text which emphasises pattern and adds to the meaning. This leads to the use of counting, shape and algebraic thinking in communicating meaning.' This does not mean of course, that working with a junior class on Haiku poetry has a strong mathematical content as the counting of the syllables, whilst being essential for the poem, but is not commensurate with the level of mathematical understanding of the children. However, recognizing and understanding the pattern of the words, the metre and rhythm, plays an important part in the enjoyment, understanding, and reading and writing of poetry. In a similar way, NCETM have an excellent article on mathematics and poetry in the online Primary Magazine – Issue 9. They recognize that poetry can be used to help to practise counting skills, recall information, develop a richer vocabulary, look for patterns and extend sequences and solve problems.

[B] Case study 1 – Year 4, a discussion between three children

Haberdasher's Puzzle was given to three children to work out together. The puzzle comprises four polygons – two triangles and two quadrilaterals. The challenge was to arrange the four pieces to make first a square then an equilateral triangle.

Child A, child B and child C randomly tried to make a square from the four pieces for 5 minutes.

Transcript of their talk:

B: I can make it if I overlap bits.
C: That's stupid; they're to all be seen. (*Children have various attempts.*)
A: Remember if it's a square it's got those square angles in the corners.
C: The corners might make right angles put together, let's find them.

(*Child held the angles against the corner of a piece of A4 photocopying paper to check they were right angles, as they had in some recent mathematical work.*)

A: Look there's one of those right angles on each shape even the triangle.
B: Put the right angles on the corners.

Puzzle completed quickly.

C: Now we've got to make a triangle. I don't think they will make a triangle, there's not enough pieces.
A: We don't know how big it's going to be.
B: We won't have those right angles on the outside, will we?
A: No you couldn't anyway. There's four, and the triangle's got three bits sticking out.
B: We can't overlap bits can we?
C: No you know we can't, you said that before.
B: We'll hide the right angles in the middle so they won't show up. She said it was an equilateral one.
A: So the sides are the same. Look for sides looking the same.
Children measure the sides against one another. After some false starts, the triangle was made.

The group decided to draw diagrams of the completed square and triangle but not to make them readily available to the other children!

Teacher's comment

Part of the reason for this activity was to assess the children's use of vocabulary for triangles and quadrilaterals and to see if the children used their knowledge of the properties of an equilateral triangle and square to solve the problem, the importance of the 90° and 60° angles and sides of equal length.

They used the A4 paper to check for right angles, a task they had done in Year 2. With the triangle, the children focused on equal length of sides and not the angles. They were very pleased with their success and said it was better than doing maths like the rest of the class!

Mathematics involved in this work

Mathematics	Objective	Activity
Using and Applying	• Find possible solutions to a puzzle and confirm them in the context of the problem. • Explore patterns, properties and relationships and propose a general statement involving the shapes.	Use understanding of the properties of equilateral triangles and squares to solve the puzzle. Use the correct mathematical vocabulary for 2-D shapes.
Shape and Space	• Describe the properties of triangles and quadrilaterals.	Explain how this knowledge was essential in finding a solution.

Other curriculum areas included in this work

Subject	Objective	Activity
English group discussion	• Actively include and respond to all members of the group use talk to organize, sequence and clarify thinking, ideas, feelings and events.	Successfully solve the puzzle together using mathematical knowledge and understanding. Plan how to explain the process to others.

Reading and writing

Wray and Lewis (1997) recognized the central importance of reading and writing across the curriculum together with opportunities to focus on English teaching in the other subject areas.

> Reading and writing can never be pigeon-holed as simply 'English' activities and children read and write in virtually all other curriculum areas. This suggests that each curriculum area offers its own opportunities for the teaching of reading and writing as well as specific content. (Wray and Lewis, 1997, p.4)

Reading

It is essential to make sure that poor reading does not mask good mathematics in the same way that the teacher must ensure that an EAL (English as an additional language) child is not incorrectly assessed because of their lack of English.

Reading ability is required to find background information or extend understanding, to follow instructions and to identify the relevant facts in word problems. Recent small-scale research by DCSF (2009) has shown that children well able to read and interpret meaning from text in English lessons do not apply these skills to mathematical problem solving.

When reading a mathematical word problem, Wray and Medwell (1991, p.153) recognize that the purpose is to understand the story in order to achieve an accurate calculation, 'calculating rather than appreciating'.

It is possible that children find it difficult to have the skills to find the mathematical calculation within the text. They argued that children have to 'ignore the flow' of the story in the word problem and 'concentrate on picking out exactly those few pieces of information which matter'.

Wray and Medwell (1991, p.155) further attest that although it could be tempting to give children 'mathematics questions in a straightforward format unembedded in text', this is not advisable as mathematics in the wider world does not come in 'neatly separated "sums" but is always embedded in real contexts'.

It is important to put into place the strategies to cope with word problems; how to eliminate unnecessary, irrelevant material, how to identify key words and if necessary use a simple model of the same type of calculation and then substitute the number facts from the problem.

It is important that a child reads word problems with understanding, as he/she cannot rely on the order of the numbers to perform the calculation. *Take 4 biscuits away from 15 biscuits* does not have the same number order as what are *15 biscuits minus 4 biscuits?* If you add to this list, what is *4 less than 15* and *what is the difference between 15 and 4,* then you also have four different sets of words for a simple subtraction.

A key point is that it is helpful if the word problem is of interest and relevance to the child and a far cry from those well-remembered problems, from our own school days, concerning the numbers of men digging holes in the ground. Who really cared how long it took them!

Word problems linked to other ongoing curriculum areas have the advantage of capturing the child's interest. The mathematics is of real use because it is an integral part of the study. In order to bake biscuits for a school sale, it is imperative that children can increase quantities, know how many biscuits will be made and work out the initial cost and profit. This is so much better than a contrived exercise and provides opportunities for the teacher to differentiate the tasks, the results of which will all contribute to reaching the task's goal.

Whilst studying charts and graphs, it is essential to understand them and use them mathematically. This will entail reading the written information on the graph as well as reading the graph itself. Failure to do this will lead to inaccuracies that will spoil a child's work.

Writing

Writing is an integral part of using and applying mathematics. It is essential when:

- planning and recording mathematical investigations
- predicting mathematical outcomes

- recounting mathematical work of various kinds
- itemizing instructions for carrying out different kinds of mathematical work
- making records of activities
- writing reports, explanations and details of observations
- making labels which have to be accurate
- writing headings for work that provide the required information for others
- offering mathematical proof.

Wray (2006, p.1004) reminds us that teachers must not expect a child to be able to write in these different text types as 'mathematics writing is not natural: it needs teaching if children eventually are to be able to write in a manner approximating that of mathematicians.'

It is therefore clearly important for the teacher to ensure that when writing, there is a purpose, which is recognized by the child, and the child will have been taught the way in which to proceed. This will prevent the situation described by Lee (2006, p.81) where children 'do too much writing and not enough thinking'.

As always, the teacher needs to ensure that the children's existing mathematical knowledge is firm. This can be done by discussion or an earlier lesson. Children also need to know how to use different sources of information be it the internet, reference books or equipment. The presentation of work can be modelled by the teacher in order for the children to see the type of writing that is expected. Work needs to be planned and drafted. There are a number of ways to help the children to structure their work. A straightforward way is to plan as a group on the board with the teacher, as the scribe, building up an outline of the main features of the work together with vocabulary, key points and the like. Learning ladders and writing frames provide a scaffold on which children can develop their work; they are supports towards the aim of independent writing.

Writing frames

Wray (2006, p.69) described a writing frame as a 'skeleton outline to scaffold the children's writing of a particular text type. The skeleton consists of different key words or phrases, according to the particular generic form.' Lewis and Wray (1995) looked at the benefits of using writing frames in non-fiction writing. These frames provided a structure and helpful prompts which enabled the child to achieve this genre. They eliminated the terror of an empty page and not knowing where or how to start the writing. They help the child to gather their thoughts and concentrate on what they want to record and report rather than getting muddled with how to present their thoughts. Wray (2006, p.69) stressed that the frames are a bridge to independent writing, and the teacher must 'constantly look for opportunities to move all your children on in their capabilities' and not rely on such support when he or she is able to write independently. The strategies learnt while using writing frames will give the child confidence.

Such methods of planning can also be done collaboratively on the board with the teacher scribing the children's agreed methods of investigation. The children are focusing on the task, thinking about what they already know and how this will be helpful in the task, and they will be confident that they know how to put their work onto paper if they wish to follow the guide provided.

Case study 2 – Year 3 instructional writing

The class were studying Malawi as part of work on contrasting localities. A teacher had recently visited the country and left some basic mathematics equipment in a village school. The children were given the photograph of the Malawian teacher using a hundred square for the first time, and their task was to write instructions to help the children in her class. These would then be sent to the class in Malawi.

These instructions were written by three 8-year-old girls.

> Instructions for how to be able to use your number square:
> First get your number square and some additions and subtractions less than 100.
> Look along a row. The numbers go up in ones.
> Look down a row. The numbers go in tens.
> Adding:
> When you add, you go down or to the right. So if you add 15,
>
> - you go down the column to add 10 and
> - go to the right on a row to add 5.
> - The number you land on is your answer.
>
> Subtracting:
> When you take away you go up the column and left on a row. To take away 15,
>
> - you go up the column to take away 10 and
> - go left on the row to take away 5.
> - Again, the number you land on is your answer.
>
> It's easy when you know how. (We wouldn't use it for multiplying and dividing.)

Teacher's comment

A learning ladder was used to help to structure a children's work and provide an opportunity for assessment of work by both the children and for me, after they had completed the task. They were concentrating on writing instructions, and I was looking at their understanding of place value and using the hundred square for efficient mental calculations. The children were very interested to think that their work was for a teacher and consequently worked well. See Table 8.1.

Table 8.1 Learning ladder for the instructional writing

Pupil	Instructions		Teacher
	Objective		
	I started by stating the goal		
	I listed the items needed		
	I wrote instructions in sequenced steps		
	I used numbers, bullet points or time connectives		
	I added additional information in a separate box		
	I put the verbs first and in the present tense		
	My instructions are written in the second person		
	I used clear, precise language		
	What could I do to improve my instructions next time?		

Mathematics included in this work

Mathematics	Objective	Activity
Using and Applying	• Describe and explain methods in writing, using diagrams	Written instructions and diagrams, how
	• Add or subtract mentally combinations of one digit and	to use a hundred square to add and
Number	two digit numbers	subtract using efficient mental
	• Demonstrate understanding of place value	calculation methods

Other curriculum areas included in this work

Subject	Objective	Activity
English	• Writing instructions	Writing instructions for the use of a hundred square and self-assessing the work
Geography	• Study of the locality and comparing/contrasting it with another part of the world	Looking at the facilities and comparing and contrasting opportunities for teaching and learning at home and in Malawi

Mathematics and modern foreign languages (MFL)

Because language is a tool for communication – comprising speaking, listening, reading and writing – learning a new language strengthens a child's command of their mother tongue. Given appropriate opportunities, they will make explicit links between the two.

Rose (DCSF, 2009, p.102)

Introduction to mathematics and MFL

While MFL is not a compulsory national curriculum subject at Key Stages 1 and 2, it is government policy that by 2010, every child in Key Stage 2 should have an entitlement to learn a language other than English.

DfES (2003) recognized that they depended on language learning being embedded in primary schools for their Languages for Learning: Languages for Life Strategy to Work. A DfES report (2004) on the provision of MFLs for Key Stage 2 says that pupils understood that the development of MFL in primary schools was starting on a low base line but felt that with more flexibility afforded by the modern curriculum, there was great potential to move forward before 2010.

It is generally accepted that schools already teaching MFL believe that the main aims of primary MFL teaching and learning are to develop enthusiasm for language learning, to develop speaking and listening skills, and to learn about/understand other cultures.

Jones and Coffey (2006, p.69) point out that 'the primary teacher is in a unique position to deliver MFL as a cross-curricular experience. Unlike her/his colleague in the secondary school, the primary teacher is already an expert in delivering whole curriculum learning and has privileged access to the global experience of the pupils' perspective. These are major assets in the process of successfully embedding MFL across the curriculum.'

Teaching MFL with a cross-curricular emphasis, embedded and integrated within other subject areas is endorsed by Sharpe (2001, p.59) who feels it would be desirable and would be '"killing two birds with one stone", or "d'une pierre deux coups", as the French say'. However, the obvious problem with planning to combine some work in MFL and mathematics is to remember that, for the mathematical content to be of value, it must be commensurate with the child's level of understanding and not merely involve counting, number rhymes, action songs or telling the time in another language. Numbers and counting tend to be one of the first things taught in MFL. All these activities are perfectly valid for the language development but not for mathematics. Making number work part of an oral mental starter could be a way of combining use of MFL and mathematics as in Jones and Coffey's (2006, p.125) description of a lesson involving a game of number bonds to ten where the numbers are spoken in French. An interesting point is made by Sharpe (2001, p.63) that MFL can provide a 'fresh start' for pupils experiencing failure in mathematics. 'Primary teachers have found that mathematics topics presented in French or another MFL can give pupils a "second chance to learn" and instances have been reported of children learning to tell the time or learning tables in MFL lessons where they had not previously mastered these skills.'

Case study – French, Year 6

The teacher provided the class with a large map of France on which the cities of the Premier French League were identified together with main road routes.

She also provided a distance chart for these towns.

Partners were given a city and found the mileage from there to Paris. They then converted that distance to kilometres. In French conversation, they then named the town and how far it was from Paris.

'J'habite a Lille et c'est kilometres de Paris.'

This was done alongside the BBC Primary French programme, *Where do I live?* (available at http://www.bbc.co.uk/schools/primaryfrench/).

Using the Smartboard, a network was built up of the key cities together with the distances between them. This network was used in a range of mathematical work:

- finding the shortest routes to different cities, using the network
- finding average distances travelled by football teams
- finding the range of the distances
- rounding the populations of the cities to the nearest 1,000
- rounding distances to the nearest 10 or 100 km.

Teacher's comment

A surprising outcome of this work was the confidence of usually reluctant French speakers to talk because they were sure of the mathematics involved. Working in pairs encouraged both mathematical and linguistic discussions.

The rounding up/down aspect of the work provided useful consolidation and assessment of rounding an integer to the nearest 10, 100 or 1,000.

Mathematics involved in the work

Subject	Objective	Activity
Using and Applying	• Solve multi-step problems involving decimals and choose and use appropriate calculation strategies at each stage' including calculator use. • Use decimal notation for tenths and hundredths, rounding up if necessary.	Conversion from miles to km and the use of this information to find distances of routes in France. Convert miles to kilometres by multiplying by 8 and dividing by 5 and rounding that number to 2 decimal places if necessary.
Number	• Use efficient written methods to add and subtract integers and decimals.	Addition and multiplication to find route totals.
Measures	• Use, read and write metric units. Know rough equivalents of miles and km. • Record estimated lengths in decimal form	Work involved in network of routes between the French towns.
Handling Data	• Construct and interpret tables and line graphs. • Describe and interpret results and solutions to problems using the, range, median and mean.	Create a conversion graph on paper and/or computer. Investigations on range and averages of distances travelled by the Football teams.

Possible misconceptions and difficulties

- There could be confusion with miles and kilometres and the units being interchanged.
- Range is the measure of the spread of a set of data and in this case will be the range of distances travelled by the teams. Compiling the required information on the board, together as a class, would be helpful so the children can concentrate on the important aspect of finding the difference between the shortest and longest distances.

Other curriculum areas included in this work

Subject	Objective	Activity
MFL	Listening and responding – to a clear model of standard language, but may need Items to be repeated	Listen to, and understand the model for the phrases
	Speaking – short, simple responses to what they see and hear – they name and describe people, places and objects.	Copy short phrases – I live, I travel to . . . – and remember the vocabulary of transport and compass points
	Reading and responding – understand short phrases presented in a familiar context – match sound to print by reading aloud single familiar words and phrases – use books or glossaries to find out the meanings of new words	Understand the emails and notes written by the other children – understand the written distances such as Nice est – kilometres de Paris
	Writing – copy familiar short phrases correctly – they write or word-process items	Send email to inform friend of where they are and travel arrangements to reach a new town
ICT	Opportunity to create a data file for a database, using a graph package and using the internet to find out information	Using conversion tables on the internet – convert £ to € and m to km
		Production of information of a French city through internet research
Geography	Use of maps and drawing of plans and maps – use of secondary sources of information including ICT	Research and production of materials connected with chosen city and its locality
Literacy	Non-chronological report writing	A written report of chosen city and football team

Other MFL topics that could involve relevant mathematics work

Always ensure that the level of mathematics is commensurate with the age and ability of the children.

- Create a shop with goods priced in the currency of the country
- Café menus with prices
- Teach a mathematics lesson entirely in the language
- Multiplication tables spoken in an MFL
- Currency and distance conversion tables
- Travel data – distances, times, costs
- Travel brochure
- Decimals using metric measures

References and further reading

Ball, G. (1990) *Talking and Learning Primary Mathematics for the National Curriculum* Oxford: Basil Blackwell.

Bottle, G. (2005) *Teaching Mathematics in the Primary School* London: Continuum.

Clausen-May, T. (2005) *Teaching Maths to Pupils with Different Learning Styles* London: Paul Chapman Publishing.

Coles, D. and Copeland, T. (2002) *Numeracy and Mathematics Across the Primary Curriculum* London: David Fulton.

Department for Children, Schools and Families (2009) *Children Who Attain Level 4 in English but not Mathematics at Key Stage 2* [Online.] Available at: http://nationalstrategies.standards.dcsf.gov.uk/node/166696?uc−force_deep (Accessed: 31 August 2009).

—Williams, P. (2008) *Independent Review of Mathematics in Early Years and Primary Schools Final Report* London: DCSF Publications.

—Rose, J. (2009) *Independent Review of the Primary Curriculum Final Report* London: DCSF Publications.

Department for Education and Employment (1999) The *National Numeracy Strategy* London: DfEE Publications.

—(2000) *The National Numeracy Strategy Mathematical Vocabulary* London: DfEE Publications

Department for Education and Skills (2002) *Languages for All: Languages for Life/A Strategy for England* London: DfES Publications.

—(2003) *Excellence and Enjoyment: A Strategy for Primary Schools* London: DfES Publications.

—(2004) *The Provision of Foreign Language Learning for Pupils at Key Stage 2* London: DfES Publications.

Fielker, D. (1997) *Extending Mathematical Ability through Whole Class Teaching* London: Hodder and Stoughton.

Holderness, J. and Lalljee, B. (1998) *An Introduction to Oracy* London: Cassell Education.

Hymer, B. and Michel, D. (2002) *Gifted and Talented Learners: Creating a Policy for Inclusion* London: David Fulton.

Jones, J. and Coffey, S. (2006) *Modern Foreign Languages 5–11* London: David Fulton.

Kyriacou, C. and Issitt, J. (2008) *Effective Teacher – Pupil Dialogue Key Stage 2 and 3 Mathematics* Research Brief DCSF EPPI – 02–08.

Lee, C. (2006) *Language for Learning Mathematics Assessment for Learning in Practice* Maidenhead: Open University Press.

Lewis, M. and Wray, D. (1995) *Developing Children's' non-fiction writing* Leamington Spa: Scholastic.

Ofsted (2008) *Mathematics: Understanding the Score* London: Ofsted.

Pimm, D. (1987) *Speaking Mathematically Communication in Mathematics Classrooms* London: Routledge Falmer.

Pratt, N. (2006) *Interactive Maths Teaching in the Primary School* London: Paul Chapman Publishing.

Sharpe, K. (2001) *Modern Foreign Languages in the Primary School: the What, Why & How of Early MFL Teaching* London: Kogan Page.

Wood, D. (1998) *How Children Think and Learn* Oxford: Blackwell Publishers.

Wray, D. (2006) *Teaching Literacy Across the Primary Curriculum* Exeter: Learning Matters.

Wray, D. and Lewis, M. (1997) *Extending Literacy Children Reading and Writing Non-fiction* London: Routledge Falmer.

Wray, D. and Medwell, J. (1991) *Literacy and Language in the Primary Years* London: Routledge Falmer.

Websites

All website addresses were accessed on 31 July 2009.

Haberdashers Puzzle. Available at: *www.daviddarling.info/.../H/Haberdashers_Puzzle.html*.

NCETM: for wide range of mathematical articles and ideas. Available at: http://www.ncetm.org.uk.

The National Literacy Trust is an independent charity that changes lives through literacy. Available at: www.literacytrust.org.uk.

National association for the teaching of English. Available at: www.nate.org.uk.

Mathematics and Understanding Physical Development, Health and Wellbeing

9

Chapter Outline

The physical development, health and wellbeing programme of learning provides opportunities for children to use and apply a range of mathematical skills including number, measurement, shape and space, graphing and data handling.

Rose (DCSF, 2009, p.70)

Mathematics and physical education (PE)

Introduction to mathematics and PE

From an early age, children learn to practise their physical skills by repeating and improving what they have already done. They work through sequences and patterns of movement and observe and copy shapes and create mirror images. At school and in the playground, they learn all about shapes and spaces, relationships, position and patterns individually and with groups of friends. They learn how to be safe in these spaces.

The National Curriculum (NC) recognizes the desirability of linking skills into sequences of movement patterns in dance and creating fluent sequences of movement in gymnastics, using the vocabulary of position, direction, shape and movement. The Rose Report (DCSF, 2009, p.16) recognizes that 'dance is a performing art which is equally at home in physical education and both are enlivened by music.'

Peter (1997, p.1) recognizes the importance of rhythm: 'Responding to life's rhythms appears to be an innate physical drive. Most of us will feel the urge to tap our feet along to the beat of some catchy tune.' It is easy to see the connection between music, dance and mathematics.

The words patterns, sequences, movement, shapes all form part of the mathematics curriculum and this is recognized in the QCA PE Schemes of Work with mathematics and PE both having a shared focus on describing and understanding spatial patterns, location, position and direction.

Recently a student teacher was observed successfully combining PE and mathematics. The ongoing mathematics work involved investigating the properties of 3-D shapes that included a cylinder, a cuboid and a triangular prism.

The student wanted the children to visualize the properties of the shapes, so during a PE lesson, the class was 'shrunk' to the size of their thumbnail. They were then instructed to enter a Smartie tube and had to imagine how this would be.

- What would it be like to feel the walls?
- What would happen if you tried to run quickly or lean on the wall?
- Where might you bang your head?

With movement, the children acted out this experience.

They then 'entered' a Toblerone packet and then a fruit gum box and discussed the different experiences these would afford. With their movements the children felt the sides, edges and corners. They demonstrated how it would be easier to run inside the Toblerone triangular prism than the Smartie cylinder. There is no doubt that the class's understanding of the properties of these shapes was greatly enhanced by this work.

Case study – triangle and square dances, Year 3

The teacher used the Standards Site Scheme of work PE Unit 8: Dance activities. The class had previously completed a module of country dancing from a radio programme.

The ideas for the dances were adapted from Holt and Dienes (1973), *Let's Play Maths*, a book that had been in the staffroom for many years. They recognized that the dances were 'problems in handling space – early geometry in fact. Seen in action, they have an intensely humorous quality. In mathematical terms the dances accurately mirror the properties of simple geometric shapes – the triangle, square and oblong' (Holt and Dienes, 1973, p.106).

In the daily mathematics lesson, the class was working on the three and four times tables. As a starter for the PE lesson, the children were asked if they could make groups of three without anyone being 'left over'. There were 24 children in the class, which was convenient. The class moved round the room and then at a signal, made groups of three as quickly as possible. They found that there were eight groups. The children all knew that $24 \div 3 = 8$ and $3 \times 8 = 24$.

Next the children listened to the chosen dance music and counted, conducted or jigged to the beat with most of them recognizing the three beats to each bar. They were then given time to work in their threes to create a triangular dance. They all had a chalked equilateral triangle to help them to keep to the triangular form of the dance. They also numbered themselves with stick-on labels on their chests to help with the general organization. Orders such as 'three swing one' were frequently heard. The exercise was repeated at a later date, this time making groups of four for square dances.

Teacher's comment

The class had previously participated in some country dancing so the concept was not new to them.

They appreciated the triangular or square outlines chalked on the floor that guided them so that they retained their 'shape' during the dance. It also helped to make a connection with the shapes when investigating the properties of equilateral triangles and squares back in the classroom. The children found that the square provided more potential for moves as they could dance diagonally from corner to corner as well as along the sides.

> Children were using the vocabulary of shape quite naturally.
> Using numbers, symbols and diagrams, the sequence of the dances were recorded.
> One group also created its own extension activity as it estimated the distance danced in one sequence using the measurements of the chalked triangle.
> One dance was chosen for all the children to perform in their groups of three. Tessellating the groups solved the organization of this in a line. See Figure 9.1.

This was repeated with one choice of 'square dance'. Video recordings were used to evaluate, adapt and develop dances.

From the point of view of country dance, the results were excellent. However, it must not be forgotten that the health and wellbeing aspect was very important as well. The dancing was very physically demanding and the children helped and supported one another while having a great deal of fun.

Figure 9.1 The organization of the groups of three for the dance.

Mathematics involved in this work

Subject	Objective	Activity
Using and Applying	• Identify patterns and relationships involving numbers or shapes, and use these to solve problems Describe and explain methods, choices and solutions to puzzles and problems orally and in writing using pictures, diagrams and symbols	Using 3 or 4 people and 3 or 4 beats in a bar and 3 or 4 sides to the shape of the dance, devise and perform a sequence of movements Record this dance so that others could perform it. Make use of appropriate symbols and provide a key Children conduct to the music thus emphasizing the three or four beats to a bar
Number	• Know by heart the three and four times tables	Mental problem-solving exercises such as 'your waltz dance has four sequences with three beats per bar, how many beats in total?
Shape and Space	• Classify 2-D shapes, referring to their properties such as reflective symmetry, number of sides, vertices etc whether or nor angles are right angles – Identify and sketch lines of symmetry.	Draw the shapes on the ground for the dancers while devising the dances In the classroom, draw, cut and fold triangles and squares to discover the properties of symmetry, internal angles etc.

Possible misconceptions or difficulties

- Children may have difficulties visualizing the shape of the dance hence the chalked outline on the floor.
- Children may have difficulties with the technique of organizing the dance so it has a recognizable sequence of moves. Careful grouping of children would help with this.
- Children may be uncertain about 'performing' the dance. Again, sensitive grouping of children will help.

Other curriculum areas included in this work

Subject	Objective	Activity
PE Dance activities	• Create and link dance phrases using a simple dance structure • Perform dances with an awareness of rhythmic, dynamic and expressive qualities in small groups	Triangle dances – work in threes as the three points of the triangle help to devise and perform a dance using the sides and the angles for the movements Square dances – work in fours as the four corners of a square to perform a dance using the sides, corners and diagonals Listen to and count the rhythm of three or four beats to a bar
ICT	• Share and exchange information using video camera	Videos taken of the movements and actions to help them to develop their ideas

Other PE topics that could involve relevant mathematics work

Always ensure that the level of mathematics is commensurate with the age and ability of the children by cross referencing the PNS objectives when at the planning stage.

- Planning a sports day – costing, timing, organization
- Planning a sports event for younger children – measurement, time, number work – division

- Record keeping of personal achievement in athletics over a term to identify improvement in performances – data handling. Measuring time and distance, estimation
- Recording of results and times at a Sports day – data handling
- Orienteering – shape and space
- Outdoor activity with maps, scales, symbols – shape and space, measurement
- Work with Roamer – measurement, shape and space, scale (don't forget the procedure to draw to scale)
- Keep fit project such as skipping, with recording of times, total skips etc. – link with national keep fit projects for Heart health awareness

Mathematics and religious education (RE)

While not part of the 'understanding physical development, health and wellbeing' area of learning, RE is a component of the basic curriculum, to be taught alongside the NC in all maintained schools. There are two general requirements in the 2002 Education Act for schools, to have a 'balanced and broadly based curriculum which promotes the spiritual, moral, cultural and physical development of pupils at the school' (Rose, DCSF, 2009, p.28).

We also felt that there were a number of important issues to discuss, hence its inclusion in this chapter.

Introduction to mathematics and RE

The connection between religious education curriculum and mathematics is not obvious and there would be a danger of 'dragging in' some mathematics in order to include the subject in a religious topic. This was stressed by Copley and Copley (1993, p.14) who stated that if RE is 'part of a topic led by another subject theme or a multi-subject or cross-curricular theme' it is important that 'tenuous connections between the topic and religion are to be avoided' and only included in the planning if 'there are genuine connections'.

Copley and Copley (1993, p.52) further warn that 'sometimes hours of work by teacher and class leading to magnificent art, drama, discussion and imaginative work are poured into what appears to be an RE topic, only to be shown on closer inspection to have no RE in it at all.'

With sensitive planning, pattern, symbolism, statistics, dates, life cycles all have relevance to both subjects. For older children the cycles of birth and death, endings and beginnings, rebirth, resurrection and reincarnation can be studied.

Looking at the patterns of nature, as well as studying mathematics and science there will surely provide opportunities for teachers and pupils to 'wonder in amazement at some fascinating aspect of the natural world and spectacular achievement and then question, realising that sense of something or someone much bigger than themselves' Farnell (2002, p.i).

Artefacts can provide a tactile and visual source of interest supporting both RE and mathematical work. Draycott (1997, p.2) believes that the use of religious artefacts could greatly enhance teaching. With sensitive use, pupils will enhance their knowledge and understanding of religious practice and belief and have the opportunity 'for personal reflection on that practice and belief'. Artefacts must not be simply part of an interesting display or a curiosity but recognized as part of 'the expression of faith' and 'one of the tangible ways in which religious experience of humankind is expressed'. That does not mean that the mathematical aspects of the symmetry of a Jewish Menorah or the Buddhist dharma wheel, the features of a Muslim prayer mat or the Christian crosses should be avoided so long as the study is sensitive to the religion.

An interesting project involving RE and mathematics is cited by Coles and Copeland (2002, p.28). They suggest a number-line ordering events through to BC from AD. 'The key mathematics of this activity involves extending the number-line to include negative integers, being able to order a set of these and calculate the difference between the two integers.' A point of interest is that 'historians do not use the Year 0 so calculations of differences across years AD to BC give results that are one more or one less than the same calculation with integers.' QCA has recognized that good teaching of RE provides pupils with opportunities to develop their key skills. Those directly relevant to mathematical skills are listed below.

Communication is not only through the development of accurate vocabulary but also through the communication of ideas.

- The application of numbers through calendrical reckoning, collecting, recording, presenting and interpreting data involving graphs, charts and statistical analysis.
- Information technology skills – using spread sheets and databases to handle and present data relevant to the study of RE.
- Problem solving through recognizing key issues to do with religious belief, practice and expression, interpreting and explaining findings and making personal decisions on religious issues ethical dilemmas and priorities in life (QCA, 2004, p.15).

Case study

Lecturers in mathematics and RE at St Martin's College (now University of Cumbria) together with some final year students visited a nearby Buddhist Temple and then planned a range of work suitable for primary children from Year 2 to Year 6.

The initial planning was done in subject areas as shown below.

The potential use of photographs and artefacts in the classroom following a visit by children was given special attention. These included photographs and statue of Buddha, photograph of the Wheel of Life, Prayer wheel, Juzu beads, prayer flags, offering bowls and incense holders.

The focus for the use of the resources was to balance the potential for mathematics and the importance of respecting their religious significance.

Planning work after the visit to the Buddhist Centre

- Religious Education
    i. facts about the Buddhist faith and Buddha and the importance of
    ii. community

    iii. the bodhi tree and meditation

    iv. the significance of the artefacts

    v. worship

- Citizenship

    i. community living and sharing

    ii. kind thoughts, non-violence, empowerment and conflict resolution

- Local history and geography

    i. the development and expansion of the Buddhist centre

    ii. the involvement of local businesses and craftsmen during the expansion of the centre

    iii. the impact of tourism on the local area

- Mathematics

    i. symmetry and pattern

    ii. artefacts with 2-D and 3-D shape

    iii. problem solving involving symmetry and pattern and shapes

- English

    i. writing of kind messages for Clootie tree, recording and reporting

    ii. writing, descriptive writing, poetry/prose of awe and wonder

- Design and Technology

    i. designing and making artefacts such as the prayer flags making and using patterns influenced by the visit

There are no objectives identified, just the activities as the planning was for a wide age range. The objective and activity would need to be adapted according to the age and ability of the children.

Mathematics potential

Subject	Activity
Using and Applying	Solving problems involving shapes Exploration of patterns Explanations of reasoning behind decisions made, using recording or discussion
Shape and Space	Work involving the symmetry of a Stupa, dharma wheel and Prayer wheel Rotational symmetry Order 8 of the dharma wheel Pattern designs 2-D and 3-D shapes Measuring and dividing fabric up to make ribbons for the Clootie tree
Measures	Measuring flags accurately so that they are all of the same size Accurate angle measuring to make Wheel of Life or dharma wheel
Data Handling	Analysis of data connected to the growth and management of the Centre Data-handling work produced by children using information from the visit

Possible misconceptions and difficulties

- Initial difficulties being confused with the colour and pattern of the artefact and not seeing the symmetry.
- Practical difficulties with measuring length – using the correct equipment and unit of measurement.
- Difficulties extracting information from leaflets, for use in data handling. This could be because the words used or the amount of detail. Simplified data could be provided.

Other curriculum areas included in this work

Subject	Activity
English	
Oral-Group discussions	Sharing ideas and reflecting on experiences resulting from the visit
Writing	Use of specialist vocabulary
	Leading a school assembly
Reading	Kind thoughts messages for the flags
	Various non-fiction genres such as recount
	Research of various aspects of the Buddhist faith
RE	
Study of Buddhism leading to understanding of the beliefs and philosophy	Recognition of the key features of Buddhism:
	• Beliefs
	• Texts
	• Religious stories
	• Significance of artefacts
	• Art
	Make links between aspects of our own lives and others' experiences
PHSE	
Respect of the differences between people	Talking to those living and working at the temple including the local community involved in some way with the temple
Recognition of the similarities and differences between people	Watching a religious ceremony, discussing the significance of the various aspect of it
	Visiting the café and exploring the grounds, especially the organic vegetable garden

References and further reading

Coles, D. and Copeland, T. (2002) *Numeracy and Mathematics Across the Primary Curriculum* London: David Fulton Publishers.

Copley, T. and Copley, G. (1993) *Religious Education at Key Stage 1* Crediton: Southgate.

Department for Children, Schools and Families Rose, J. (2009) *Independent Review of the Primary Curriculum Final Report* London: DCSF Publications.

Draycott, P. (1997) *Religious Artefacts Why, What, How?* Derby: Christian Education Movement.

Farnell, A. (2002) *Opening Windows: Spiritual development in the Primary School.* Nottingham: The Stapleford Centre.

Holt, M. and Dienes, Z. (1973) *Let's Play Maths* Harmondsworth: Penguin.

Peter, M. (1997) *Making Dance Special* London: David Fulton Publishers.

Qualifications and Curriculum Authority (2004) *Religious Education, the Non Statutory National Framework* London: QCA.

Wishey, A. S. (1980) *Music as the Source of Learning* Lancaster: MTP Press.

Websites

All website addresses were accessed on 31 July 2009.

The British Heart association has a number of children's websites for education and activities to do with having a healthy life style. Available at: www.bhf.org.uk

The Use of Open-Ended Resources to Develop Children's Mathematical Thinking in the Early Years

10

Lin Savage and Rachel Wilby

Chapter Outline

Babies' and children's mathematical development occurs as they seek patterns, make connections and recognise relationships through finding out about and working with numbers and counting, with sorting and matching and with shape, space and measures.

Children use their knowledge and skills in these areas to solve problems, generate new questions and make connections across other areas of Learning and Development.

(DCSF, 2007)

Introduction to the Early Years Foundation Stage (EYFS)

The last decade has seen a plethora of research and initiatives related to curriculum and pedagogy for the foundation stage child and practitioner. The Effective Provision of Preschool Education Project (EPPE) (Sylva et al. 2003) and The Researching Effective Pedagogy in the Early Years Report (REPEY) (Siraj-Blatchford et al. 2002), have provided criteria which can be used to assess quality of early years provision. These developments have informed the new statutory EYFS, which is underpinned by a principled and play-based curriculum that responds to children's interests and involves a balance of child-initiated activity and structured adult-led learning experiences, supported by knowledgeable adults who have secure levels of conceptual understanding and a sound understanding of how young children learn.

The significance of developing children's thinking skills in the EYFS curriculum has been highlighted in the findings of the REPEY Report (Siraj-Blatchford et al. 2002) and the concept of 'sustained shared thinking' and the skills and conditions that enable it to occur are a central concern for the foundation stage practitioner.

The report defines shared thinking as:

> An episode in which two or more individuals 'work together' in an intellectual way to solve a problem, clarify a concept, evaluate activities, extend a narrative etc. Both parties must contribute to the thinking and it must develop and extend. Siraj-Blatchford et al. (2002, p.8)

This will focus the child as their thinking becomes extended through interaction with others during the talk and experimentation of play.

EYFS planning

The work of Athey (1990, 2007) is based on a development of Piaget's (1969) work on schematic thinking and has influenced the delivery of the foundation stage curriculum in many settings over the last decade.

The new EYFS document (DCSF, 2008a) and DCSF (2008b) confirm the central role of observation in the planning cycle for foundation stage provision. Observation of children's investigations and explorations, while using open-ended resources, will reveal to the skilled practitioner, the interests and concepts that particularly motivate specific children. This will facilitate the planning of next steps developed from personalized, individual and group preoccupations of the children thus creating 'meaningful experiences that inspire and provoke problem-solving, reasoning and creative thinking' (DCSF, 2008b, p.8). An example of this is the following conversation between a teacher and Child A and Child B while working with boxes.

Child 1 and 2 were playing with the boxes in the outdoor area.

> Child 1: We're playing parcels. *Tried to fit smaller boxes into the largest box.*
> Child 2: Will they fit?
> Teacher: Why don't you try and find out.
>
> Child A and B did this.

Teacher: How many small boxes did you fit in the biggest box?
Child B: 7.
Child A: No 8.
Teacher: Lets count and check together.
Child 1 & 2: 7.
Teacher: How many boxes do you think you could fit in the middle-sized box?

This dialogue demonstrates how young children's mathematical thinking and reasoning can be extended by adults posing open questions, and the children use this scaffolding to extend their mathematical thinking and reasoning further. The teacher recognizes their interest in the boxes and uses this information to plan further work.

Possible lines of development (PLOD)

PLOD is a model developed at the Pen Green Children's Centre by Whalley (2001) in which the interests of the children are mapped out and subsequently supported and developed. This results in a curriculum delivery which is built around the observed schematic interests of children. Practitioners add comments to the original PLOD so that development of the child's thinking and areas of learning can be seen.

Developments specifically related to developing children's mathematical thinking and skills

The decision to change the name of the area of learning, previously known as Mathematical Development to Problem Solving, Reasoning and Numeracy (PSRN) gives a clear message to EYFS practitioners concerning the breadth and range of learning experiences for which they need to plan in order to promote mathematical thinking in a variety of contexts.

The William's Report (2008c) devotes chapter 3 to the EYFS. This confirms the message of the EYFS in advocating the importance of a play-based approach to learning for young children and states:

> Central to effective mathematical pedagogy in the early years is fostering children's natural interest in numeracy, problem solving, reasoning, shapes and measures. Children should be given opportunities in a broad range of contexts, both indoors and outdoors, to explore, enjoy, learn, practise and talk about their developing mathematical understanding. Such experiences develop a child's confidence in tackling problem solving, asking probing questions, and pondering and reasoning answers across their learning. Vitally important is ensuring that children's mathematical experiences are fun, meaningful and build confidence. (Williams, DCSF, 2008c, p.34)

There are two significant recommendations in the William's Report (DCSF, 2008c): the inclusion of capacity and time within the Early Learning Goals and increased opportunities for young children to engage in emergent mathematical mark making.

Mark making

DCSF (2008b, p.30) recognized the elements necessary to support children's mathematical marks:

- an environment that gives children many opportunities to explore mark making
- assessment that is positive and responsive to children's marks and informs the next steps of learning
- adults who model mathematics in meaningful contexts
- adults who understand and can therefore value children's marks.

The necessary tools should be readily available for the children to select and use to encourage mathematical mark making and recording. This is important as mark making can arise spontaneously. Implements can be outside and inside; chalk, paint brushes, clip boards, large pieces of paper and other interesting writing tools will encourage children to make mathematical recordings. Mathematical language and numbers can also be on display, both outdoors and indoors, to support children with prompts and to model mathematical symbols and vocabulary.

Resources

The creative use of well-organized resources is crucial. They can:

- support mathematical concepts.
- add interest/relevance to the task (for both child and practitioner!)
- facilitate exploration of a learning experience in a practical context
- demonstrate the real life purpose of mathematics
- develop early investigative work through play
- allow children to pose their own questions and investigate possible answers through play
- enable collaborative work with other children

The role of parents

The 2007 Children's Plan stresses the significant role of families and parents in their children's education. A key message is the practitioner's role in supporting every child to reach their potential, particularly those from less resourced homes, plus a timely reminder about making learning and childhood fun.

This necessitates the need for good dialogues between practitioners and parents through diaries and formal and informal meetings. This facilitates a two-way exchange of information about the child's interests and needs.

The Rose Report (2009) recognized that parents are more likely to meet teachers when taking young children to Nursery, so the importance of building trust and awareness between school and home at this stage is crucial.

Case study – boxes and bags, buckets and buttons

We have chosen to focus on this selection of specific resources to exemplify how children's thinking can be extended, how they can be introduced to concepts which will support them in achieving the Early Learning Goals and so create secure foundations for later mathematical development.

Boxes, bags, buckets and buttons are readily available and inexpensive and are everyday items to be found in any home and could be:

- used freely by children without cost implications
- used by the children in a variety of ways to develop a range of mathematical ideas that they might be interested in
- used by a variety of practitioners in a range of settings
- used by practitioners to extend mathematical vocabulary.

The following table details the range of resources used to support and extend children's mathematical vocabulary and learning. See Table 10.1.

The resources outlined in the Table 10.1 can be used in different contexts and be adapted to provide a range of learning experiences both for use within continuous provision, or as an enhanced or focused activity. Many of the experiences lend themselves to the outdoors, using large boxes and transporting buckets full of sand and water, for example. The use of the large cardboard boxes outside encouraged the children to work on a bigger scale, giving them the opportunity to measure in larger units. This has particularly interested the boys in the reception class.

The parents of the reception-class children, who were involved in the work, were encouraged to talk about and repeat some of the learning experiences at home and develop ideas of their own. This transferred into everyday family experiences such as shopping and the size of bag needed for all their items.

We used PLOD planning and mindful of the specific recommendations of the Williams Report (DCSF, 2008c) the concepts of time and capacity and the provision of mark-making opportunities were considered in our planning. See Figure 10.1.

In order to demonstrate the potential learning experiences of these resources we have presented our ideas in tabular form, linking experiences with concepts, schema and Early Learning Goals. Those objectives printed in bold, are Early Learning Goals which have been met during the work.

Our planning is covered in the following tables of learning experiences:

- numbers as labels for counting
- calculating
- shape, space and measures

Table 10.1 Table of resources

Boxes	Bags	Buckets	Buttons
▪ Egg boxes	▪ Hand bags	▪ Small buckets	▪ Clothes buttons – different sizes, shapes, colours and patterns
▪ Food boxes and nets, e.g. Toblerone	▪ Money bags	▪ Large buckets	
▪ Gift boxes	▪ Gift bags	▪ Shaped buckets (castles, sea animals)	▪ Buttons to thread
▪ Large boxes, e.g. crisps. fridge, washing machine etc.	▪ Packaging bags	▪ Buckets made from different materials-plastic, metal	▪ Chocolate buttons
▪ Money boxes	▪ Grow bags		▪ William Accorsi's 10 Button Book (Board book) by *William Accorsi*
▪ Post box	▪ Shopping bags	▪ Packaging buckets – from kitchen	
▪ Jack in the box	▪ Bags made of different materials	▪ Bucket balance	
▪ Chocolate boxes	▪ Bags with different patterns	▪ Books	
▪ Telephone Boxes	▪ Bags in a range of sizes	▪ Billy's Bucket by Kes Gray and Garry Parsons (Paperback – 3 June 2004)	
▪ Books: 'My cat likes to hide in boxes' book. *My Cat Likes to Hide in Boxes* (Picture Puffin) by Eve Sutton (Spiral bound 30 August 2001)	▪ Purses and Money		
	▪ Books	▪ **Harry and the Bucketful of Dinosaurs (Harry and the Dinosaurs)** Ian Whybrow and Adrian Reynolds (**Paperback –** 7 May 2009)	
	▪ *The Shopping Basket* (Red Fox picture book) by John Burningham		
▪ The Box (Books for Life) (Paperback) by *Martha Lightfoot*			
▪ **Spot's Toy Box: Board Book (Little Spot Board Books)** by Eric Hill (Hardcover – 30 April 1998)			
▪ *Kipper's Toybox* by Mick Inkpen (Paperback – 18 March 1993)			

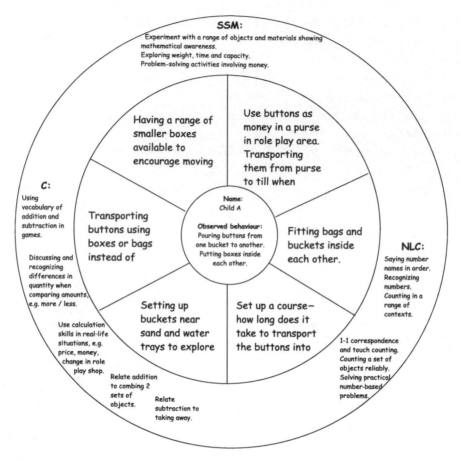

Figure 10.1 Possible lines of development observation.

Supporting the 'numbers as labels for counting' strand

The following table exemplifies learning experiences which took place to meet key objectives from the 'numbers as labels for counting' strand. See Table 10.2.

Having taught this, we found that sometimes resources needed to be adapted to enable children to access the activities, for example by sticking numbers to the buckets. Adult-led activities were used to help support these concepts.

Supporting the 'numbers as labels for calculating' strand

The following table draws upon key experiences which aimed to support the calculating strand of the EYFS. See Table 10.3.

We found that practitioners needed to help the children with the vocabulary and resources to enable them to access these learning experiences and reach their potential. Children also

Table 10.2 Use of boxes, bags, buckets and buttons to support and enhance 'numbers as labels for counting' objectives

Resource/Learning experience	Mathematical thinking	Key experience/ Objective
■ Counting how many spaces of sand, small buckets of sand, etc., will fit in different buckets? ■ How many buckets of soil do we need to fill a grow bag? ■ How many seeds could we plant in a grow bag? ■ How many grow bags could we fit in the garden? ■ How many small bags, buckets or boxes can we fit into a larger bag, bucket or box? ■ Counting bucketfuls of water ■ Basic – counting how many missed/landed in the bucket/bag/box ■ How many children can we fit in a large bucket/bag/box? ■ Collect as many objects as possible in a bucket / bag / box	■ Transporting schema – moving sand, soil to different bags ■ Enclosure schema – filling empty buckets, boxes, bags ■ Trajectory schema – throwing objects into bucket, bag, box ■ 1–1 correspondence ■ Touch counting ■ Capacity	■ **Say some number names in familiar contexts** ■ **Say number names in order** ■ **Count reliably up to 10 objects** ■ **Use developing mathematical ideas and methods to solve problems (EYFS, p.68)** ■ Know that numbers identify how many objects are in a set ■ Count aloud in ones, twos, fives, tens
■ Could we make up our own tune to a nursery rhyme we know – how many times do we need to hit each bucket to play the tune? ■ How many jumps in a sack does in take to complete the obstacle course?	■ Patterns using sound ■ 1–1 correspondence ■ Follow mathematical mark makes	■ Count aloud in ones ■ **Count reliably up to 10 everyday objects (EYFS, p.68)**
■ Buckets/bags/boxes with numbers on them in the correct order ■ Hide inflatable numbers in boxes – challenge children to feel and guess the number	■ Positioning schema – ordering and organizing objects ■ Enclosure schema- hiding objects in boxes, buckets or bags	■ Orders numbers up to 10 ■ Recognizes, orders, counts and uses numbers up to 20
■ Collect 5 leaves, 6 objects, 7 sticks, in a bucket/box/bag ■ Find hidden boxes, buckets, or bags ■ Use bean bags or quoits (extend to balls) to aim and throw into numbered buckets / boxes	■ Transporting schema – collecting and moving objects ■ 1–1 correspondence ■ Trajectory schema – throwing and aiming ■ Connection schema – distributing and collecting objects	■ Know that numbers identify how many objects are in a set ■ Count reliably up to 10 everyday objects (EYFS, p. 68) ■ Recognize numerals 1–9 and beyond. (EYFS p.68)
■ Use money boxes in role play area to count money and solve real life problems ■ Use telephone boxes in role play area to encourage number recognition, and recording numbers	■ Coin recognition ■ Enclosure schema – coins in box ■ Number recognition ■ Explore mark making methods	■ Recognize and discuss value of coins ■ Solve real life money problems ■ **Recognize numerals 1–9** ■ **Say number names in order** ■ **Say some number names in familiar contexts (EYFS, p. 68)**

Table 10.3 Use of boxes, bags, buckets and buttons to support and enhance 'calculating' objectives

Resource / Learning experience	Mathematical thinking	Key experience/Objective
■ Sort and categorize buttons of different size, shape, patterns, number of holes into groups according to their properties	■ Sorting ■ Categorizing ■ Mathematical reasoning	■ Categorize according to properties
■ Extension – point scoring – score 3 points if you get the bag into the bucket with the number 3 on it etc. – Use tally and recording to compare and record scores of each child	■ Time ■ Calculating ■ Problem solving ■ Mathematical recording	■ **In practical activities and discussion, begin to use the vocabulary involved in adding and subtracting (EYFS, p.70)** ■ Use the vocabulary or 'more' and 'less' to compare two numbers
■ Calculating, adding, subtracting challenges with buttons ■ Exploring and investigating number bonds to 10 with a set of 10 buttons by splitting set of buttons into 2 groups ■ Collect 2 buttons from the blue bucket and 4 from the yellow bucket – How many buttons have you got altogether?	■ Problem solving ■ Calculating ■ Pattern ■ Colour ■ Number bonds	■ **In practical activities and discussion, begin to use the vocabulary involved in adding and subtracting** **Use the vocabulary or 'more' and 'less' to compare two numbers (EYFS, p.70)**
■ Use purses and money in role play situations, e.g. a shop – Write prices on objects and explore paying for items, and giving change – Write receipts	■ Real-life problem-solving contexts ■ Calculating ■ Coin recognition ■ Reading and recognizing numbers	■ Investigate number bonds to 10 **Use developing mathematical ideas and methods to solve practical problems (EYFS, p.68)** **Recognize numerals 1–9 (EYFS p.68)**
■ Use chocolate boxes in role play area and investigate number of chocolates that fit in a box – What shape chocolates need to be to fit in certain compartments – How many of each chocolate we would include in a box.	■ Sorting ■ Organizing ■ Problem solving ■ Counting and calculation	■ Explore numerical mark making methods **Use developing mathematical ideas and methods to solve practical problems (EYFS, p.70)** ■ Use and apply reasoning, sorting and organizational skills ■ Calculate the difference between 2 numbers ■ Use vocabulary of more and less

required adult support to access the child-initiated experiences. Adult-led activities and group experiences gave the children the ideas they needed to access these concepts independently during continuous provision.

Supporting the 'shape, space and measures' strand

This last table exemplifies the wide range of shape, space and measure-based learning experiences which these resources enable to be accessed. See Table 10.4.

This was the strand which was drawn upon in most activities. Through teacher observation of the children it became clear that children accessed these activities, related key vocabulary and learning experiences independently, particularly with the larger-scale resources outside.

Obviously there are many more ideas which could have been included to use these resources in different ways. These tables are offered as a starting point, but can be developed further in your own setting.

The adult-led activity plan

The Adult Led Activity Plan is linked directly to the PLOD observation which showed Child A's observed behaviour in the centre. It aims to demonstrate how mathematical concepts and ideas can be developed and extended through adult led play-based activities. See Table 10.5.

From this, other possible learning experiences have been identified and then possible links to PSRN objectives have been identified.

Continuous provision learning opportunities plan

The 'Continuous Provision Learning Opportunities Plan' highlights opportunities for child-initiated play during continuous provision. Here, possible learning objectives are listed, but these are obviously dependent upon how the individual child uses and develops their mathematical understanding with the available resources. The possible activity ideas here are again linked to the PLOD of Child A, demonstrating how opportunities for the child to initiate and develop their own mathematical understanding can be planned for and incorporated into continuous provision opportunities. See Table 10.6.

The learning experiences in the plans offer ideas of how mathematical thinking can be developed from the child's interest. These formats can be used to develop and plan for any number of experiences based on a specific child's interest in PSNR and the other 5 areas of learning in the EYFS.

Table 10.4 Use of boxes, bags, buckets and buttons to support and enhance 'shape, space and measures' objectives

Resource/Learning experience	Mathematical thinking	Key experience/Objective
Shape:		
■ Making sand castles of different shapes ■ Feely bag – hide, describe, guess the shape / object	■ Shape ■ Capacity ■ Pattern	■ **Use language such as 'circle' or 'bigger' to describe the shape and size of solid and flat shapes (EYFS, p.74)** ■ Recognize and name basic 2-D and 3-D shapes ■ **Talk about, recognize and recreate simple patterns (EYFS, p.74)**
■ Explore, compare and recreate patterns on gift bags	■ Rotation schema- spinning around to make large scale patterns	■ Attempt to re-create basic 2d shapes and explore designing own shapes
■ Put a small hole in the bottom of a bucket and fill it with water, sand, salt etc. – Walk around with the bucket to make a range of shape and patterns – Could be done with paint on large paper	■ Pattern ■ Large scale mathematical mark making	■ **Use developing mathematical ideas and methods to solve practical problems (EYFS, p.74)**
■ Explore jack in the boxes – Challenge children to make the net for a box to fit the jack in	■ Problem-solving skills ■ Estimation, checking, measuring ■ Enclosure / containing schema	■ Estimate and measure using standard and non-standard units of measure ■ **Use everyday words to describe position (EYFS, p.74)**
Space:		
■ Use the buckets or boxes to create an obstacle course for the children to take it in turns to travel round, e.g. climbing / jumping over, walking on bucket stilts, carrying a bucket of sand, collecting objects in an empty bucket along the way, building a tower using 3 boxes, climbing through a box tunnel, directing a blindfolded partner	■ Positioning schema ■ Instructional, directional and positional vocabulary	■ Follow instructions containing positional vocabulary
■ Use post boxes in role play area to explore positioning, size and measure concepts, e.g. which envelope do I need to fit this letter in? How many times do I need to fold my letter to fit it in the envelope? Will this parcel fit inside this post box?	■ Problem-solving skills ■ Estimation of shape, space, position and size	■ **Use developing mathematical ideas and methods to solve practical problems (EYFS, p.74)** ■ Use positional and size based comparative vocabulary
Measures:		
■ Comparing different sized sand castles and bucket moulds	■ Transporting schema – moving sand and water from one place to another	■ Use language such as bigger, smaller, higher, to compare sand castles
■ Capacity – how many buckets of water will it take to fill a larger bucket? The water tray?	■ Containing schema – filling up different containers	■ Use language of capacity to solve a practical problem

- Bucket relay – groups of 4 children, each with a bucket. Challenge to transfer a bucket of water from one end of the course to the other, by pouring and carrying between each team member. Winning team that with most water left at the end – comparing capacity.
  - Planning, problem solving – working as a team
    - Use vocabulary of 'most', 'least' to compare capacity
    - Order items by capacity

- Use the buckets as drums, with sticks as beaters. How does the size of the bucket affect the sound?
  - Sound patterns
  - Writing and interpreting mathematical mark makes
    - Talk about the effects of the size of buckets on the sound made when it is hit – Use vocabulary such as bigger, smaller, taller, shorter

- Who can build the highest: bucket or box tower?
- Arrange boxes / buckets / bags in order of size, height and length.
  - Height
  - Problem solving
  - Shape and space related vocabulary
    - Order items by height
    - Use vocabulary of tallest, shortest, highest, lowest to compare tower heights

- Who can make the longest bucket / bag / box snake?
  - Estimation
  - Predicting
  - Checking
  - Recording
  - Distance
    - Order items by length
    - Use vocabulary of longest, shortest to compare snake length

- How many small buckets / bags / boxes can we fit in a large bucket?
    - Use vocabulary of smaller, larger, bigger

- Use the boxes / buckets / bags as non-standard units of measure to measure the playground, bench etc. Discuss the concept of how to select which size object to use to measure different distances.
    - Develop understanding of non-standard units of measure

- Den building – mathematical discussion and problem solving. What shape should we build the den? What part of the den should we use each materia for? How many children could we fit in? How big do we need to make the den for 6 children to fit in?
  - Positional and size related vocabulary and problem-solving tasks
  - Estimating, predicting and checking
    - **Use developing mathematical ideas and methods to solve practical problems (EYFS, p.74)**

- Obstacle course time how long it takes each child to complete the obstacle course using a stop watch. Record times. Add time penalties as an extension for if any items fall or are hit to develop problem-solving skills in using and applying addition and subtraction skills/
  - Time
  - Mathematical recordings
  - Positioning schema of moving around, over, under various obstacles
  - Number recognition
  - Units of measure, e.g. seconds, minutes.
    - Estimate, measure and use the vocabulary of time

Table 10.5 Adult led activity plan linked to PLOD

Adult-led activity plan linked to PLOD

Key Experience / Focused activity:

Transporting Schema – using child A's interest in transporting buttons from one bucket to another as staring point. Set up an obstacle course and time how long it takes to transport buttons from one end to the other, passing through all of the buckets.

Main Learning Intentions:

PSRN

- Estimate, measure and use the vocabulary of time
- Apply problem solving and reasoning skills from all 3 strands
- Recognize numerals
- Develop skills in mathematical mark making
- Use language of shape, space and measure

Key Vocabulary:

- Time
- Seconds
- Minutes
- Longer
- Shorter
- More
- Most
- Least
- Quickest
- Less
- Fastest
- Slowest

Key Questions:

- What was the quickest time?
- What would happen if we added time penalties for any dropped buttons?
- How many buckets did the buttons get transported through?
- How could we record the different times?

Adapting the experience for individual children:

- Develop from child's personal interests, e.g. adapt how could we transport sand, water, toy car?
- Differentiated by questioning
- Support through adult and peer modelling

Resources:

- Variety of different size and shaped buckets
- Range of different sized and shaped buttons
- Stop watch
- Recording materials
- Cones / obstacles to manoeuvre around

Children for whom this activity is particularly appropriate:

Children with an interest / demonstrating behaviours related to transporting schema.

Session:

Structure:

- Adult-led activity to take place during continuous provision
- Children who are interested have the choice to join in
- Focus for observed children who show behaviours related to transporting schema

Activity:

- Explain to children the problem that we need to transport all of the buttons from one end of the obstacle course to another
- Explain conditions, e.g. the buttons must pass through all of the buckets
- Set up and discuss course, bucket layout as group (Diagram of layout of buckets / course could be produced to encourage mark making / recording.)
- Share how to use stop watch – Teacher to demonstrate completion of obstacle course (Teacher to spill some of the buttons) – Lead to discussion of penalties for if buttons are dropped / spilt to extend more able children and develop calculation skills

Children's Involvement:

- Planning / setting up and designing course of travel
- Decision making, e.g. how many buckets do the buttons have to travel through? How many buttons will we transport? How will we record the times?
- Turn taking each to have a turn at completing course and recording
- Respond to questions and share ideas

Adult role:

- Develop children's transporting schema interest
- Adapt activity for individual interests
- Question children to develop their understanding of concepts involved
- Scaffolding and pole-bridging
- Allow for spontaneous response and children's ideas
- Encourage and ensure all children participate / are involved
- Assess and plan for further learning opportunities

Conclusion:

- Key questions, e.g. who completed the course in the quickest time? How did we record the times? How could we make the course more challenging? What other resources / materials could we transport around the course? What was the difference between the quickest time and the slowest time? How did the penalties for dropped buttons impact on overall times / scores?

Table 10.6 Continuous provision learning opportunities for problem solving, reasoning and numeracy

Potential learning objective	Brief description of key experience	Experience area	Opportunities for assessment	Resources
▪ Use language such as 'circle' or 'bigger' to describe the shape and size of solid and flat shapes ▪ Counting the number of small buckets of sand / water to fill a larger bucket	▪ Develop transporting schema to using sand and water rather than buckets ▪ Making sand castles of different shapes	▪ Outdoor sand tray ▪ Outdoor water tray	▪ Informal observations of use of mathematical vocabulary used and problem-solving approaches developed.	▪ Small buckets ▪ Large buckets ▪ Shaped buckets (castles, sea animals) ▪ Buckets made from different materials – plastic, metal ▪ Sand tray ▪ Water tray
▪ Correspondence ▪ Estimate, measure and use the vocabulary of time ▪ Apply problem solving and reasoning skills from all 3 strands ▪ Recognize numerals ▪ Develop skills in mathematical mark making ▪ Use language of shape, space and measure	▪ Set up similar obstacle course to adult led activity and allow children to develop and extend through child initiated ideas ▪ A range of resources, e.g. boxes, bucket, bags, buttons available for children to choose from	▪ Outdoor area	▪ Informal observations of mathematical vocabulary used, peer modelling / coaching, numeral recognition, counting skills, use of mathematical recordings.	▪ Range of buckets, bags, boxes, buttons ▪ Range of objects and materials to create obstacles of child's choice ▪ Stop watch ▪ Range of mark making materials for mathematical recordings
▪ Correspondence ▪ Touch counting ▪ Counting reliably a set of objects ▪ Numeral recognition	▪ Have a range of boxes and buckets available with a range of numbers stuck on them ▪ Children to transport the number of buttons given on the bucket / bag / box	▪ Number area	▪ Informal observations to assess numeral recognition, reliability in counting a set of objects, touch counting, use of number based mathematical vocabulary used.	▪ Numbered buckets, bags, boxes ▪ Range of buttons

References and further reading

Athey, C. (1990) *Extending Thought in Young Children: A Parent-Teacher Partnership* London: Sage.

—(2007) (2nd edn) *Extending Thought in Young Children: A Parent-Teacher Partnership* London: Sage.

Department for Children, Schools and Families (2007) *Areas of Learning and Development: Problem Solving, Reasoning and Numeracy* London: DFES Publications. [Online.] Available at: http://nationalstrategies.standards.dcsf.gov.uk/earlyyears (Accessed 26/01/10).

—(2008a) *The Early Years Foundation Stage* London: DFES Publications.

—(2008b) *Mark Making Matters: Young Children Making Meaning in All Areas of Learning and Development* London: DFES Publications.

—Williams, P. (2008c) *Independent Review of Mathematics Teaching in Early Years Settings and Primary Schools Final Report* London: DCSF Publications.

—Rose, J. (2009) *Report Independent Review of the Primary Curriculum: Final Report* London: DCSF Publications.

Piaget, J. (1969) *The Mechanisms of Perception* London: Routledge and Kegan Paul.

Siraj-Blatchford, I., Sylva, K., Mullock, S., Gilden, R. and Bell, D. (2002) *Researching Effective Pedagogy in the Early Years* London: DFES Publications.

Sylva, K., Melhuish, E., Sammons, P., Siraj-Blatchford, I. and Taggart, B. (2003) *The Effective Provision of Pre-School Education* (EPPE Project) London: DFES Publications.

Whalley, M. (2001) *Involving Parents in their Children's Learning* London: Paul Chapman Publishing.

11

The Impact of Extended Services on the Teaching and Learning of Mathematics

The United Kingdom is still one of the few advanced nations where it is socially acceptable – fashionable, even – to profess an inability to cope with the subject. A parent expressing such sentiments can hardly be conducive to a learning environment at home in which mathematics is seen by children as an essential and rewarding part of their everyday lives.

Williams (DCSF, 2008b, p.3)

Introduction to mathematics and extended schools facilities

Every Child Matters (DfES, 2004b) is the Government's vision for children and young people from birth to nineteen. Its five aims are to ensure that every child, whatever their background or circumstances, should have the support needed to be healthy, stay safe, enjoy and achieve, make a positive contribution and achieve economic wellbeing.

The Government requires all organizations involved in providing services to children and young people to work together to meet these aims. They therefore need to be considered in everything a school does and reinforced through every aspect of its curriculum – lessons, events, routines, the environment in which children learn and what they do out of school. *Excellence and Enjoyment* (DfES, 2004a) recognizes that it is essential to think beyond the normal school day and extend provision for the children to have the best possible opportunities from their learning.

It is through Extended Schools that provision is made for young people, their families and the local community to access a wide range of facilities often beyond the normal school day. As such, this becomes part of the plans for Local Authorities (LAs)and Children's Trusts to deliver the five aims of *Every Child Matters*.

The provision of such services will differ from one school to another according to local need, but will include a range of out-of-school-hours learning activities, childcare, adult education and family learning, and ICT access. The presence of child care can be essential for the parents with young children to be able to use the facilities on offer: breakfast clubs, after school clubs and activities and the like. The Government intends that by 2010 all schools should become 'extended', offering courses and activities designed to enrich and support the experience of children and young people and parents and remove any barriers to their achievements. Legislation for this is in the White Paper (2009b) in which LAs, in their role between the national level and the schools, must ensure the delivery of the Pupil Guarantee. This guarantee will ensure the 'effective early intervention and wider support for children, young people and their families'. Schools may choose to provide these services themselves but are more likely to offer than through clustering arrangements, using the expertise of third-party providers from the private, voluntary and community sectors.

Extended schools support can help to raise mathematics standards:

- by improving the parents' attitude towards and understanding of mathematics. With a widely accepted expression of an inability to cope with mathematics, there is a need to improve the attitude of many parents so that they will have the interest and confidence both in the subject itself and working with their children on mathematical activities. This in turn will help children to have a positive attitude to the subject.
- by providing children with the best possible mathematics education that can be supported through extended school opportunities. 'In-school' and 'out-of-school' mathematics will merge in the child's understanding.

Examples of the range of mathematical support and activities available

Examples of the range of mathematical support and activities available have been categorized in the book as follows:

- Study Support
- Family learning – courses for parents of pre-school children

  courses for parents of Key Stage 1 children
  courses for parents of Key Stage 2 children

- Provision of resources – for fathers with young children

  for parents by a group of primary schools.

Study support

One aspect of the extended schools is a range of activities often referred to as Study Support. It is also known as 'Out-of-School-Hours Learning' as it covers activities which take place outside the normal school day and which have a learning focus. These activities can take place before or after the school day, at lunch and break times, at weekends and during school holidays. Participation is voluntary and in many cases is free of charge. It is intended that children and young people should enjoy taking part in Study Support. The atmosphere should be relaxed as this will help participants to relate to both the focus subject and to their peers and adults in a new way. Even the most reluctant learners will not feel that they are 'in school'. In successful Study Support sessions, there can be significant benefits in terms of attainment. Tutors enjoy the opportunity to get to know the young people in informal surroundings. They also have the freedom to experiment with new ways of working away from the confines of the classroom though not all Study Support sessions are led by teachers. Following relevant training, teaching assistants, volunteers and students can be involved and have the advantage of not being 'mathematics specialists' and the unfavourable connections that may have with the learner. A relaxed and enjoyable approach with little or no pressure is the key to experiencing success and raising achievement.

There is considerable evidence that participation in Study Support leads to improvement in young people's self-esteem, achievement, attitudes to learning, classroom behaviour and school attendance. They also have fun while developing new skills, mix with different groups of pupils and adults and have the opportunity to learn at their own pace. MacBeath (2001) found that secondary students who took part regularly in Study Support activities did better by an average of 3.5 extra grades or one extra A–C pass, than those who did not participate. Ofsted has frequently highlighted a strong relationship between the provision of extra-curricular activities and pupil attitude and attendance and suggests that extended services are helping to enhance self-confidence, improve relationships, raise aspirations and produce better attitudes to learning.

Within this setting of Study Support, maths clubs have been established to encourage children and young people to become more confident learners. It is important that such a club offers activities that are complementary to the curriculum but at the same time avoiding duplicity. Hence the focus could be a practical, problem-solving club emphasizing success, fun and enjoyment. Alternatively, Study Support programmes can be an essential component of personalized learning. This is one of the aims of DfES (2005) where all children can have access to extra support or tuition in different subject areas through an exciting range of opportunities and activities, beyond the school day. This will allow children and young people to follow their interests, broaden their horizons, remove barriers to learning and to be motivated to greater achievement enabling them to take greater responsibility for their own learning and development.

Study centres based on professional football clubs provide examples of Study Support. These study centres were established by the DfEE with the Professional Footballers' Association to provide 'first class IT facilities and focus on the improving of literacy, numeracy and IT skills for Key Stages 2 and 3 pupils using the medium and environment of football as motivators and curriculum tools' (DfEE, 2000a). They provide opportunities for children to learn in a relaxed environment and away from school. It was hoped that the link with the football club would engage young people who otherwise might not have participated in maths clubs.

Case study – a mathematics trail based at a study support centre attached to League 1 Football Club

A mathematics trail was developed with the aim of providing real experiences for the development of core skills in mathematics. It was suitable for Years 5, 6 and 7 and was a mixture of mental calculations, pencil-and-paper procedures, problems to solve and investigations to develop.

Both primary and secondary school pupils attend the centre during the day with sessions organized with schools. There are also after-school sessions run by the permanent staff and volunteers.

The trail involved children completing 15 'tasks'.

Example: Task 1

Find the cost of entry to the Paddock area for tickets bought on the day.
1 adult (a)

1 concession (c)

Once the children had completed the 15 tasks of information they had been set, their next challenge was in the study centre. Here, they were given a set of questions relating to the 15 tasks. There was a choice of questions of graded difficulty so the pupils could choose those they felt comfortable in tackling. Working together and supporting each other was encouraged.

For Task 1, the following questions were given:

Choose one of the questions

(a) Please complete the table

1 adult + 1 concession

1a + 1c	2a + 2c	3a + 3c	4a + 4c	-- - --
£...+ £....= £..	....	....	....	....

or

(b) Increase the entry fee by 10%

Original entry fee for adult –   New entry fee for adult –
Original entry fee for concession –   New entry fee for concession –

or

(c) The total paid for the number of tickets bought on the day, including both adult and concession at the current price is £110. . .
What tickets could have been bought?

Example: Task 2

Draw an aerial (bird's eye) view of a water carrier for the player's water bottles showing the number of sections in it (they are in the trainer's room).

Activity when back at the centre.

Choose one of the questions:

(a) Check that you have drawn a water carrier with 6 sections – (3 × 2) How many water carriers would you have to take out to training for 16 players, manager, coach and physiotherapist? You can draw the carriers if it helps!

or

(b) What is the perimeter of a carrier?

NOTE – Each of the sections is 12 cm^2

or

(c) Imagine a large carrier that is 6 sections by 4 so it holds 24 bottles.
There are 18 bottles to be put in it.
Can you place the bottles so that there is an *even* number in each row and column?

Is there more than one way of doing this?

NOTE – there is a 6 × 4 grid and 18 bottle tops that are available to help you if you wish.

The questions provided encouraged children to build mathematical understanding, applying higher order thinking skills such as reasoning and problem solving, in different contexts to those of previous school-based work. A choice of questions based upon the tasks also gave children ownership of their work.

Family learning

Family learning is another aspect of extended schools provision. It broadly refers to approaches that engage parents and children jointly in learning. This includes family literacy and numeracy programmes to improve the basic skills of parents and thus their willingness to engage with their children in mathematical activity.

One of the five principles of the Children's Plan (2007b) is that it is the parents and not the government who bring up children, so there is a need for the government to do more to actively back parents and families. Parents must be an integral part of any development planned to improve children's education.

This was already recognized in *Excellence and Enjoyment* (DfES, 2003a) with the statement that 'parents have a huge influence in setting aspirations and expectations for their children, and in stimulating their learning.' It was again revisited in Williams (DCSF, 2008b, p.73), 'parents are central to their child's life, development and attainment. They cannot be ignored or sidelined but should be a critical element in any practitioner's plans for the education of children.'

Similarly, DCSF (2007a and 2008a) repeat the importance of the influence of parents throughout childhood and adolescence on their children's learning. The problem arises when the parents have neither the understanding nor the confidence to work with their children.

While it is common for parents to be confident in helping the child with reading, they can baulk at the idea of mathematics at home. They possibly remember their own school experiences where they could well have been taught without understanding the methods employed resulting in a mathematical switch off.

These concerns were again highlighted by The Parents as Partners in Early Learning (PPEL) project, which began in October 2006. Its aim was to review current provision with an initial baseline audit of policy and practice across 150 LAs in England. Its final audit report recognizes a range of barriers to involvement by parents. Key messages from the report stressed the need for 'greater precision and clarity in the definitions of "parental support," "parental engagement" and "parental involvement" as part of strategy development'. Also, although there were programmes involving parents developed in LAs, they tended to be as a response to localized initiatives rather than a coherent authority-wide strategy on parental involvement. The report recognizes that barriers to parental involvement include communication problems, difficulties with the parents' own skills, knowledge and understanding together with lack of understanding of the importance of their involvement in the child's education.

These are two-way barriers towards the development of mathematical progress.

- Parents are aware of their lack of understanding of the professional jargon and vocabulary used by teachers. They may have low self-esteem and feel uncomfortable with teachers, and this was seen to be a particular issue for fathers and male carers. They may also place a low value on education because of their own 'failure' at school.
- Teachers may find it difficult to relate to parents and lack the confidence to work meaningfully with them. The negative attitude could well be as a result of previous unsuccessful attempts to engage with the parents or the teacher may not be convinced of the importance of the role of the parent.

These issues need to be addressed by teachers and agencies concerned with developing parent partnership. An obvious key factor in family learning sessions is to encourage both enjoyment and success with mathematics and an explanation of the methods used in the daily mathematics lesson, thus breaking the parents' cycle of fear and apprehension.

An evaluation of numeracy programmes, which examined achievement before and after the courses found a significant improvement in the understanding of numeracy. As well as an improvement in the subject, 'communications between parents and children were also found to improve markedly, and parents also reported being more confident in helping their child at home and communicating with the teacher at school' (DCSF, 2008a, p.7).

The following case studies describe work completed with parents and children in a range of situations. The aims were to engage the parents in mathematical work and to encourage mathematical talk and activity between parent and child.

Case study – course for parents of pre-school children

The course (organized by Sure Start) was part of a wider programme of working with parents of young children in a Nursery setting.

The tutor was employed to work with 11 mothers and a grandmother for 2 hour sessions. A family support worker brought one of the mothers to the course. She then chose to stay and participate for her own enjoyment and to share the experience with her client.

The parents worked with the tutor in one room and the pre-school children from 1–4 years of age were in a crèche/nursery in the same building. During the sessions, the parents developed tasks and activities and experimented with them before taking them home.

The aims of the course were planned with the tutor and the nursery leader. Remembering that mathematical development was the focus of the course, the expressed objectives were that the participants would:

- enjoy the course
- share ideas and experiences

- have increased confidence in their abilities to help with their child's development
- have increased understanding of the value and importance of a rich range of experiences which will help the child to develop varied interests and skills
- make a personalized resource for home focused on the child's interests
- have better understanding of early years' work in school – in preparation for the child starting Nursery and Reception classes.

The parents/carers were encouraged to be aware of the opportunities to develop experiences through the home and the environment. While there was an emphasis on numeracy, as early education is holistic, other important areas of education were discussed.

Teacher's comment

Initially there was a degree of uncertainty of the unknown. I aimed to engage the mums in their child's learning by recognizing the value of play, story, rhyme and talk. I wished them to see that they need not fear mathematics as there were no 'sums' but just practical activity and a lot of talking and listening.

Coffee breaks and informal seating were important to create the right atmosphere. I spent a lot of time listening to the discussions and chatting informally about general child issues as well as mathematics. Without exception, the participants were nervous that they wouldn't understand the content of the course and they had 'hated' mathematics at school. There were also concerns about their child's behaviour and worries about forthcoming school. Those with older children were keen to discuss their schooling too.

Work was planned remembering that at all times, the participants were to feel comfortable such as never to be in a position to be required to read as some members were not literate.

Stories were carefully chosen so that they reflected the mathematics of the session with humour. The mothers enjoyed being read to as if they were young children, and after initial embarrassment, most of them joined in with the actions and repetitions.

Week 1

Mathematical content – Shapes and Patterns and the vocabulary of shapes and position.
Stories – *My Mum and Dad Make Me Laugh*, a story about spots and stripes and *How Many Bugs in a Box*—a book of 3-D shapes.
Home resource – Wooden jigsaw board with teddies and a range of interchangeable patterned clothing.

To start with, the focus was on helping the mothers to realize the importance of working with the child during practical activity and the centrality of play and talk. When the building bricks were introduced in the first week, one of the mothers commented that she did not like them. She described how she had emptied bricks onto the floor and the child had just put them back in the box. She clearly had not 'played' with him.

During the morning, the mothers built the tallest tower, a bridge for a boat to go under, a bridge for a car to go over, a fairy castle and a block of flats. There was a good response to some gentle questioning. Which bricks would balance? Which would roll? Which were larger/smaller? Which had the same shape but were of a different size? There was also a lot of laughter and possibly relief as there was not a number in sight.

Spots and stripes were printed using wine bottle corks: rolled for the stripes and the circular face for the spots.

The jigsaw boards were used, with the mothers looking at the different patterns, sizes and shapes. They all felt that their child would enjoy this game and the different activities that they had tried out with me.

Week 2

Mathematical content – measuring
Stories – *Guess How Much I Love You*
Home resource – Play-doh made during the session

The vocabulary of measures was discussed with the mums while they were estimating and then comparing length of teddies and ordering them according to their height.

Discussions of mathematical opportunities during bath time were considered with toy containers being full, half full or empty.

Making the play-doh was interesting. The recipe involved measuring out the ingredients, mixing them and cooking them in a microwave. Measurements were found using cups and tablespoons. Some mothers were not confident but working in pairs helped this. The different coloured balls of play-doh were shared out fairly. Changing their shape provoked discussion about the conservation of mass. Was the long sausage of play-doh the same as the ball if nothing had been added or taken away?

Week 3

Mathematical content – Sorting and sets
Story – *Goldilocks*
Home resource – A choice of sets of people, dinosaurs, farm animals or cars.

I made sure that the sorting equipment for the session was all from a home setting and was not 'mathematical' equipment. We sorted buttons, clothes pegs, spoons, toys, jewellery and plastic bottle tops always looking for what was the same and what was different about the groups. We sorted according to size, colour, shape, what it was made of and the like.

I sorted collections into two sets using hoops to secure the groups. The mothers had to find the criteria for my choice. Negative criteria were introduced: that set is made of wood, and the other set is NOT made of wood. The group then developed the game so that each mother put an object from her bag on the table, and these were then sorted into two groups by one member, and the others had to find the chosen criteria.

Weeks 4 and 5

Mathematical content – counting, combining and taking away groups of objects
Stories – Range of counting books, songs and rhymes. 1–5, 5–1, 1–10, 10–1
Home resources – 5 ducks and 2 'ponds' (blue face flannels). Home made Counting story book.

I felt I could now work with numbers. Reading from a range of counting books was very important in these sessions. Some books had numbers from 1 to 5, some from 5 to 1, some from 1 to 10 and others counted down from 10 to 1 or zero. Ordinal numbers were introduced through poetry.

The mothers counted a small group of objects in different ways but always came to the same total. The importance of the visual impact was demonstrated by setting out two rows with the same number of counters but with one row more spread out. See Figure 11.1.

It is easy to think that there are more counters in the second row.

The mothers were interested to try an experiment with building bricks at home. They were to count out 5 and build them into a tower. They were then to build the same five bricks into something different – and ask the child how many bricks there were. They found the result was that the child counted them again even though nothing had been added or removed. This is a normal stage in the development of young children.

We talked about the importance of not confusing the ability to 'count' up to large numbers with real mathematical activity. The chanting of numbers can merely be a form of memorizing words with no mathematical rationale. It is so much more important to count and point, thus understanding that each object counted has its own number name and that the last number counted is the total of the group.

Informally the group was learning the counting laws:

- that number names are always said in the some order
- that each object in the group to be counted only has one counting name as it is only counted once
- that the last number counted represents the total of the set.

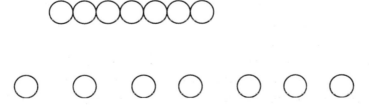

Figure 11.1 The visual impact of placing the counters close together and spread apart.

- that the order of counting does not matter but it can be made easier/harder to ensure that we don't miss any out depending on how logically we count the objects
- that there should be a reason for counting the otherwise there it has no purpose to the activity.

At all times, we discussed how the work could be continued at home. 'I'll line them up when we go to the car and say, you go first, you're the second and I'm third' suggested one of the mothers.

Enacting the Five Little Ducks poem, the five plastic ducks were put on one pond and counted, pointing to each one as the number name was said.

One duck went to the other pond making four on one pond and one on the other. The total was still 5. As the poem developed the mothers saw that $5 + 0 = 5$, $4 + 1 = 5$, $3 + 2 = 5$, $2 + 3 = 5$, $1 + 5 = 5$ and $0 + 5 = 5$. There was a heated discussion as to whether $1 + 4$ was the same as $4 + 1$.

As the group was beginning to add together two amounts, this was the time to introduce the dog puppet. He was not very good at counting and often made mistakes that needed rectifying. This was helpful as it took any pressure away from a mother possibly worrying about making a mistake herself.

We compiled lists about using numbers and counting at home from the following prompts.
Numbers

- When do you *talk* about numbers at home?
- Where do you *use* numbers at home?
- Where do you find numbers to *see* at home? These may well be big numbers but are still part of the child's life.

Counting

- Name things that you can count that can be put in different positions – such as toys?
- Name things that you can count that can be touched but not moved – such as light switches
- Name things that you can count that can be seen but not touched – such as cars passing the house
- Name sounds that you can count – such as claps
- Name physical movements that you can count – such as jumps
- Name occasions where you can count out a required number – such as plates for tea

A 0 to 5 counting book was made with pictures of the child's interests printed out from clip art. The front page was individually designed with the child's name and appropriate patterns or photographs. The pages were then laminated and ring bound together. The mothers were immensely proud of these books and felt a sense of achievement.

Attendance was good. The 'free gifts' were undoubtedly a bonus. An evaluation of the course concluded that there was a marked increase in both interest and confidence as the weeks progressed. There was surprise that mathematics was not something difficult and special done in school but was everywhere and part of everyday life. As such, they, as parents had a role to play in their child's education.

Two school-based courses involving parents

Case study – course for parents and children, Key Stage 1

For half the morning the parents worked with the tutor and their children worked separately with the teacher from the school. For the second part, the children joined the parents. They then worked together on an activity prepared earlier and the session finished with a story read to everyone by the tutor or teacher. Each week the teacher produced a light-hearted newsletter with details of the previous week's work and photographs. This was very popular.

The parents made and used simple games and activities and discussed the mathematics involved before working with the children. They made tens and units arrow cards, Kim's game cards to reinforce number bonds, digit cards and simple board games involving dice for addition and subtraction. These were then laminated before taking home.

Three-dimensional work involved making a photographic shapes trail round the school that would be used by the children.

Two-dimensional work involved printing with the different faces of boxes with the children. The parents made tessellating patterns in the style of Escher and a 'stained glass window' of 2-D shapes from empty CD cases and glass paint.

Counting and number sequences involved finding missing numbers in sequences, odd and even games and snakes and ladders with multiples of 2 and 5.

Work on sorting and sets was extended to simple graph work.

During work on place value, addition and subtraction, parents made arrow cards and used them to partition 2-digit numbers. Fan cards formed the basis of a range of games with parent and child working as partners. Number tracks were used together with games involving number bonds to 10. A domino investigation took place with the spots added and sorted into those with the same total and placed in the form of a block graph. The parents were fascinated with the result and discussed why this had happened. This was repeated with subtraction remembering to put the larger number first.

There was a trip to a nearby train station for parents and children. The children bought their own tickets at a slot machine, caught the train back to town and then a minibus back to the school. This was quality time for parent and child. The parents were briefed to involve the child in discussions looking for numbers and shapes as well as general observations of interest.

The measuring session with the parents involved the use of the range of vocabulary and the progress for non-standard to standard measures in Key Stage 1. 10-cm long centi-snakes and angle munching monsters with $90°$ mouths were made in preparation for accurate estimation and measuring of length and finding right angles in the room.

During the course, art work and photographs were used to create a mathematics display on the Parents' notice board. This showed the range of work on the course. Understanding of place value had been an important aspect of the course, and the photographs included some of the parents wearing H, T or U hats and holding large digit cards as they made the largest, smallest, odd or even numbers from the three digits. That aspect of the display was a talking point for some time!

An evaluation of the course showed that the parents were appreciative of their increased understanding of the National Curriculum and the PNS together with the methods used to teach mathematics, particularly mental calculation strategies.

Case study – an evening course in primary school for parents of Key Stage 2 children

The Head-teacher had requested the course as a result of numerous queries from parents about the daily mathematics lesson, the PNS and SATs tests. It was to introduce the parents to the ways in which their children are taught, the resources that were used and the structure of the PNS. This would give them more confidence to support their children at home.

There was a very wide range of mathematical competence and confidence but all parents wanted to find out how they could help their child. The sessions were a blend of practical information about the mathematics requirements for the children and games and activities to illustrate good practice. They took the format of a conventional daily mathematics lesson with an oral and mental starter, the main part of the session with group and individual work followed by a whole group introduction. During the plenary the issues from the session were discussed.

As with the previous course, the parents made resources and games to take home, the most popular being a set of Napier's Rods for multiplication and a set of thousands, hundreds, tens and units arrow cards. The head teacher would visit the session for a short time each week and join in the work.

Outline plan of the course:

Week 1   Parents and NC and good practice
          Introduction to classroom mathematical resources
          Mental calculation – efficient methods
          Features of Using and Applying mathematics

Week 2   Place value and ordering
          Knowing what each number represents
          Understanding partitioning
          Using hundred squares and Gettagno place value charts
          Making and using games involving understanding of place value

Week 3	Addition and subtraction
	Understanding the range of vocabulary
	Recognizing the importance of knowing and using known number facts and number bonds
	Understanding that subtraction is the reverse of addition
	Discussion of the principles of the commutative and associative laws
Week 4	Multiplication and division
	Understanding of multiplication as repeated addition
	Multiplication a division by 10 and 100 – the decimal point does not move – honestly!
	Division – grouping or sharing
Week 5	*Measures*
	Recognizing the importance of the correct vocabulary
	Estimation
	Using measures and suitable units at home and other curriculum areas. Conversion charts
	Conservation of length, volume and mass
	Problem solving involving area and perimeter
Week 6	Handling data
	Recognizing attributes for sets and sorting for Venn and Carroll diagrams
	Practical work followed by discussion of the data handling cycle. – how the data was collected, recorded and interrogated and what might be developed from it
	Different types graphs
	Use of ICT in mathematics

Homework was given in a light hearted way and became a highpoint of the course!! This included questions from *Mathematical Challenges for Able Pupils in Key Stages 1 and 2* (DfEE, 2000b) that provided excellent examples of using and applying mathematics while problem solving. A memorable piece of homework came from a father, an ICT specialist, who solved the problem while at work using a sophisticated spread sheet and then challenged his colleagues to complete it.

Provision of mathematical resources for parents and children

Resources for fathers and young children

DCSF have stressed that a father's interest in a child's schooling is strongly linked to educational outcomes of the child. 'Research shows that a father's early involvement in their child's life can lead to a positive educational achievement later on, and a good parent child relationship in adolescence' (DCSF, 2007a, p.10). The quality of the time that fathers spend with their children is more important than the amount of time.

This work did not take the form of a course but in the preparation of resources for fathers who were finding it difficult to have a positive approach to playing with their children in a way that was helpful to the child's learning. They lacked both confidence and understanding

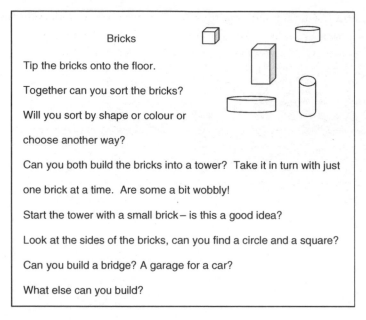

Bricks

Tip the bricks onto the floor.

Together can you sort the bricks?

Will you sort by shape or colour or

choose another way?

Can you both build the bricks into a tower? Take it in turn with just

one brick at a time. Are some a bit wobbly!

Start the tower with a small brick – is this a good idea?

Look at the sides of the bricks, can you find a circle and a square?

Can you build a bridge? A garage for a car?

What else can you build?

Figure 11.2 Support sheet from the 'building' box.

of the needs of young children and sometimes only had access to the children for set periods of time through access arrangements.

A range of resource boxes was made that would at first be used with a social worker and the fathers together so they could become familiar with the contents and the way to use them. Then the fathers could borrow them for home use.

The boxes contained toys and books with a main theme and some simple suggestions about how to make good use of them. The content of the boxes had a mathematical focus within play, and the aim was for the father and child to enjoy them together. One such box featured 'building' and contained bricks, a digger lorry, story books, a toy tool set and photographs of tools. There were simple suggestions for play activity involving sorting, counting and working with 3 dimensional bricks. See Figure 11.2.

Other boxes dealt with bedtime issues and cooking, areas in which fathers may not be comfortable. Though the focus on play and activity, the father could build a purposeful relationship with the child and look forward to their times together.

Resources for parents of a group of primary schools

'It is apparent that a guide to the primary curriculum, in plain language, would be of considerable help to parents and enable them to give more support at home for their children's learning' Rose (DCSF, 2009a, p.19). It is important that parents have the confidence to work with their children at home. For this they need to have some understanding of both the curriculum taught in school and recognition of the value of play in learning.

The boxes provide a practical resource with books and equipment in everyday use and easily bought on the High Street. They contain practical activities to work though without a worksheet in sight and a guide booklet for support for the parent.

Case study of the use of boxes for the parents organized by the extended schools co-ordinator of a cluster of primary schools

The collection of boxes covered the Foundation Stage and Key Stages 1 and 2. They all had themes of interest to children and contained a story book and a non-fiction book and four or five games or activities linked with the theme. With the younger children there was also a suitable toy. An information booklet gave the parents straightforward information about how to use the books and possible areas for discussion; how to make good use of the resources, possible questions to ask and relevant vocabulary. There was also a contents list that proved invaluable in preventing loss of contents.

Example of a foundation stage box for parents to take home

The theme was *Trains*. The aims of the box were set out in the parents' booklet. They were for the child to be able to

- say and use the number names in order in familiar contexts
- count up to 5 (and then 10)
- recognize numerals 1–5 (and then 10)
- use developing mathematical ideas and methods to solve practical problems
- begin to use the vocabulary involved in addition
- begin to relate addition to combining two groups of objects
- begin to understand and use ordinal numbers
- sort and match objects justifying the decisions made
- use everyday words to describe position; follow and give instructions about positions
- use language such as circle to describe the shape of solids and flat shapes.

The books to read together were *Choo Choo Clickerty-Clack* by Margaret Mayo and *Terrific Trains* by Tony Mitton. There were instructions for the games and activities together with mathematical vocabulary to use.

1. A wooden train pulling a wagon full of bricks provided an opportunity to talk about the important features of 3-D shapes, to sort according to colour or shape and to challenge the child to find more circles on the train and the room and build and make patterns with the bricks.
2. A train 1–10 jigsaw with each carriage having a digit and that number of passengers.

3. A box of wooden shapes: aeroplane, hot air balloon, car, lorry, bus, bicycle, motor-bicycle, boat, yacht, tanker to sort according to different criteria.
4. A set of magnetic trains and wagons used in a counting game with a 0–5 die.

The examples have shown the importance of shared understanding of how children learn mathematics, together with the breaking of parental barriers of mathematical fear. This is summed up in the Rose Report (2009a, p 18) 'Children thrive best when parenting, the curriculum and pedagogy are all of a high quality. In other words, children benefit most when their home lives and school lives establish similar values and expectations for their learning, behaviour and wellbeing.' Schools working with parents, be it a course or resource, will undoubtedly have positive fallout well beyond mathematics.

The White Paper (DCSF, 2009b) has introduced *the 21st Century School Parent Guarantee* that will ensure that every child goes to a school that has high aspirations for them and is given the opportunity to do the best they possibly can to succeed in school and in adult life. It will also ensure that schools work with mothers, fathers and other carers as full partners in their child's learning and wider development. 'To make this happen: every parent will have opportunities, information and support to exercise choice with and on behalf of their child; every parent will have a Home School Agreement outlining their rights and responsibilities for their child's schooling; every parent will have the opportunity, information and support they need to be involved and engaged in their child's learning and development; and every parent will have access to extended services including support and advice on parenting' (DCSF, 2009c).

References and further reading

Arenson, R. (1998) *One Two Skip a Few – First Number Rhymes* Bristol: Barefoot Books.

Department for Children, Schools and Families (2007a) *Every Parent Matters* London: DCSF Publications.

—(2007b) *The Children's Plan: Building Brighter Futures* London: DCSF Publications.

—(2008a) *The Impact of Parental Involvement on Children's Education* London: DCSF Publications.

—Williams, P. (2008b) *Independent Report of Mathematics Teaching in Early Years Settings and Primary Schools* London: DCSF Publications.

—Rose, J. (2009a) *Independent Review of the Primary Curriculum Final Report* London: DCSF Publications.

—(2009b) The White Paper *Your Child, Your School, Our Future: Building a 21st Century Schools System* London: DCSF Publications.

—(2009c) *Your Child, Your School, Our Future: Building a 21st Century Schools System – The Parent Guarantee* [Online.] Available at: http://publications.dcsf.gov.uk/default.aspx?PageFunction=productdetails&PageMode=publications&ProductId=DCSF-00681–2009 (Accessed: 1 July 2009)

Department for Education and Employment (2000a) *Playing for Success Learning F.C.* London: DfEE Publications.

—(2000b) *Mathematical Challenges for Able Pupils in Key Stages 1 and 2* London: DfEE Publications.

Department for Education and Skills (2004a) *Excellence and Enjoyment* London: DfES Publications.

—(2004b) *Every Child Matters – Summary* London: DfES Publications.

—(2005) *Higher Standards, Better Schools for All: More Choice for Parents and Pupils* London: DfES Publications.

MacBeath, J. (2001) *The Impact of Study Support,* DfES Research Report 273 London: DfES Publications.

Mayo, M. (2005) *Choo Choo Clickerty-Clack* London: Hodder and Stoughton.

Mitton, T. (2000) *Terrific Trains* London: Pan Macmillan.

Williams, B., Williams, J. and Ullman, A. (2002) *Parental Involvement in Education,* DfES Research report 322 London: DfES Publications.

Websites

All website addresses were accessed on 31 July 2009.

Graphics from Revelation Natural Art. Available at: http://www.logo.com/logotron.html

Information on how to use a Gettagno place value chart. Available at: http://www.ncetm.org.uk/mathemapedia/Ways+of +working+with+a+Place+Value+Chart

The National Literacy Trust is an independent charity that changes lives through literacy. Available at: www.literacytrust. org.uk

Sure Start (2006) *Parents as Partners in Early Learning (PPEL) Parental Involvement – a Snapshot of Policy and Practice Phase 1 Report.* Available at: *www.dcsf.gov.uk/research/data/uploadfiles/DCSF-RR039.pdf*

Appendices

Appendix 1

Table A1.1 Table of educational developments since 1989 and their mathematical implications

Date	Document	Mathematical Implications
1989	*National Curriculum for England and Wales* was introduced in separate curriculum files.	The first statutory requirements for teaching primary mathematics. There was a separate Attainment Target for using and applying mathematics suggesting that this was not part of every aspect of mathematics.
1999 DfEE	*The National Curriculum Handbook for Primary Teachers in England* was introduced in one document. It provided the legal requirements of the National Curriculum in England for 5–11 year olds.	Using and applying mathematics – problem solving, communicating and reasoning was built into the first section of all parts of the mathematics programme of study together with suggestions for cross-curricular links.
1999 DfEE	*National Numeracy Strategy –Framework for Teaching Mathematics from Reception to Year 6* Together with the Literacy Strategy, they were to provide an educational foundation for the twenty-first century.	This provided a framework and support for teachers, helping them to plan and teach mathematics effectively. A key element was the structured daily mathematics lesson. It was central to the government's target for 2002 for 75% of 11-year-olds to reach level 4. The focus was very much on number and calculations and children were not necessarily given the opportunity to develop their mathematical thinking through discussion, group work and challenging tasks. Using and applying was within a broad heading of solving problems – making decisions, reasoning and generalizing about numbers and shapes and problems involving 'real life' and money.

(Continued)

Table A1.1 Continued

Date	Document	Mathematical Implications
2002 QCA	*Curriculum Guidance for the Foundation Stage* This provided comprehensive guidance for early years education in six areas of learning	One of the areas was Mathematical Development – Number as labels for counting, calculating and shape, space and measures. Early learning goals were the same as the key objectives of the NNS in Reception thus ensuring a smooth transition
2003 DfES	*Every Child Matters* This was a vision of how professionals should work together to provide children's care in a more integrated and effective way. It states that every child, whatever their background or circumstances, should have the support they need to: be healthy, stay safe, enjoy and achieve, make a positive contribution and achieve economic wellbeing These five outcomes are to be at the heart of everything a school does and reinforced through every aspect of its curriculum – lessons, events, routines, the environment in which children learn and what they do out of school.	Every child should experience mathematical success and enjoy their work in school. This necessitates the provision of a carefully planned, challenging, progressive and relevant curriculum. This should be by well trained and inspirational mathematics teachers who are capable of building problem solving, investigations, creativity, and real-life experiences into the mathematics lessons through their teaching and their awareness of the potential for developing mathematics work throughout the curriculum. Parental involvement should be developed.
2004	Children's Act provided the legislative spine for the 10-year *Children's Plan: Building a Brighter Future* together with the agenda of *Every Child Matters* (2003)	As above
2003 DfES	*Excellence and Enjoyment: A Strategy for Primary Schools* This was aimed at ensuring that all children had the life chances they deserved. The document focused on: school character and innovation, excellent teaching, learning with a focus on individual children, partnership beyond the classroom, leadership issues and workforce reform.	Schools were encouraged to use the National Numeracy Strategy as a springboard for teaching and not a constraint, with the mathematical priorities to: 'Build on and apply their mathematical knowledge and skills Become numerate thinkers Apply their knowledge and skills to solve increasingly complex problems Use mathematics to reason and explain' (p.28) The principles of good teaching must obviously be applied so that teachers plan to build on what the child already knows so that learning is 'vivid and real' and an 'enjoyable and challenging experience' (p.29). The benefit of high-quality discrete teaching and meaningful work across the curriculum is also featured as is the importance of working with parents.
2004 DfES	*Every Child Matters: Change for Children in Schools* This set out in more detail the implications of *Every Child Matters* (DfES, 2003) for schools and their children. Pupil performance and wellbeing go hand in hand. Pupils can't learn if they don't feel safe or if health problems are allowed to create barriers.	Its aims listed below gave clear implications for mathematics teaching and learning: attend and enjoy school achieve stretching National Standards at Primary School achieve personal and social development and enjoy recreation stretching national educational standards at secondary school Parents, carers and families to support learning.

(Continued)

Table A1.1 Continued

Date	Document	Mathematical Implications
2006 DfES	*Primary National Strategy Primary Framework for Literacy and Mathematics* This embeds the principles of both *Every Child Matters: Change for Children in Schools* (2004) and the principles of *Excellence and Enjoyment: Learning and Teaching in the Primary Years* (2004)	There was a greater emphasis on planning for progression. The objectives were simplified into seven core areas of learning (strands), one of which was using and applying. The objectives for every year group included progression in communication, representing, reasoning, enquiry and problem solving. These themes related directly to the three subdivisions of the using and applying programmes of study in the National Curriculum.
2007 DfES	*The Early Years Foundation Stage. Setting the Standards for Learning, Development and Care for Children from Birth to Five* These were the legal requirements of the EYFS relating to Learning, Development and Welfare of children from birth to five. This became statutory in 2008.	'Problem Solving, Reasoning and Numeracy' was one of the six areas of learning, as in the 2002 document. Early learning goals of this document were highlighted in the Core learning in mathematics for the Foundation Stage in the *Primary National Strategy Primary Framework for Literacy and Mathematics* (DfES, 2006) thus ensuring a smooth transition from the Early Years to Primary education.
2007 DCSF	*The Children's Plan: Building a Brighter Future* sets out in five main principles how the DCSF plans to make this country the best place in the world for children and young people to grow up, by putting the needs of families, children and young people at the centre. *It* describes a vision of improving outcomes for all children and young people, reducing inequalities and narrowing the gap between those who do well and those who do not. This is a 10-year plan is based on the development of *Every Child Matters* (DfES, 2003) and the principles of *Excellence and Enjoyment – A Strategy for Primary Schools* (DfES 2003).	The aim is for every child to be ready for and be successful in all phases of education from the Foundation Stage through to the Secondary Education. There is a specific mention of the importance of the 'transition points' in the children's lives. Its three principles clearly apply to mathematics: • 'all children have the potential to succeed and should go as far as their talents can take them;' • 'children need to enjoy their childhood as well as grow up prepared for adult life;' • 'it is always better to prevent failure than tackle a crisis later.' (DCSF, 2007, p.4) Specific mention of mathematics – 'More time for basics so children achieve a good grounding in reading, writing and mathematics'(p.9) There is continued awareness of the importance of parental involvement.
2008	The updated *Every Child Matters Outcomes Framework* provides an overview of the ECM outcomes and aims which the CYPP (Children and Young People's Plan) will cover. The document demonstrates how the national *Children's Plan* fits with *Every Child Matters*	

(Continued)

Table A1.1 Continued

Date	Document	Mathematical Implications
2008 DCSF	*Williams Review of Mathematics Teaching in Primary Schools and Early-Years Settings* The most effective pedagogy of teaching mathematics and the range of provision in schools was studied. The intervention programmes for children failing to master the basics of numeracy were looked at. The mathematical conceptual and subject knowledge of teachers was a key point together with the most effective design and sequencing of the mathematics curriculum How parents can be helped to support their children's mathematical development was looked at.	There needs to be a focus on the use and application of mathematics. The importance of quality classroom discussion in mathematics is stressed. *Every Child Counts* programmes must be introduced for underachieving children. There must be a focus on the effectiveness of ITT and CPD to ensure teachers' mathematical competence. There should be at least one mathematics specialist in each primary school in post within 10 years, with deep pedagogical mathematical subject knowledge. He/she should be found from the existing school staff.
2009 DCSF	The Rose Report – Independent Review of the Primary Curriculum The aim was to look at the curriculum and decide how it should be developed in order to 'foster children's different and developing abilities during the primary years' (sect 1.2). This forms a springboard for building a curriculum of high standards both in for classroom and for personal development. Strong links and overlaps between EYFS and Key Stage 1 and then Key Stages 2 and 3 ensure smooth transition.	High standards are to be secured through both high-quality direct mathematics teaching and through this content being used and applied in cross-curricular studies. There are six areas of learning: (with the separate NC subjects clearly visible within them) 1. understanding English, communication and language, 2. mathematical understanding, 3. science and technological understanding, 4. historical, geographical and social understanding, 5. understanding physical development, health and wellbeing, 6. understanding the arts. Mathematics is a core subject along with literacy and ICT and personal development. The National Curriculum remains the statutory requirement with the 8 level scales. The PNS is part of the planning and delivery of mathematics.
2009 DCSF	Government White Paper *Your Child, Your Schools, Our Future: Building a 21st Century Schools System* – summary. 'We want every child to succeed, we will never give up on any child' (p.1). There are entitlements for all pupils and parents, which reflect the best of what schools are now doing. There is a move away from centrally managed contracts to schools working as federations to ensure delivery of the Act as they move forward with the curriculum.	There is a continued role for extended school partnerships to support children's needs including mathematics. The daily mathematics lesson continues together with the use of the PNS but there is flexibility to adapt and 'tailor provision to the circumstances and needs of the children in the school. There are individual pupil and parent guarantees ensuring the best possible education for the child and good liaison between school and home.

Appendix 2

Table A2.1 NCETM exemplification of TDA standards (as they apply to mathematics) for Qualified Teacher Status

Professional Standard	Professional Standard (TDA)	Exemplification (NCETM)
Q1	Have high mathematical expectations of children and young people including a commitment to ensuring that they can achieve their full educational potential and to establishing fair, respectful, trusting, supportive and constructive relationships with them.	1. Understand that all children and young people can achieve in mathematics, with understanding, at an appropriate level, and that appropriate expectations need to be flexible in the light of the range of evidence available to the teacher and student. Share suitably high expectations with learners. 2. Understand that the development of new cognitive frameworks such as those required in mathematics, depends on the learner feeling secure and respected in their environment. Begin to establish, and expect, such an environment.
Q2	Through their teaching of mathematics, demonstrate the positive values, attitudes and behaviour they expect from children and young people.	1. Understand that all young people can enjoy mathematics at an appropriate level, especially when they feel supported, valued and encouraged by those with whom they learn. 2. Share your confidence to enjoy, and be challenged by, mathematics with learners. 3. Model support and encouragement of learners trying to make sense of new ideas in mathematics. 4. Model positive and constructive attitudes to mathematics, e.g. through checking whether answers make sense, seeking and welcoming conjectures, encouraging perseverance, evaluating a solution to a problem or progress towards a solution, attempting to make links between different parts of mathematics, using a variety of written, verbal and physical means of communication of mathematical ideas.
Q3a	Be aware of the professional duties of teachers of mathematics and the statutory framework within which they work.	1. Be aware of the current teachers' pay and conditions document and any current workforce agreements as they apply to your status as a teacher. 2. Be aware of the National Curriculum that defines programmes of study for mathematics for each key stage, attainment targets and arrangements for end of key stage testing and reporting. 3. Understand how the programmes of study for mathematics define a minimum of mathematical experiences for all learners over a key stage and how they facilitate longer run planning. 4. Understand how the level descriptions set out in the attainment targets for mathematics facilitate judgements of learners' overall levels of mathematical attainment at the end of each key stage.

5. Understand how, on a daily basis, you use your knowledge of mathematics alongside your knowledge of learners' own current understanding of and proficiency in the subject to plan sequences of learning opportunities that motivate and enable learners to gain in mathematical confidence, understanding and proficiency.

6. Be aware of the wider statutory frameworks that guide your practice as a teacher of mathematics, e.g., legislation that refers to:

   o health and safety
   o equality of opportunity
   o discrimination
   o data protection
   o freedom of information

Q3b

Be aware of the policies and practices of the workplace and share in collective responsibility for their implementation.

1. Be aware of workplace policies and practices that guide your practice as a teacher of mathematics, e.g., policies and practices that refer to:

   o planning and teaching;
   o inclusion
   o behaviour management;
   o assessment and record keeping;
   o special educational needs;
   o gifted and talented.

2. Be aware of any expectations set out in your job description and the Teacher Development Agency professional standards for teachers, as exemplified for teachers of mathematics, that you are required to achieve and demonstrate by virtue of your particular status.

3. Be aware of your annual performance objectives and the help available in your workplace, such as guidance, coaching or mentoring, to support your achievement of them.

Q4

Communicate effectively within and about mathematics with children, young people and colleagues.

1. Understand how mathematical ideas, patterns and relationships may be communicated in a number of ways such as orally, in writing, symbols or pictures, or with physical or practical demonstration, and that students learn these best when they are exposed to a variety of means of communication that makes links with existing knowledge and structures.

2. Understand that mathematical symbols, vocabulary and conventions are precise and that learners need support in moving towards their accurate use.

3. Begin to select the most appropriate form(s) of mathematical communication for groups or individuals, including parents/carers and colleagues

4. Encourage learners to communicate about mathematics with each other and with parents/ carers and any other adult with whom they spend time.

(Continued)

Table A2.1 Continued

Professional Standard	Professional Standard (TDA)	Exemplification (NCETM)
Q5	Recognize and respect the contribution that colleagues, parents and carers can make to the development and wellbeing of children and young people and to raising their levels of mathematical attainment.	1. Recognize that learners experience mathematics and attitudes towards mathematics, in a variety of contexts that affect their own attitudes and confidence and that can be built on. 2. Recognize that parents/carers and colleagues know learners in ways which will influence how they learn mathematics, and meet them in contexts which offer opportunities to use and talk about mathematics; start to communicate about and build on these.
Q6	Have a commitment to collaboration and co-operative working on their own and others' learning and teaching of mathematics.	1. Recognize that an effective teacher of mathematics is an active learner and communicator of mathematics at an appropriate level. 2. Share work on mathematics and mathematics education with colleagues, recognizing that collaborative talk enhances understanding.
Q7a	Reflect on and improve their practice in the teaching of mathematics, and take responsibility for identifying and meeting their professional development needs.	1. After each teaching session assess the extent to which the mathematics that you planned to be learnt was learnt by all groups of learners. 2. Think about your answers to the questions below and, in response to your thinking, plan how you might develop your practice further. For example: o Did you check that learners understood any explanations you gave? And did they? o Were learners given opportunities to ask questions and discuss their work? And did they? o Did the session engage all groups of learners? o Did you cater for different learning preferences? o Did any materials you used, including ICT, enhance your teaching? o Were all learners clear about what they were expected to achieve and do? o Did any materials used in the session, including ICT, enhance learners' understanding? o Did you identify any learning blocks or breakthroughs? What were they? And who were the learners? o Did you feel sufficiently confident with your own mathematics to enable all learners to make progress and connect the mathematics they were working on to other areas of mathematics they had previously experienced? Talk with your tutor, mentor or coach about your own assessment of your strengths and areas in need of further development; check to see if your assessment coincides with theirs; agree how they may help you work through your areas in need of further development.

Q7b

Identify priorities for their early professional development in the context of induction

1. At the start of your career, and in the light of your career entry profile, discuss with your mentor areas you feel you need to work on.
2. With regard to the induction standards and based on the assessments of your strengths and areas for further development, identify appropriate professional targets.
3. Discuss with your mentor the learning journey you intend to take to achieve your professional targets, drawn from the induction standards, and discuss how that journey will be made.
4. Include in your early professional development opportunities to develop further your own mathematics.

Q8

Have a creative and constructively critical approach in the teaching of mathematics towards innovation; being prepared to adapt their practice where benefits and improvements are identified.

1. Be aware of a variety of approaches to, and resources for, learning mathematics. Be able to select appropriately for a given group of learners, showing some flexibility of use.
2. Be able to use a variety of learning styles, groupings, tools and materials over a period of time, adapting them to the learning response and evaluating their impact.

Q9

Act upon advice and feedback on their teaching of mathematics and be open to coaching and mentoring.

1. Evidence progression of quality of planning and practice of your teaching of mathematics in the light of observation and feedback.
2. Establish a constructive response to interaction with any colleague acting in a mentoring or coaching capacity.

Q10

Have a knowledge and understanding of a range of teaching and learning approaches in mathematics and behaviour management strategies and know how to use and adapt them, including how to personalize learning and provide opportunities for all learners to achieve their potential.

1. Understand that similar ideas and relationships in mathematics can be communicated in different ways and build on different pre-learning; that contexts which are familiar to, or of particular interest to, learners, including recreational contexts, are likely to enhance the learning of mathematics, and that particular learners may have a preference for a particular mode of learning or context.
2. Understand that optimum learning of mathematics occurs when learners are confident, interested, affirmed and challenged, and that there are a variety of ways to establish such a culture.
3. Begin to know how to provide mathematical learning opportunities that engage and challenge all learners, including those for whom English is a second language, and those with special educational needs.

(Continued)

Table A2.1 Continued

Professional Standard	Professional Standard (TDA)	Exemplification (NCETM)
		4. As expressed in "Mathematics Counts", Dr W H Cockcroft, HMSO 1982, understand how mathematics teaching should include opportunities for:
		o exposition by the teacher;
		o discussion between teacher and learners and between learners themselves;
		o appropriate practical work;
		o consolidation and practice of fundamental skills and routines;
		o problem solving, including the application of mathematics to everyday and/or work-based situations;
		o investigational work.
		5. As expressed in 'Better Mathematics' Afzal Ahmed, HMSO 1987, understand how to interpret the assertion that mathematics is effectively learnt only by experimenting, questioning, reflecting, discovering, inventing and discussing.
Q11	Know the assessment requirements and arrangements for mathematics including those relating to public examinations and qualifications	1. Be aware of the scope, nature and mode of any required national arrangements for the summative assessment of learners within the age-range which you are trained to teach, including some understanding of available special arrangements.
		2. Be aware of any national attainment standards in mathematics, which may be expressed as success criteria, aspects, profiles, specifications, level or grade descriptions that relate to the age-range for which you are trained to teach.
		3. For each national attainment standard in mathematics that relates to the age-range for which you are trained to teach, know what learner evidence you need to look for and how such evidence is best demonstrated and collected.
		4. Know how to collect and collate evidence, both formal and informal, suitable for making accurate, valid and reliable judgements of learners' mathematical performance in relation to relevant national standards.

| Q12 | Know a range of approaches to assessment of mathematics, including the importance of formative assessment | 1. Be aware of the different ways that learners may choose and use to communicate their skills, knowledge and understanding of mathematics, for example:
○ orally
○ in written or symbolic form
○ diagrammatically, pictorially or graphically
○ through application – solving problems, describing and modelling situations within and beyond mathematics;
○ through constructions.
and that each of these different ways of communicating mathematical skills, knowledge and understanding presents opportunities for assessment and evaluation by both teacher and learner.
2. Begin to know how to build opportunities for assessment into discussions and interactions with learners, encouraging them to develop an awareness of their own learning, their mathematical achievements and areas on which they should focus to ensure progression in their learning.
3. Begin to be able to use your knowledge of mathematics and your knowledge of learners' positions on the curriculum map of mathematics to plan learners' next steps.
4. Be aware of the 'relative value of written comments and dialogue and know when to use these, and when to use marks and grades, as effective feedback to inform learning. |
| Q13 | Know how to use local and national statistical information to evaluate the effectiveness of their mathematics teaching, to monitor the mathematical progress of those they teach and to raise levels of attainment. | 1. Have some understanding of the nationally agreed attainment standards in mathematics relevant to the age range of learners you teach, for example:
○ Early learning goals;
○ Foundation Stage Profile;
○ National Curriculum level descriptions;
○ Public examination grade descriptors;
○ Key skills level specifications;
○ NQF levels specifications.
2. Begin to know how to use your assessment evidence of individual learners to judge the best match with particular attainment standards. |

(Continued)

Table A2.1 Continued

Professional Standard	Professional Standard (TDA)	Exemplification (NCETM)
		3. Be familiar with the scope and nature of nationally available data on learners' attainments in mathematics and know how to use this to compare the mathematical attainment of learners in your workplace, including particular groups such as those in public care, with special educational needs, with English as a second language, or by gender
		4. Begin to be able to use the nationally available progress data to compare the progress of learners in your own workplace. For example, those that measure progress of students with similar attainment on entry, or the progress of particular sub-groups of students, including some comparisons with progress in other subjects, particularly English, Science and ICT.
		5. Based on your analyses of attainments and progress in mathematics compared with those nationally, begin to know how to identify any groups of learners who may be underperforming, and start to formulate necessary remedial and improvement strategies.
Q14	Have a secure knowledge and understanding of mathematics and related pedagogy to enable them to teach effectively across the age and ability range for which they are trained.	1. Understand how the different components of mathematics inter-relate and be able to use this personal understanding to help learners build their own progressive lattices of mathematical understanding.
		2. Know about the origins of mathematical knowledge, practices and conventions and be able to use this to enrich teaching and to help learners understand the human and multi-cultural roots of mathematics.
		3. Use mathematical language, symbols and vocabulary precisely.
		4. Be sufficiently mathematically aware and confident to recognize the nature of possible learner misconceptions or insights and be able to plan the next steps in their learning.
		5. Be aware of the applications of mathematics to other subjects and real-life situations and be able to use these to motivate learners' confidence and understanding.
Q15	Know and understand the relevant statutory and non-statutory curricula, frameworks, including those provided through the National Strategies, for mathematics, and other relevant initiatives across the age and ability range for which they are trained to teach.	1. Understand that the statutory curriculum is a minimum entitlement for all learners and know how to use this to plan a sequence of mathematical learning opportunities that engage and stretch each individual, selecting appropriately from the range and scope stated and beyond where this will enhance learning.
		2. Begin to understand the common threads across the statutory curriculum and any national strategies relevant to the age you teach, and in particular the references to or opportunities for using mathematics in other areas of the curriculum; build on these where appropriate.

Q16 Have passed the professional skills tests in numeracy, literacy and information and communication technology (ICT).

Q17 Know how to use skills in literacy, numeracy and ICT to support their teaching and wider professional activities.

1. Understand how to model the positive use of these core skills in your workplace, with learners and, where appropriate, with colleagues. For example:

2. Know how to help learners acquire the necessary mathematical vocabulary and conventional symbolism in order to classify mathematical objects, understand mathematical ideas, and to develop and communicate their mathematical reasoning.

3. Know how to help learners understand the precision on of meaning of mathematical words, especially when those words may have different or more general meanings in everyday language.

4. Know how to support learners' development of literacy skills within the context of learning mathematics.

5. Know how to help learners understand when and how to apply their mathematical skills, knowledge and understanding to:
   o describe, interpret and understand everyday and/or work-based situations;
   o solve 'everyday' problems and make predictions.

6. Know how to use, and support learners in using, ICT to demonstrate and communicate mathematical ideas and relationships, to pursue lines of mathematical enquiry, to model and to solve problems.

7. Know how to help learners to use ICT to communicate mathematical ideas and relationships, to pursue lines of mathematical enquiry, to model situations and to solve problems.

8. Know how to find, evaluate and use appropriate software and electronic information to support and enhance a variety of mathematics learning contexts.

9. Know how to use ICT and numeracy skills to chart learners' progress in mathematics and to evaluate the effectiveness of your mathematics teaching.

Q18 Understand how children and young people develop and that progress in learning mathematics and wellbeing of learners is affected by a range of developmental, social, religious, ethnic, cultural and linguistic influences.

1. Understand that learners bring with them their prior influences that may be used as contributions to a positive climate for learning mathematics.

2. Begin to be aware of learners' prior influences, and to know how to plan to build constructive and engaging mathematics learning experiences on them.

3. Understand that learners continue to develop at different rates and in different ways, often building their own maps of mathematical interrelationships, so that continuous evaluation of learning is needed to optimize progress.

(Continued)

Table A2.1 Continued

Professional Standard	Professional Standard (TDA)	Exemplification (NCETM)
Q19	Know how to make effective personalized provision in learning mathematics for those they teach, including those for whom English is an additional language or who have special educational needs or disabilities, and how to take practical account of diversity and promote equality and inclusion in their teaching.	1. Begin to understand the cultural diversity of the roots of mathematics, and of learners of mathematics and start to harness this to plan suitably engaging mathematics learning experiences. 2. Begin to understand a variety of ways to harness interests and inclinations among learners when planning mathematics learning opportunities. 3. Understand and be able to recognize and plan for addressing, the common misconceptions in the mathematics appropriate to the age range and situation in which you teach. 4. Have sufficient knowledge of, and confidence in, mathematics, to be able to encourage learners to investigate and make sense of their own learning. 5. Begin to recognize, understand and be able to provide appropriately for the most common special educational needs and the most able in mathematics.
Q20	In planning learning opportunities in mathematics know and understand the roles of colleagues with specific responsibilities, including those with responsibility for learners with special educational needs and disabilities and other individual learning needs.	1. Begin to understand the roles of colleagues within your workplace, and partners beyond, who have specific responsibilities for supporting particular learner needs, and the protocols used for enlisting their support. 2. Understand when and how it is appropriate to approach such colleagues for help in addressing particular learning needs. 3. Begin to be able to plan for the constructive and full use of any available in-class support.
Q21a	Be aware of current legal requirements, national policy and guidance on the safeguarding and wellbeing of children and young people.	
Q21b	Know how to identify and support children and young people whose progress, development or wellbeing is affected by changes or difficulties in their personal circumstances, and when to refer them to colleagues for specialist support.	

Q22	Plan for progression in the learning of mathematics across the age and ability range for which they are trained, designing effective learning sequences within lessons and across series of lessons and demonstrating secure mathematical and curriculum knowledge.	1. Use a range of data and tools to plan for learners' access and progression over a sequence of lessons. 2. Over time, demonstrate planning that gives experience of: o exposition by the teacher; o discussion between teacher and learners and between learners themselves; o appropriate practical work; o consolidation and practice of fundamental skills and routines; o problem solving, including the application of mathematics to everyday situations; o investigational work; and allows learners opportunities to be engaged in experimenting, questioning, reflecting, discovering, inventing and discussing. 3. Demonstrate approaches to teaching that allow learning in a variety of styles and builds on learner interests and motivations. 4. Demonstrate planning that shows awareness of a variety of links and relationships within the subject and across the curriculum, and encourages learners to develop and exhibit these for themselves.
Q23	Design opportunities for learners to develop their literacy, numeracy and ICT skills	1. When planning, identify opportunities for learners to read and interpret written contexts for mathematics. 2. Plan for learners to use mathematical symbols, vocabulary and syntax appropriately and precisely. 3. Demonstrate, and allow learners to experience, the appropriate use of a variety of ICT resources to enhance the learning and communication of mathematical ideas and relationships.
Q24	Plan homework or other out-of-class mathematics tasks to sustain learners' progress and to extend and consolidate their learning.	1. Plan home works that can be seen by learners to connect with, consolidate and/or extend mathematics which they have already met. 2. Where possible, plan to relate the mathematics you are teaching to everyday, wider curriculum and/or interest contexts so that they recognize and can use opportunities to transfer skills and understanding. 3. Plan opportunities for learners to research and investigate new areas or applications of mathematics.

(Continued)

Table A2.1 Continued

Professional Standard	Professional Standard (TDA)	Exemplification (NCETM)
Q25a	Teach lessons and sequences of lessons in mathematics across the age and ability range for which they are trained in which they use a range of teaching strategies and resources for mathematics, including e-learning, taking practical account of diversity and promoting equality and inclusion.	1. Over a sequence of lessons, use a variety of teaching strategies and give opportunities for learners to be engaged in experimenting, questioning, reflecting, discovering, inventing and discussing. 2. Over a sequence of lessons, use and allow learners to use, a variety of appropriate resources, including electronic, to support their learning and model and demonstrate mathematical relationships. 3. Build on learners' prior learning, culture and interests in order to motivate them and encourage appropriate progression. 4. Make suitable provision within your teaching to allow learners for whom English is a second language, or others with special educational needs, including the most able, to access learning and make progress.
Q25b	Teach lessons and sequences of lessons in mathematics across the age and ability range for which they are trained in which they build on prior mathematical knowledge, develop concepts and processes, enable learners to apply new knowledge, understanding and skills and meet learning objectives.	1. Use your knowledge of mathematics, and of the mathematics curriculum and any appropriate frameworks, to enable access to new learning and develop understanding of links and relationships between mathematical skills, concepts and processes. 2. Support learners in becoming able to apply known and emergent skills, concepts and processes in a variety of situations and to demonstrate and recognize new learning.
Q25c	Teach lessons and sequences of lessons in mathematics across the age and ability range for which they are trained in which they adapt their language to suit the learners they teach, introducing new ideas and concepts clearly, and using explanations, questions, discussions and plenaries effectively.	1. Use your understanding of the variety of ways in which mathematics can be communicated, to choose appropriately for your learners and the mathematics involved. 2. Use mathematical language, symbols and syntax precisely and accurately, building on and making overt links with, learners' current knowledge. 3. Enable learners to communicate mathematics in a variety of ways to each other and the teacher, for example orally, pictorially, electronically, in words or symbols, graphically or diagrammatically, supporting them in developing precision and in moving from everyday usage where this differs. 4. Use a variety of open and closed questions and discussions to draw out and enhance mathematical thinking from a range of learners, giving adequate thinking time and adopting varied strategies, e.g. 'think-pair-share', group exposition of main learning points, individual or group mind-maps. 5. Use your understanding of the mathematics curriculum to draw out and make clear the main learning points from an episode, lesson or sequence of lessons.

Q25d	Teach lessons and sequences of lessons in mathematics across the age and ability range for which they are trained in which they demonstrate the ability to manage the learning of individuals, groups and whole classes, modifying their teaching to suit the stage of the lesson	1. Over a lesson or sequence of lessons, give opportunities for learners to experience a variety of individual, group and whole-class learning as appropriate to the task and the learners, ensuring that all learners are engaged in making mathematics.
		2. Use your knowledge of the progression of and conditions for learning to organize groupings which vary according to learning need.
		3. Use your understanding of the benefits and drawbacks of different types of groupings ie.g. size, near/far ability), to allow access to confidence and progress for all.
		4. Begin to use groupings flexibly, .e.g. responding to unforeseen difficulties, as a lesson or sequence of lessons progresses.
Q26a	Make effective use of a range of assessment, monitoring and recording strategies.	1. Recognize that learners may demonstrate or communicate their skills, knowledge and understanding in a large variety of ways, including orally, electronically, in writing or symbols, pictorially, diagrammatically or graphically, through construction or application.
		2. Use, and support learners in using, these as a means of assessment and evaluation of progress and position on the curriculum map.
		3. Use your understanding of the mathematics curriculum to translate and assist learners in translating, this knowledge into appropriate next steps.
		4. Understand that learners are likely to focus on grades or marks if any are provided, rather than on formative written or oral comments; use this knowledge to make considered judgements about when to use different forms of feedback.
		5. Begin to develop recording strategies which support your own, learners' and colleagues' judgements about learners' attainments, progression and appropriate next steps, and enable you to evidence these to appropriate parties.
Q26b	Assess the mathematical learning needs of those they teach and set challenging learning objectives.	1. Harness a variety of opportunities for assessment for learning, e.g discussion, making of models, formal and informal written work, to inform your own and learners' understanding of their position on the curriculum map and appropriate next learning.
		2. Choose a variety of questions and rich tasks which probe understanding, build links and promote deep learning, evaluating the responses so that lessons and sequences of lessons become feedback loops supporting confidence and appropriate challenge.

(Continued)

Table A2.1 Continued

Professional Standard	Professional Standard (TDA)	Exemplification (NCETM)
Q27	Provide timely, accurate and constructive feedback on learners' mathematical attainment, progress and areas of development in mathematics	1. Use your knowledge of the mathematics curriculum map and learners' places on that, to communicate with learners about their progress and priority areas for development, helping them to appreciate their achievements and suitable targets. 2. Structure lessons and sequences of lessons to give learners opportunities to develop their own understanding and evaluation of their learning. 3. Begin to use your understanding of the mathematics curriculum and the variety of available data, local and national, to evaluate learner attainment and areas for development, sharing these at suitable times and in suitable ways with learners, colleagues and/or parents/carers. 4. Begin to develop skills in identification of learners who may be falling behind expected rates of progress, or are capable of exceeding them, and make appropriate provision.
Q28	Support and guide learners to reflect on their mathematics learning, identify the progress they have made and identify their emerging learning needs.	1. Encourage a supportive and reflective environment in which discussion and evaluation are valued, leading to the identification of learning and of misconceptions by learners, peers, teacher or other adult. 2. Structure your lessons and sequences of lessons to provide opportunities for learners to reflect on their understanding, appreciate progress relative to stated learning objectives, and identify areas for development, e.g. through peer or pupil-teacher discussion or informal or formal written contribution. 3. Use your knowledge of mathematics and of the mathematics curriculum to identify appropriate success criteria that learners can use to support their evaluation of learning, including making links with previous learning.
Q29	Evaluate the impact of their mathematics teaching on the progress of all learners and modify their planning and classroom where practice necessary	1. After each learning session, evaluate the impact of the session in relation to planned learning, across the range of learners, using a range of tools and identifying misconceptions. You might include consideration of the impacts of grouping, lesson structure, timing, questioning, resources e.g.: could any of these have been used differently to enhance learning further, for all or for particular groups of learners? 2. Using your knowledge of mathematics and of the mathematics curriculum, plan to address over time any shortfall in assessment information or learning. 3. Communicate with colleagues, particularly observers or mentors, about ways to evaluate and improve your teaching of mathematics.

Q30 Establish a purposeful and safe learning environment conducive to learning mathematics and identify opportunities for learners to learn in out-of-school contexts.

1. Use your understanding of what constitutes a supportive, safe and challenging environment for learning mathematics, to establish a learning area which is:
   - physically safe and allows for appropriate groupings, access to space, people and resources, and sightlines
   - emotionally secure, accepting and valuing all present and all contributions
   - intellectually motivating, stimulating and engaging
   - conforms to locally agreed Health and Safety measures

2. Provide regular occasions for learners to recognize and appreciate opportunities to use their mathematics at home, work or other activities, including other areas of the curriculum, and to make those links and that transference of skills.

Q31 Establish a clear framework for classroom discipline to manage learners' behaviour constructively and promote their self-control and independence when learning mathematics.

1. Use your familiarity with local behaviour expectations, rewards and sanctions, to establish routines which are consistent with those of other teachers and consistent between learning sessions, recognizing that clearly planned and engaging mathematical learning is in itself a catalyst for constructive behaviour.

2. Explain your expectations clearly and calmly, affirming constructive behaviour and dealing consistently with aberrations.

3. Promote positive self-worth by establishing a secure and supportive classroom ethos in which all participants and all contributions are valued.

4. Support learners in moving towards independent learning, e.g. by giving choice, providing appropriate access to resources, developing skills of self- and peer assessment.

Q32 Work as a team member and identify opportunities for working with colleagues, sharing the development of effective practice in the teaching of mathematics with them.

1. Engage with colleagues to discuss the different ways in which different aspects of mathematics may be introduced and taught.

2. Share with colleagues those teaching approaches in mathematics that you evaluated to have been particularly successful and those that you evaluated to be in need of development. Contribute to and benefit from your team's pool of successful practices.

3. Ensure that interactions with colleagues benefit your own and each other's development as teachers of mathematics.

4. Observe and learn from your coach or mentor's practice in planning, teaching and assessing mathematics.

Q33 Ensure that colleagues working with them are appropriately involved in supporting the learning of mathematics and understanding the roles they are expected to fulfil.

1. Incorporate the appropriate negotiated use of other available adults or older students into your planning, ensuring that learners are also aware of their role.

2. Ensure that support staff are wherever possible sufficiently informed about the plans for the lesson or lesson sequence, and the associated mathematical content in advance, so that they can fulfil their role effectively; and that there is an appropriate opportunity for feedback and other communication, including any assessments made, after the learning session.

The NCETM's presentation of the professional standards for teachers', as they apply to mathematics, is available at http://content.ncetm.org.uk/tda/ and contains additional materials and advice. While the content of this appendix considers only QTS, the online material contains exemplification of standards for core, post threshold, excellent teacher and AST status. [Online material accessed: 1 February 2009]

Appendix 3

Opportunities to use ICT within the National Curriculum for Mathematics

Programmes of study (in addition to Handling Data Key Stage 2)
Key Stage 1

MA2 Number

1f: *Communicate in spoken, pictorial and written form, first using informal language and recording, the mathematical language and symbols.*

ICT can be used to create the mathematical symbols.

Ma3 Shape, space and measures

1b: *Select and use appropriate mathematical equipment when solving problems involving measures or measurement.*

ICT resources in the form of digital and analogue devices can be used to measure weight or time.

2c: *'Create "2D and 3D" shapes'.*

There is a wide range of software to support this work.

3a, b, c: *Understanding of properties of position and movement*

A programmable resource such as PIP or Roamer provide the opportunities to 'observe, visualise and describe positions, directions and movements using common words'.

Breadth of study

1f: *Pupils should be taught the knowledge, skills and understanding through exploring and using a variety of resources and materials, including ICT.*

Key Stage 2

Ma2 Number

1c: *Select and use appropriate mathematical equipment, including ICT.*

4d: *Recognise, represent and interpret simple number relationships, constructing and using formulae in words then symbols (for example, c = 15n is the cost, in pence, of n articles at 15p each).*

Programs such as Excel can be deployed to construct and use a formula to transform one list of data to another.

3k: *Use a calculator for calculations involving several digits, including decimals; use a calculator to solve number problems; know how to enter and interpret money calculations and fractions; know how to select the correct key sequence for calculations with more than one operation.*

Ma3 Shape, space and measures

1c: *Approach spatial problems flexibly, including trying alternative approaches to overcome difficulties.* A wide range of software can be used to create repeating patterns, such as tessellations.

2c: *Make and draw with increasing accuracy 2-D and 3-D shapes and patterns; recognise reflective symmetry in regular polygons; recognise their geometrical features and properties including angles, faces, pairs of parallel lines and symmetry, and use these to classify shapes and solve problems.*

Pupils can use software to create repeating patterns, such as tessellations, patterns of reflective and rotational symmetry.

2c: *Make and draw with increasing accuracy 2-D and 3-D shapes and patterns; recognise reflective symmetry in regular polygons; recognise their geometrical features and properties including angles, faces, pairs of parallel lines and symmetry, and use these to classify shapes and solve problems.*

3b: *Transform objects in practical situations; transform images using ICT; visualise and predict the position of a shape following a rotation, reflection or translation.*

Ma4 Handling data

2c: *Represent and interpret discrete data using graphs and diagrams, including pictograms, bar charts and line graphs, then interpret a wider range of graphs and diagrams, using ICT where appropriate.*

Breadth of Study

c. Use patterns and relationships to explore simple algebraic ideas
d. Apply measuring skills on a range of context
e. Draw inferences from data in practical activities, and recognize the difference between meaningful and misleading representations of data

f. Explore and use a variety of resources and materials including ICT

g. Decide when the use of calculators is appropriate and then use them effectively.

Appendix 4

Examples of story books to inspire, enhance and inform mathematical work

Counting

(1998) *One, Two, Skip a Few! First Number Rhymes* Bristol: Barefoot Books. This Early Year book has a wealth of poems, many linked with counting and number.

Cave K and Roddell C (2006) *Out for the Count* Frances Lincoln. This book involves counting to 100 and has fun examples of arrays such as counting seven groups of ten vampire bats. Definitely not for the feint hearted.

Wilson A and Bartlett A (1999) *Over the Grasslands* Macmillan. Counting poem up to 10 of grasslands animals.

Piers H and Giffard H (1996) *Is there Room on the Bus?* Frances Lincoln. This is a round the world counting book of triangular numbers up to 10. 1 + 2 + 3 etc. as the animals try to squeeze into a bus.

Shape and space

Sharratt N (1994) *My Mum and Dad Make Me Laugh* Walker Books. This book has glorious pictures of spots and stripes, also known as circles and rectangles.

Carter D (1990) *How Many Bugs in a Box and More Bugs in Boxes* Orchard Books. The book has a wealth of pop-up polyhedra.

Tang G (2003) *Math-terpieces The Art of Problem Solving* Scholastic Press. Art work by 12 painters such as Degas and Warhol is used to inspire simple counting.

Money

Wells R (1997) *Bunny Money* Doubleday. The book brings working with money to life. The story involves giving change as well as opening up discussions about the wise use of money.

Inkpen M (1998) *The Great Pet Sale* Hodder. The story involves a shop sale in which the total cost of the animals is exactly £1. Can the children write a Sweet Shop or Sports shop version where the total goods add up to £1 or £20 or £100?

Burningham J (1980) *The Shopping Basket* Red Fox. This provides an introduction to triangular numbers.

Rowling J K (1997) *Harry Potter and the Philosopher's Stone* Bloomsbury – an interesting monetary system – 29 Knuts = 1 sickle 17 sickles = 1 galleon

Addition and repeated addition

Sayre A (2003) *One is a Snail Ten is a Crab* Walker Book. This is a wonderful book involving the addition of the feet of animals. Surely it is far more interesting to add the feet of an insect and a snail to make 7 than to see 6 + 1 =. Similarly, 60 = 6 crabs or 10 insects has more interest than 60 = 6 × 10 or 10 × 6.

Measurement of length

Briggs R (1970) *Jim and the Beanstalk* Puffin Books. This book involves a lot of measuring with a tape measure and is a good stimulus for practical work. So think beyond standard mathematical resources. Do the school resources for the measurement of length go beyond ruler, tape measure and trundle wheel? There should also be carpenters folding measures, steel rules, calipers, surveyors' tapes and dressmakers' retractable tapes.

Rowling J K *Harry Potter and the Philosopher's Stone* Bloomsbury. Convert the wands from inches to centimetres.

Morpurgo M (1989) *Why the Whales Came* Heinemann. This is an adventure story based in the Scilly Isles. The map of the area is included in the book and provides a good source of scale and directional work for Key Stage 2.

McBratney S (1994) *Guess How Much I Love You* Walker Books. Estimation of measurement of length is part of the story.

Manning M and Granstom B (1997) *What's Up* Franklin Watts. The book starts with a child climbing on shoulders to be bigger and ends with space travel – lots of comparative vocabulary.

Ridley P (1995) *Dakota of the White Flatts* Puffin – for older juniors. It includes measurements in terms of fruit and vegetables.

Measurement of time

Sharratt N and Tucker S (1998) *The Time It Took Tom* Scholastic Press. This is a 'time classic' dealing with the passing of time from seconds to years.

Carle E (1982) *The Bad Tempered Ladybird* Picture Puffin. There is a clock on each page. This records what he is doing through the day, an idea easily copied by the children to show the key parts of their day.

Browne E and Parking D (1993) *Tick Tock* Walker Books. This is a truly funny book to include in a time topic.

Dunbar J (1996) *Tick Tock* Franklin Watts. This book measures time from a second to years, seasons, calendars and the time of the dinosaurs, millions of years ago.

Fractions

Scieszka J (1995) *Maths Curse* Viking. This contains lots of fractions and much more for top juniors. The teacher is called Mrs Fibonacci!

Norton Juster (1995) *The Phantom Tollbooth* Collins – for top Juniors. Adventures in Digitopolis with the 'mathemagician' Humbug with fractions, averages and a lot more.

Murphy S J (1999) *Give Me Half* HarperCollins. This is part of the Mathstart Series and is useful as it deals with halving single items, multiples such as packet of biscuits and liquids.

Early years specifically

Featherstone S (2005) The little book of Maths from Stories. Husbands Bosworth: Featherstone Education Ltd.

Index